# Critical Theory and Economics

This book expands upon a range of economic insights within the overall context of critical theory, particularly with respect to the question of socioeconomic inequalities, and presents an explanation of how critical theory provides a number of interesting perspectives for economists.

Economic agents, deliberately imprisoned in their instrumental rationality as a means to survive under competitive relationships, are microscopic constituents of systemic forces which exist beyond their will. Despite the subjective rationality of such agents in terms of formally logical transitivity and consistency, aggregate market distributional mechanisms also display non-rational patterns. The crucial aspect of the dynamics of this system consists of the paralysing effect of the high level of socioeconomic inequality, which is driven by a permanent struggle for self-preservation under competitive rules; it is a reminiscence of natural, uncivilised relationships that constituted the reproduction process of the whole.

These reified agents thus become instruments of their socially constructed powers on the one hand, and objects of their existential conditionality on the other. Hence, the dialectical approach adopted by the author aims to uncover the way in which structurally genetic market forces govern individual behaviour, as well as how individual behaviour shapes these structurally genetic forces, which, together, form the transcending principles of unequal distribution.

This book will be of particular interest to scholars of the political economy, philosophy and the methodology of the social sciences, especially those concerned with inequality issues. The preface for this book was written by Professor Martin Jay.

**Robin Maialeh**, Director of Research Institute for Labour and Social Affairs, Prague, Czech Republic.

## Routledge Frontiers of Political Economy

**Modern Money and the Rise and Fall of Capitalist Finance**
The Institutionalization of Trusts, Personae, and Indebtedness
*Jongchul Kim*

**Innovation, Complexity and Economic Evolution**
From Theory to Policy
*Pier Paolo Saviotti*

**Economic Growth and Inequality**
The Economist's Dilemma
*Laurent Dobuzinskis*

**Wellbeing, Nature and Moral Values in Economics**
How Modern Economic Analysis Faces the Challenges Ahead
*Heinz Welsch*

**Why are Presidential Regimes Bad for the Economy?**
Understanding the Link between Forms of Government and Economic Outcomes
*Richard McManus and Gulcin Ozkan*

**Critical Theory and Economics**
Philosophical Notes on Contemporary Inequality
*Robin Maialeh*

**Corporate Financialization**
*An Economic Sociology Perspective*
*Marcelo José do Carmo, Mário Sacomano Neto and Julio Cesar Donadone*

For more information about this series, please visit: www.routledge.com/Routledge-Frontiers-of-Political-Economy/book-series/SE0345

# Critical Theory and Economics

## Philosophical Notes on Contemporary Inequality

**Robin Maialeh**

Routledge
Taylor & Francis Group
LONDON AND NEW YORK

First published 2023
by Routledge
4 Park Square, Milton Park, Abingdon, Oxon OX14 4RN

and by Routledge
605 Third Avenue, New York, NY 10158

*Routledge is an imprint of the Taylor & Francis Group, an informa business*



*British Library Cataloguing-in-Publication Data*
A catalogue record for this book is available from the British Library

ISBN: 978-0-367-22220-8 (hbk)
ISBN: 978-1-032-43782-8 (pbk)
ISBN: 978-0-429-27384-1 (ebk)

DOI: 10.4324/9780429273841

Typeset in Bembo
by Apex CoVantage, LLC

**This book was partly supported by institutional support for the long-term conceptual development of the research organisation for the years 2018–2022 provided by MoLSA.**

# Contents

*Preface* ix

**Introduction** 1

1 **Prolegomena to Critical Theory** 5
*The History of Critical Theory 5*
*Critical and Traditional Theory 11*
*Critical Theory and Economics 16*

2 **Prolegomena to Economic Theory** 29
*Foundations of Contemporary Economics 29*
*Distributional Theories 37*
*The Impotence of the Behavioural "Critique" 44*

3 **Dialectical-Critical Reflection** 70
*A Critique of Positivism: From Metaphysical Ontologism to Mathematical Formalism 70*
*Dialectics as a Reaction to Positivism 78*
*Dialectical Totality and the Pseudoconcrete 84*

4 **Subject and Reason** 93
*Instrumental Reason and Contemporary Economics 93*
*Rational Attitude Towards Self-Preservation 97*
*Metamorphosis of the Subject and Its Objectification 101*

5 **Immanence and the Transcendence of Contemporary Inequality** 108

*On the Worthiness of De-ontologised Positivism 108*

*Heteronomous Agents and the Transcendence of the Market Economy 114*

*The Immanence of Unequal Distribution 124*

**Conclusion** 135

*Index* 138

# Preface

"The Revolution against *Capital*", the provocative title of Antonio Gramsci's 1917 essay on the Bolshevik Revolution, has become the canonical formula to characterise the larger meaning of the revolutionaries' audacity in overthrowing the Russian autocracy. It signalled a paradigm shift in Marxist praxis, the exercise of subjective will and collective action against the economic determinism of the "orthodox" Marxists of the Second International, who waited patiently for the ripening of "objective contradictions" to reach a crisis point in the most advanced capitalist countries. Implying the "primacy of the political" over the economic mode of production, it led to the adoption of a more efficacious organisational model – the vanguard party – to accelerate the pace of radical change.

The formula could, however, also be invoked to signify something very different in the development of what came to be known as Western Marxism. Here it referred to a shift of emphasis from political economy to cultural critique in the larger totality of relations that explain the persistence of capitalism beyond its allegedly terminal crises. Over time, this "culturalist" turn in Marxist theory led to a growing pessimism about the possibility of meaningful political action as well as economic crisis in an ideologically permeated culture that successfully integrates the victims of the capitalist mode of production into the system that victimises them.

Gramsci himself sought heroically to combine the two meanings, remaining a stalwart of the Italian Communist Party even during the incarceration of his last years in Mussolini's prison, while at the same time producing a rich and detailed analysis of the ways in which the battle over cultural "hegemony" would define class struggle in the 20th century. Other Western Marxists, however, most notably those who came to be known as "the Frankfurt School", gradually lost hope both in the explosive potential of the objective contradictions of the capitalist economy and in the possibility of radical political action. Not only had the militancy and solidarity of the working class waned as the revolutionary moment receded into the past, but also the vanguard party, once in power, had descended into an authoritarian dictatorship over the proletariat (and everyone else under its rule).

In reaction, the Frankfurt School abandoned any meaningful attempt to solve the challenge of effective political organisation, retreating into what Jürgen Habermas called a "strategy of hibernation". Occasional expressions of nostalgia for the council communist movement notwithstanding,[1] they concentrated their energies on exploring the "affirmative" power of the "culture industry", the social-psychological pathologies of the "authoritarian personality", and the erosion of critical resistance in an "administered world" or "one-dimensional society". Ironically, returning to the policy of patience of the Second International "orthodox" Marxists, they did so without any of their naïve optimism about the ripening of objective contradictions that would inexorably cause the collapse of capitalism.

Economic questions, to be sure, were never entirely forgotten by the Frankfurt School, or more precisely by the Institute of Social Research in its more inclusive form. In the period before their American exile, its members were cautiously hopeful that the planned transition from capitalism to socialism attempted by the Soviet "experiment" might succeed.[2] Henryk Grossman, an early Institute collaborator, and protégé of its first director, Carl Grünberg, continued to focus on the unresolvable contradictions of capitalism.[3] Even after the unanticipated rise of fascism, Franz Neumann grounded his analysis of Nazism, *Behemoth*, on the expansionist imperatives of monopoly capitalism.[4]

But once the alternative model of "state capitalism" was introduced by Friedrich Pollock during the Second World War to explain the convergence between fascist, Soviet and New Deal versions of a crisis-proof, stabilised system, critical theory's interest in political economy waned.[5] Ironically, the primacy of the political, which for Gramsci signalled subjective revolutionary initiative from below, now came to mean the counter-revolutionary control of the economy from above. Marx's analysis of the commodity form and the pervasive power of exchange value in capitalist society may have continued to inform many Frankfurt School analyses of cultural phenomena, but it served more as a background assumption than an actively developed focus of their work. Suspicious of the productivist focus of traditional Marxism, they envisaged the utopian goal of critique less in terms of overcoming alienated labour and more in terms of technologically enabled, aesthetically infused play. Although in many respects they differed from the structuralist Marxism of Louis Althusser, whose Leninist politics they rejected, it might be said that they implicitly shared his paradoxical assumption that the economy "was determinant in the last instance", but "the last instance never comes".

Or at least so it seemed for a long time. With the collapse of the totalitarian versions of state capitalism and the erosion of the Keynesian consensus of post-war liberal democracies, a new stage in capitalist development emerged, which soon took on the label of neo-liberalism. Although it remains to be seen if the still unresolved "contradictions" of capitalism will lead to a terminal crisis of the system, the neo-liberal turn certainly has exacerbated some of the tensions that Pollock thought had been successfully contained. The alarming inequality gap between rich and poor and the populist resistance to globalisation are only two signs that economic questions are once again front and centre. No less pressing is the alarming threat of climate change, which cannot be met by blithely continuing the expanded production and the technological exploitation of natural resources underpinning developmental economics, whether driven by private or public interests.

Accordingly, there have been a number of recent attempts to rethink the relationship between critical theory and the critique of political economy.[6] Most of them are informed by a revitalised faith in traditional Marxist arguments, whose relevance once again seems compelling. But what if the "science" of political economy that Marx had so powerfully criticised has itself changed in the interim? What if both "late capitalism" and the theoretical attempts to explain its workings have themselves evolved? What if critical theory could be employed to engage with contemporary non-Marxist economics rather than simply reasserting the enduring superiority of traditional Marxism?

Robin Maialeh, drawing on his training in mainstream economic theory, takes on these urgent questions. The author of an earlier study that combines empirical and theoretical research with cutting-edge quantitative analysis to explore the role market dynamics plays in fostering economic inequality,[7] he now steps back and interrogates the underlying assumptions that still inform economic reasoning today. Against the comforting illusion that imperfections in market relations can be successfully corrected through traditional fiscal or monetary policy, he argues that basic structural problems account for the dysfunction of the system as a whole. Neither mainstream economics nor its behavioural complements can address the deeper sources of the ever more apparent instability of global capitalist relations. Relying on outmoded models of rational self-interest defined by the logic of the market cannot explain the sources of increasing inequality, let alone provide a meaningful antidote. Only a more comprehensive approach that draws on all the resources of critical theory can hope to meet the challenges of a world that threatens to spin out of control. Robin Maialeh's *Critical Theory and Economics* provides us the tools to begin that most daunting and exigent of tasks.

Martin Jay
Sidney Hellman Ehrman Professor Emeritus
History Department
U. of California, Berkeley

## Notes

1 Perhaps the last expression of this hope was Max Horkheimer's 1940 essay, The authoritarian state. *Telos*, 15 (1973).

2 F. Pollock (1932). Die gegenwärtige Lage des Kapitalismus und die Aussichten einer planwirtschaftlichen Neuordnung. *Zeitschrift für Sozialforschung*, 1(1). The issue of planning remained on the table for the Institute even after their move, for example in the work of Pollock's assistants K. Mandelbaum and G. Meyer (1934). Zur Theorie der Planwirtschaft. *Zeitschrift für Sozialforschung*, 2(2). It should also be noted that the *Zeitschrift's* review section always had an extensive section devoted to new economic works.

3 H. Grossman (1992). *The law of accumulation and breakdown of the capitalist system*. London: Pluto Press. This is an abridged version of the original of 1929, which was reprinted as *Die Akkumulations- und Zusammenbruchsgesetz des kapitalistischen systems*. Frankfurt, 1970. For a sympathetic account of his career, including his years at the Institute, see R. Kuhn (2007). *Henryk Grossman and the recovery of Marxism*. Urbana and Champagne, IL: University of Illinois Press. Although he was supported in New York by the Institute, Grossman was increasingly marginalised, in part because of his defense of the Soviet Union.

4 F. Neumann (1944). *Behemoth: the structure and practice of national socialism, 1933–1944*. New York: Oxford University Press. There is a substantial literature discussing Neumann's argument and its place in his career, with the most notable recent addition being D. Kettler and T. Wheatland (2019). *Learning from Franz L. Neumann: law, theory and the Brute facts of political life*. London: Anthem Press.

5 Pollock was not the only advocate of the model of "state capitalism," which had also been developed by Rudolf Hilferding, Ante Ciliga and other anti-Soviet Marxists, but his version had the greatest impact in the development of Critical Theory. For an account of the initial controversy and ultimate success of the theory in mainstream Frankfurt School thinking, see M. Gangl (2016). The controversy over Friedrich Pollock's state capitalism. *History of the Human Sciences*, 29(2). This special issue is devoted to "The Frankfurt School: Philosophy and (political) economy".

6 See, for example, W. Bonefeld (2014). *Critical theory and the critique of political economy: on subversion and negative reason*. London: Bloomsbury; C.A. Prusik (2020). *Adorno and neoliberalism: the critique of exchange society*. London: Bloomsbury; J.F. Dorahy (2021). Habermas and political economy. *Philosophy and Social Criticism*, 47(6).

7 Robin Maialeh (2020). *Dynamic models of inequality: the role of the market mechanism in economic distribution*. Cham, Switzerland: Springer.

# Introduction

It is rare that critical theory and economics are studied side-by-side in the same research publication. In the eyes of economists, philosophy is often perceived, however mistakenly, as speculative metaphysics and unprovable poetry. Philosophers, on the other hand, often use the term "economics" pejoratively when describing a narrow-minded reason or an issue based on "merchant logic". Critical theory is so close to economics and yet so distant for economists. And conversely, economics, which is from numerous perspectives seen as the antithesis of critical theory, may represent the missing element in the mosaic of truly critical research. This book attempts to present critical theory and economics as complementary subjects that act to enrich each other, and to provide new perspectives on selected aspects of the subject matter of these two disciplines without lapsing into a form of artificial theoretical "cross-fertilisation". Since this is one of the few attempts to date to create a mutual platform for critical theory and economics, it necessarily implies a more general than a detailed approach. Thus, compromises were required in order to allow for these two disciplines to communicate with each other. Hence, the level of abstraction and the depth of thought that is usually attributed to critical theory has, to a certain extent, been restricted while, conversely, these aspects of economics have been assigned elevated prominence. Therefore, I kindly ask readers from the field of critical theory to accept a certain degree of "shallowness" in terms of the approach to communication with economics; a field that would otherwise remain impenetrable for critical theory. Conversely, I also ask readers from the field of economics to relax their requirements concerning formal accuracy, and to accept the "essayistic" approach and "aphoristic" style as both a potential source of knowledge of the real world and a means of communicating with critical theory.

The major difference between these two disciplines is that economics has often been fetishised as the highest order of reality – the ultimate source of everything, the further questioning of which is prohibited. The book concentrates on providing an inspection of the fundamental aspects of socioeconomic reproduction, which manifests itself in the form of self-propelling economic forces, and its consequences for inequality. These forces closely follow the behaviour of the agents involved, and are seen as both external forces that are independent

DOI: 10.4324/9780429273841-1

of the agent's will and the manifestation of the aggregate conscious actions of individual agents. While social scientists have already contributed substantially to their demystification, this book aims to elaborate these forces beyond the traditional explicative concepts of fetishism and reification. The understanding of the principles proposed herein incorporates new contextual nuances that are pushed to a point from which these subjective research attributes metamorphose into a new, specific definition of the subject under research. In particular, the book accentuates the role of the essential elements of socioeconomic self-production, and, inspired by the dialectical legacy, it strives to reveal the essence of the production process in its inner antagonistic form.

Despite the diversity of studies on critical theory, I considered sources that corresponded principally to the emancipatory objectives related to the sphere of the "economy", including returning to the theoretical roots that led to the critique of the core questions of contemporary economics. In other words, the book revives and elaborates upon the materialist origins of critical theory and implicitly raises the question of a return to the primacy of the economy. Therefore, rather than the collection of knowledge on critical theory presented in the book being a random collection of thought, it has been carefully selected with a view to targeting the fundamental questions of contemporary economics. The critique of positivism, instrumental reason and the consequences of inequality forms the core of my approach. Economic inequality is thus seen not as an epiphenomenon of the production process, as is common in contemporary economic research, but as the immanent element of modern economic relationships and social contradictions.

How should economics be addressed by critical theorists? How can economists be inspired by critical theory? And, more specifically, how is critical theory able to contribute towards explaining economic inequality? In order to answer these questions, the book was divided into five chapters. Chapter 1 introduces critical theory. Following a brief outline of the history of critical theory, I present the fundamental theses of the thinking of critical theory. The aim is to remind the reader of its intellectual origins and to demonstrate the ambivalent attitude towards metaphysical categories such as materialism and idealism, as well as towards the more politically defined Marxism. It demonstrates the insufficiency of specialised sciences and mere interdisciplinarity, which are unable to overcome the limits of individual scientific branches. Critical theory combines a philosophical focus on the essential and universal with the expert insights of the specialised sciences. The aim is to attain a state in which scientific methods are applied to serious scientific problems with a universal significance as opposed to the posing of frivolous questions on fragments of our immediate and banal existence, which is frequently examined through scientific methods in economics.

Chapter 2 presents the main inspiration for modern economics, which served to reshape the foundations of the classical period. It introduces general relationships based on the marginalist framework and clarifies certain fundamental economic categories such as utility, price formation, competition and exchange. Despite the numerous theoretical approaches to these categories, I present those that formed the foundations for the economic analytical apparatus that are intended to capture the principles of human behaviour, as well as the basis of modern economic thought with respect to the rules of distribution. Economics as a logical science with a strong deductive methodology assumes these patterns and infers claims concerning how scarce resources *should* be distributed. Moreover, this chapter considers the hidden distributive normativity of mainstream economics in tandem with other aspects such as innate abilities and obtained competencies, and, from a different perspective, the chapter investigates the linkages between wants, needs and preferences aimed at examining the type of distribution that is designated by competitive markets. The final part of this chapter addresses the behavioural critique of neoclassical economics. It is argued that due to the nature of scientific investigation in the social sciences, the behavioural approach makes only a limited contribution to the epistemology of economics. The importance of this chapter relates to the fact that not only mainstream economics but also the mainstream critique of mainstream economics is faced with significant challenges in terms of gathering knowledge and explaining various economic phenomena.

Chapter 3 is dominated by the dialectical focus of critical theory. The chapter provides a critique of positivism as the main methodological background for contemporary economics. Questions are raised concerning whether the scientised positivist approach, accompanied by the division of scientific labour, is reliable in terms of examining objective reality as are questions on the impossibility of the valuelessness of positivism, the selectivity and impossibility of gathering empirical findings and, finally, the advantages of positivism in terms of demystifying "medieval obscurantism". Dialectics is meant to deal with most of these deficiencies. The truth of an object upon inspection, according to dialectical-critical theorists, relies on the systemic context and processual nature of social reality. It is meant to overcome mere inductive-statistical and formally deductive modes of inquiry in order to reach beyond the mere appearance and separateness of social phenomena and to ascertain their essence through a genetically dynamic conception of totality.

Chapter 4 addresses the question of which types of reasoning are connected to the modern subject. It focuses mainly on the role of instrumental reason that embodies rationality, as adopted in economics. At the same time, instrumental rationality comprised one of the main objects of criticism for the first generation of critical theorists, which stemmed from the ontologised positivism that lies behind scientised and value-neutral research in the social sciences. Subjective rationality, which is of an instrumental nature, is then reduced to a permanent struggle for self-preservation, which then becomes the sole, universally shared goal in the competitive market societies and the driver of the reproduction of the socioeconomic system as such. This serves to harm the formation of individual subjectivity and genuinely free human behaviour. Conversely, critical theory is meant to elucidate the pre-formation of the subject's consciousness and to contribute to truly emancipatory behaviour.

Chapter 5 commences, once more, with the role of positivism. Questions are raised as to why and how positivist analytical constructions, despite the extensive criticism thereof, could be helpful for dialectical analysis. It is discussed whether the methodological confrontation between critical theory and economics can help to uncover the abstract structurally genetic patterns behind the law of socioeconomic motion. Since social theory as asserted by the Frankfurt scholars concerned the transcending of the abstract antithesis between totalistic philosophy and the analytic empirical research, the objective is to prepare the ground for a theory that exceeds the two methodological pillars of "truth" in modern economics – empirical falsification and simplifying rationalism. I further consider general economic categories such as production, economic distribution, exchange and consumption in the context of abstract categories such as freedom and responsibility and their transcending power over individual agents. The final part of the book outlines how unequal distribution is immanent to the interaction of agents as governed by markets. This permanent drive towards inequality is explained via systemic forces and their dialectical interconnection with the supposedly free behaviour of agents. The representative agent orientation of this book, as inspired by traditional economic methodology, circumvents the approach of critical theory (or the generally Marxian approach) to questions of the class society and its exploitative nature. Since the question of class is, today, so fragmented, I provide a perspective in which socioeconomic inequalities, rather than being embedded in class relationships, are immanent to the abstract principles and the functioning of markets even before one considers the class analysis perspective.

It is also worth providing a few remarks on the terminology used in the book. In those places where the context requires distinguishing between different economic schools of thought, I refer mostly to "neoclassical" economics, the assumptions, methods and themes of which constitute the foundations for "mainstream" economics, which is the term I use to embrace conventional approaches in economics and, especially, with concern to the academic environment. In order to grasp the more general aspects of economics, including their historical background, I use the term "contemporary" economics, which encompasses the dominating tendencies in economics over the past hundred years or more since its separation from the political economy. Nevertheless, despite the slight contextual differences, the terms can be used, in view of their partly synonymous nature and semantic overlaps, almost interchangeably. Finally, I use *femininum*, *maskulinum* and *neutrum* either according to the original author or according to the contextual suitability, but always with the genuine intention of applying an approach that is dignified and which fully respects the principles of equality.

# 1 Prolegomena to Critical Theory

## The History of Critical Theory

Although this book does not intend to provide a detailed examination of the term "critical theory", partly in an attempt to avoid the accusation of alibism, it was thought that the clarification of the meaning of critical theory in this publication would be useful to the reader. Firstly, the etymology of the word "critical" originates from the Ancient Greek word "*krinein*" (κρίνειν), which means "to separate" or to "distinguish between two or more things". Critical theory is, therefore, understood as a perspective from which notions such as being and appearance, essence and phenomenon, general and specific, and constant and variable must be distinguished. Conversely, it refers to an intellectual perspective from which already separated notions such as subject and object should be understood as mutually interlaced. Of what critical theory is critical is not a legitimate consideration – no commonly shared view exists on what the subject of critique should be and the methods that should be employed when examining the subject. Critical theory, therefore, differs from previous critical philosophies. It goes beyond both the Cartesian and Kantian "critique" and endeavours to overcome their insufficiencies. Concerning this publication, the intention, among others, is to critically examine the Cartesian "enlightened" *cogito* as one of the methodological fundaments in economic theory. Critical theory, as it is understood in this book, does not differ from the normal perception of critical theory in its broader sense, that is, as a thought flow(s) originating from the political philosophy and sociology of the Frankfurt School. The difference lies, however, in terms of the context to which critical theory is applied since its combination with economics is relatively rare. As a result, the rejection of false rationalism by critical theory serves as an intellectual tool for scepticism towards fetishised rationalism and dogmatism in economics. For Kant, the activity of critique was applied to relating the perception of objects in the mind (phenomena) and our rational, conceptual grasp of those objects (noumena). Marx, too, saw critique as relating the isolated phenomena of the material-economic world (commodities) with various aspects of the systems of production (those structured by capital) from which they were constituted, as well as with the community that produced them. And Freud adopted a similar

DOI: 10.4324/9780429273841-2

approach in order to peer beneath apparent forms of human behaviour and the underlying rational structures of the unconscious that produced them. Based on the theoretical foundations of these and other critical thinkers, critical theory develops its critique in order to unmask what appears to us and to explore the rational structures that grant us rational access to the world.

The difficulties associated with mapping and fundamentally grasping critical theory[1] are enormous. It is widely considered to be the most difficult school of thought to understand (e.g. Nichols and Allen-Brown 1997) with its combination of the demanding continental philosophies of Hegel, Marx and Kant (Smith 1993). In narrow terms, critical theory is equivalent to the Frankfurt School – the school of thought established by Carl Grünberg (1861–1940) and founded upon the *Institut für Sozialforschung* at the Johann Wolfgang Goethe-Universität in Frankfurt am Main in the early 1920s. Compared to its more orthodox contemporaries, the Institute began to include the broader dimension of critical social research under the leadership of Max Horkheimer (1895–1973) as early as in the early 1930s. Grünberg's era, characterised principally by empirical-historical studies, was replaced by Horkheimer's vision of a materialist supra-disciplinary social theory which differed from eastern Marxism to a greater extent than it did during Grünberg's era. This shift represented a salient moment for critical theory since it diverted the research focus of the Institute away from somewhat orthodox, scientific Marxism (Jay 1973) to new perspectives on critical social research, a direction that continues up to the present time – for instance, Honneth's theory of recognition involves a return to the idealism of Mead and Dewey. When dealing with domination, Honneth (e.g. 1995) appeals for a move away from the Marxian foundations followed by the first generation, to focus on social phenomena independently of economic logic. Some of the most prominent figures around Max Horkheimer included, in particular, Theodor Adorno (1903–1969), Herbert Marcuse (1898–1979), Walter Benjamin (1892–1940), Friedrich Pollock (1894–1970), Leo Löwenthal (1900–1993) and Erich Fromm (1900–1980). Most of the Institute's scholars managed to emigrate when the Nazis came to power in 1933 followed by their occupation of the Institute (Löwenthal 1981; Jay 1973). In 1934, an arrangement was made to re-establish the Institute of Social Research at Columbia University in New York. Although the Institute's members became dispersed during the war period, especially the leading figures of Horkheimer and Adorno, whose insights were eternalised in their magnum opus *Dialectics of Enlightenment*, they still managed to sketch out new perspectives on various branches of the humanities, social sciences and social research.

Some of the scholars of the former Institute returned to Germany after the war. Interestingly, the scholars who remained in exile, especially Erich Fromm and Herbert Marcuse (and, to a lesser extent, Leo Löwenthal), partly due to an upswing in interest in the psycho-analytical field at the time, enjoyed even greater worldwide attention in the following decades than did their fellows in Frankfurt. The second generation of critical theory was led by Jürgen Habermas, with Axel Honneth subsequently succeeding him as the leading figure of the third, current, generation of the Frankfurt School. It is notable that critical theorists are no longer exclusively concentrated around the Institute in Frankfurt; indeed, the legacy of the early Frankfurt School was adopted by many scholars globally, with reputable departments on every continent and in diverse academic fields continuing to fulfil the vision of the Institute's founders of the interwar period by conducting powerful critical social research.

In the broader sense, critical theory is also understood as an umbrella term for various kinds of radical philosophy. This definition views critical theory as constituting a variety of differing positions for which it is difficult to define a single critical theory (Piccone 1980). This approach comprises authors who, at least to a certain extent, adopted the general views of the founders of the Frankfurt School. Löwenthal (1981) himself, as one such author, supposedly had to rely on Jay's research in order to assess the main characteristics of the school, finally concluding that critical theory is nothing more than a collective denominator.

Pearson aptly portrayed the Frankfurt School as "a tendency in contemporary social thought which everyone 'knows' and nobody reads" (1974, p. 111). Connerton (1976) and Antonio (1983) concluded that critical theory resists any attempts to provide a brief summary. The latter claimed that it is difficult to characterise critical theory via a particular set of methodological techniques and theoretical propositions. Despite this uneasiness, theoreticians have continued to attempt to identify a common denominator, as already indicated by the example of Löwenthal. Antonio (1983) further points out that critical theory can be defined on the basis of meta-assumptions that derive from Hegel's dialectics and Marx's materialist critique, which stress the immanent principles of contradiction, change and movement, and which oppose the formal and static nature of Kantianism. Löwenthal (1981) argues that the aim of critical theory is to criticise and refashion Marxian theory in the light of changed historical situations. Geuss describes the Frankfurt School as "a reflective theory which gives agents a kind of knowledge inherently productive of enlightenment and emancipation" (1981, p. 2). The idea of Enlightenment plays the crucial role in critical theory – it inspires the utilisation of reason to free humans from their objectified position within unwitting conditions and to make them subjects of social processes.

Horkheimer suggests that critical theory is not a "storehouse of hypotheses" but rather that it "constructs a developing picture of society" (1972 [1937], p. 239) that deals, according to Antonio (1983, p. 331), with "the prevailing system of domination, expresses its contradictions, assesses its potential for emancipatory change, and criticises the system in order to promote that change". Horkheimer adds that critical theory is a part of the development of the society and its critical standpoint – the idea of the reasonable organisation of society that will meet the needs of the whole community – is immanent in human work. Thompson adopts a similar approach by not presenting critical theory as a set of a priori values and ideals in the social sphere, but as a school of thought that unravels the contradictions that already exist within society – a school that makes "evident an emancipatory insight into the very fabric of what we take as given, as basic to our social world" (2017, p. 3).

Fuchs (2016) accentuates the system of domination as the main normative concern. Critical theory aims for a domination-free society through a dialectical critique in the tradition of Kantian enlightenment, refined by the Marxian requirement for abolishing all forms of slavery and degradation. An inclination towards the Marxian tradition suggests that the general Kantian approach to science and enlightenment as comprising critical and liberating categories is insufficient or even misleading – that a significant part of science is far from being critical; that it also plays administrative and legitimising roles that serve to maintain the functioning of the system of domination. As regards the level of content, Fuchs defines six dimensions. The first concerns epistemological questions of how knowledge and theoretical concepts are constituted. These questions are answered by critical theorists through dialectical reason. The next three dimensions are ontological. Critical theorists focus on three fields of critique aimed at determining how reality is organised: political economy, domination and exploitation, and ideology. The last two dimensions are praxeological and relate to critical ethics and struggles in political practice.

A negative delimitation, typical for critical theorists, relies on the fact that critical theory "has no specific influence on its side, except concern for the abolition of social injustice". In abstract terms, critical theory represents "the materialist content of the idealist concept of reason" (Horkheimer 1972 [1937], pp. 213, 229). Piccone (1980) identifies a single shared fundamental objective: to come to terms with new emerging forms of organised capitalism and to reconstitute the project of human emancipation. Howard (1974) defines critical theory in a similar way to Horkheimer, that is, as an approach to understanding the social world, which concerns emancipatory action. Antonio summarises that critical theory focuses on contradictions between ideology and reality. His explanation states that ideology portrays "a false unity of the ideal and real", where the greater the distortion, the deeper are the contradictions it reflects and the higher the sensitivity of the system to criticism (1983, p. 331). The role of ideology is crucial for Antonio: "the immanent critique points at the social structure from the perspective of its own legitimations by criticising ideology from the perspective of history" and "contrasting emancipatory aspects of ideological claims with social reality". The aim is to "turn legitimations against their context, transforming them into weapons against false consciousness" (1983, p. 338). Critical theory thus contributes to the subjective dimension of emancipation by clarifying historically based immanent emancipatory goals, and it demystifies reification that opposes free human action (1983, pp. 331–332). Briefly, critical theory should elucidate the pre-formation of the consciousness of the subject. This feature of critical theory embodies one of the main motives thereof that relates to class consciousness and the legacy of one of its most important inspirators György Lukács – specifically to determine why the working class has not yet been transformed into the revolutionary class; a class that is aware of its historical role ("*der Klasse für sich*"). Such questions were behind the influential infusion of Freudian psychoanalysis into the traditional Marxian framework, which has become one of the trademarks of critical theory.

To continue with this general specification, Keucheyan (2014) posits that critical theories[2] challenge the existing social order from a higher perspective since they do not concern any particular aspects of the order such as the composition of the tax system or pension reforms. Hrubec (2013), when mapping a history of critical theory, underlines that it concerns long-term trends in society; Pullmann (2013) adds that it reveals the universal grammar of human action. That is not to say that critical theory neglects particular phenomena, but rather that it treats them in terms of their interrelatedness to the Outside.

Kellner (1975) sees the roots of the Frankfurt School in the Marxist critique of the political economy and the historical dialectic aimed at revolutionary change. Critical theory undoubtedly follows up on the Marxian "categoric imperative" so as to dispense with all those conditions that serve to debase and enslave man (Marx 1994 [1844]). Translated into political terms, through the demonstration of the potential of society, it strives for radical liberation that goes beyond mere political democracy. Kellner further clarifies that critical theory[3] is based on the Hegelian-Marxist dialectic and historical materialism. His position emphasises the Marxist thrust of critical theory through which he questions Jay's "underestimation" of the Marxist legacy. However, it is worth remarking that Jay presented justifiable reasons for diminishing the view of critical theory as based solely on Marxian foundations. For instance, Horkheimer (1972 [1937]), based on his conviction that the general intellectual level of the great masses is rapidly declining, opposes the idea of the orthodox view of the proletariat, which is, he claims, no guarantee of true knowledge. This position was also shared by the most prominent critical theorist of the second generation, Habermas (1981), who does not describe any collective agent of emancipation that might constitute new normative structures. It is possible to list several other examples that diminish the role of orthodox Marxism in critical theory, for example, as proposed by thinkers from the former Eastern bloc. Despite their often adopting (or being forced to adopt) a perverted soviet form of Marxian thought, they demonstrate how far critical theory is from dominant (at that time) Marxian theorising. One might recall for instance Czechoslovakia, where the Frankfurt School was labelled as a "bourgeois socio-philosophic school" (Javůrek et al. 1976) or, later, as the "Frankfurt caricature of 'Marxism'" that strives for "would-be Marxist dialectics" (Zelený 1982, p. 126). Others included, for example, Rainko (1976), von Heiseler (1970) and Steigerwald (1969). It is suggested that the greatest difference between the standpoints of orthodox Marxism and critical theory comprises the role of class, since most critical theorists do not reduce humans to mere class individuals, as was often the case of their (pro-)soviet Marxist contemporaries.

Moreover, Horkheimer (2018 [1931]), in his inaugural address, distances his vision of the Institute's social research from crude Marxian materialism. Under his leadership, the role of the Institute was not, despite its obvious materialist background (as will be expanded upon later), to firmly subscribe to a specific metaphysical category such as materialism or idealism when addressing social issues. Such monism was perceived as philosophical reductionism, which was rejected as "bad Spinozaism". Since the illusion that everything originates from the "Idea" is a misunderstanding on the part of Hegel, and the consideration of pure material conditions as the only source of being is a misunderstanding on the part of Marx, such naïve absolutes can only be overcome through dialectical reasoning. Dubiel (1985) notes that critical theorists redirect terms such as "materialism" and the "economic theory of society" towards their own understanding of Marxian theory. Such an understanding primarily distances itself from various vulgar forms of determinism, economism and mechanical materialism for which economic activity is the sole determining factor, as previously criticised by Marx and Engels in *The Holy Family*. Nevertheless, the clash between these two absolutes – idealism and materialism – is highly imbalanced for critical theorists. Critical theory openly inclines towards a form of materialistic view that was not sufficiently expanded upon prior to the existence of critical theory. According to Kellner (1990), the materialist foundations of critical theory, free from the mechanistic metaphysics and positivist forms of materialism, lead to materialism in terms of material conditions, human needs and the struggle against oppression. Taken from the non-dogmatic perspective, the materialism of critical theory takes different forms depending on the context. Following Horkheimer's *Materialism and Metaphysics* (1972 [1937]), one observes hostility to the totalising of metaphysical systems as a source of knowledge. As demonstrated via the example of religious faith, the criticism of such dogma may play a decisive role at a particular time and place, while under differing circumstances, it is unimportant for the complex of materialist views. Both theoretical and practical activity must reflect ever-changing reality so that theories and concepts change to reflect changing historical conditions; they should not be presented as stand-alone and absolute sources of knowledge.[4]

In summary, critical theory simply aims to refine the relationship between the base and the superstructure in terms of their dialectical interconnections. It is also important to note that the former division between the base and the superstructure is considered to be reductionist in itself, which is one of the reasons that the dialectical totality is intended to overcome the strict division between these two spheres. As underlined by Postone (2006), theorists of the Frankfurt School viewed the various economic, social, political, legal and cultural dimensions as interrelated. The new perspectives raised by the first generation adopted a more philosophical, non-dogmatic approach that was open to diverse intellectual currents (Jay 1973). Critical theory thus opens up a new narrative horizon involving the radical liberation of humankind, which opposes both dogmatic Marxian views and the views of modern pro-capitalists. On the other hand, since they are in opposition to the bourgeois approaches characterised by the fragmentation of the sciences, they fail to grasp the critique of the political economy from a truly economistic (and, thus, reductionist) perspective and, thus, the critique does not allow for the challenging of economic questions by those same economic theoretical tools and concepts.

Nevertheless, neither critical theory nor any other school of thought can exist without internal tensions. Although critical theorists generally agree on the establishment of supra-disciplinary research and on deriving knowledge from various fields of philosophy and the social sciences with the aim of the radical emancipation of human beings, different scholars assign differing degrees of emphasis to different disciplines. Concerning the two main theoretical strands of the first generation, while scholars close to Horkheimer tended to see the social sciences as the main source of knowledge on society, scholars who adhered to the Adornian and Benjaminian lines of thought favoured philosophy and culture. From today's perspective, it can be concluded that the cultural aspect prevails over more scientific approaches. However, in this respect, it is important to recall that economic deprivation among the masses was not a major consideration in the West during the three "golden" decades following the end of the Second World War, during which critical theory experienced its greatest boom. At this time, economic wellbeing in the United States and Western Europe reached relatively high levels. However, on the other hand, one should bear in mind that this was the period in which, for example, African Americans did not fully enjoy the right to vote and in which homosexuality was diagnosed as a mental illness and homosexuals were banned from public office (see e.g. Eisenhower's Executive Order 10450). The struggle for liberation at this time thus naturally inclined towards these political questions and their cultural manifestations. Today, perhaps more than ever, it is important to reflect that the misfortune and social exclusion of the masses in the West are principally of a historical-material nature. In order to determine the core of current "non-freedoms", one should rather focus on various types of laws; that is, reconsider the all-embracing economic laws that affect humans via their general characterisation as the prime determinant of both momentary success and failure and a general precondition for human liberation.

## Critical and Traditional Theory

This subchapter considers critical theory as distinct from more traditional theoretical viewpoints, and further expands upon the critical approach. Before embarking on a definition of the distinction between the two approaches, it was thought appropriate to briefly introduce the concept of "critique" as viewed by critical theory. Following Thompson (2017), critique is understood as an approach to relating subject and object. Inspired by Hegel's *Phenomenology of Spirit*, it acknowledges that the subject undergoes transformation as the result of possessing a deepened knowledge of the object. Such knowledge is, however, constituted through the being of the object itself, as well as through subjective factors that serve to mediate the knowledge of the object. Critical theory, therefore, aims to unmask the conditions under which the subject relates to the object and *vice versa*. As will be seen later, a further aspect of critique refers to not merely understanding the object but also transforming the nature of the subject in the real world in a liberating way; to transform the Whole to its greater end.

Perhaps not surprisingly, critique as a method of producing knowledge is considered to be superior to other scientific methods, for which Thompson (2017) summarises three distinct reasons: Firstly, the critical account is more comprehensive in the sense that it is "able to grasp the systemic, dynamic features of reality as well as their internal and external relations with other aspects of the social totality in order to derive knowledge of the essential processes that constitute reality". Secondly, it overcomes the conflict between facts and values, in place of which it provides "an epistemic framework that would synthesise cognitive and evaluative claims about the social world". And, thirdly, knowledge, as the product of applied critique, is not intended to be merely accumulated; rather, it should be evaluated based on its transformative capacity. The aim is "the transformation not only of the vantage point of the subject", but also the "metamorphosis of the subject from a passive, contemplative analyst to an active, rational agent in the world".[5] The basic pillars of the critical method are thus as follows: Firstly, the nature of reality is dynamic and processual rather than static and discrete. Further, factual and normative (or evaluative) knowledge claims are unified. And, lastly, the critical method problematises the relationship between essence and appearance in the understanding of social reality (2017, pp. 231–232). As we will see, all these aspects play an important role in the investigation of contemporary economics.

Max Horkheimer most aptly defined the direction of early critical theory. In his inaugural address as the managing director of the Institute, delivered on January 24, 1931 and entitled "The State of Social Philosophy and the Tasks of an Institute for Social Research" (Bronner and Kellner 1989, pp. 25–36), Horkheimer urges an approach to the fate of human beings in terms of the entire material and spiritual culture of humanity. In line with Horkheimer's attempt to synthetise the social sciences and philosophy, humans are not seen as mere individuals, but as a part of a community with all the accompanying determining aspects such as the state, the legal system and the economy. In terms of the sociological context, this contradicts the positivist traditions of Comte and Durkheim who rejected any reference to the importance of philosophy in social theory due to its uncontrollability and general inability to be subjected to scientific procedures such as experimental investigation and verification/falsification. Horkheimer, conversely, strives for a dialectical mutuality between philosophy and the praxis of individual disciplines in social theory.

Separated social sciences neglect the general structure and organisation of society as a whole and are limited to particular viewpoints on social experience. The division of academic labour leads to epistemological and metaphysical problems in terms of neglecting the interconnectedness of phenomena in the world (Kellner 1990). Critical theory attempts to overcome the deficiencies of the division of academic disciplines via exceeding their established disciplinary boundaries and providing new discourses. In his essay *Materialism and Metaphysics* (1972 [1937]), Horkheimer rejects both of these concepts of science. His objection is that both of these concepts posit the invariability of natural laws, which renders them unhistorical. Despite positivism and materialism sharing the same view that reality is knowable through the senses, the materialism of critical theory also claims that the sense experience is mediated through concepts, which are naturally subject to change depending on the social, economic and political conditions. The pure division of cognition and the senses is dismissed: the materialism of critical theory not only claims that objective material conditions form our thoughts and knowledge but also acknowledges that cognition and theory may determine our perception of the objective world. Naturally, it is possible to dispute the meaning of "objectivity". Gramsci, another great inspirator for critical theorists, mentions in this respect that the objective always relates to humans, so that the objective can also be understood as the "universal subjective", that is, as something "real for the whole human race *historically* unified in a single unitary cultural system" (2003, 445). In any case, the dialectical interweaving outlined earlier positions itself against the two absolutes and ensures that the results are context-dependent.

The beginnings of critical theory are known for combining philosophical inclinations towards the universal and the essential, with expert insights into the immediate world provided by individual disciplines. The aim is to apply the most advanced scientific methods while aiming to address the great philosophical questions. This arrangement enables specialised scientific fields not to lose sight of the universal; moreover, philosophy also refines its questions with regard to current social praxis. The supra-disciplinary approach of critical theory is, thus, anchored in the inability to grasp the whole by specialised scientific disciplines and in the insufficiency of traditional philosophical schools to utilise the knowledge provided by a fragmented social existence. This means that interdisciplinarity alone is insufficient since it fails to confront the alleged self-sufficiency of individual disciplines. This feature was specifically described by Adorno (2000 [1968]) thus:

> What I have in mind here might perhaps be expressed in terms of the following thesis: the strict moats dug between the differentiated scientific disciplines cause the intrinsic interest of these disciplines to disappear; and this interest cannot be restored by retrospective cooperation or integration – for example, by mutually explaining findings or discovering formal agreements between the structures identified, say, by sociology and economics. This is simply because something secondary, assembled after the event from factors (as they're called), is made to appear as what is decisive and concrete; and the purpose of science, ultimately – as the positivists in particular ought to admit – is to engage with social concreteness, and not to gratify itself with schematic classifications.

The clearest distinction between the traditional and critical approaches to theorising is provided in Horkheimer's famous essay "Traditional and Critical Theory". Moreover, the essay also poses fundamental economic questions which are of importance for the purposes of this book. Typically, Horkheimer begins by clarifying his own position through opposing other positions. Kantian social philosophy is inadequate since it is based on individual faculties and experiences. Hegelian social philosophy is criticised for its fixation on the status quo. Similarly, more recent phenomenological and existential philosophies are attacked for their speculative metaphysics and their adoration of higher transcendental dimensions over the real world. And, most notably, positivism is rejected for its dependence on isolated facts and methodological presuppositions. Postone refers to this essay as "the immanent dialectical critique" (2006, p. 183). The discussion is expanded by questioning the very nature of theory. Horkheimer discusses the sum-total of inter-linked propositions on a subject, which then allows for the derivation of the rest: "The general goal of all theory is a universal systematic science, not limited to any particular subject matter but embracing all possible objects" (1972 [1937], pp. 188–189). Theoreticians are thus expected to present their results in accordance with their theoretical concept. This requires the integration of facts into conceptual frameworks, subsequently confirmed by experiments in such a way that they fit into the theory as currently accepted. The scientist's task is to provide an explanation for a subject in the respective specialist discipline in as much detail as possible via the synthesis and analysis of masses of data. The critical point thus concerns the dualism of thought and being, understanding and perception, all of which constitute the "second nature" to the scientist. Traditional theory thus speaks not of what theory means in human life, but only of what it means in the isolated sphere in which it comes into existence. While the division of labour favours such isolation, this does not mean that scientific branches actually become self-sufficient and independent: "They are particular instances . . ., moments in the social process of production" (Horkheimer 1972 [1937], p. 197).

One could be forgiven for being curious about the hostility of critical theory to the description or traditional theorising of specialised sciences that celebrated enormous success over the past century. Critical theory begins with the simple exchange of commodities and then defines the idea with the help of universal concepts. It moves further by using knowledge from the research of all the relevant specialised areas. Here, the political economy in its very broad sense plays the key role since; in combination with critical theory, it is tasked with exposing how an exchange economy, given the changing conditions of humankind, must necessarily lead to the exacerbation of social tensions. The basic form of the commodity economy contains, per se, both internal and external tensions, while the commodity exchange process generates such tensions in an increasingly heightened form. This progressively regressive process then experiences periods of the development in terms of human powers, individual emancipation and the enormous extension of human control over nature; however, it also drives "humanity into a new barbarism" (Horkheimer 1972 [1937], p. 227).

When critical thinkers speak about theory, they bear in mind that theory presupposes the reproduction of life: "Its element is freedom, its theme oppression". The language of theory, by definition, thus can be neither neutral nor practical. Insisting on the positive aspects without considering the negative whole creates its opposite: violence (Adorno and Horkheimer 2002 [1944]).

Horkheimer subsequently concludes that "[t]he special sciences, and especially contemporary political economics, are unable to derive practical profit from the fragmentary questions they discuss" (1972 [1937], p. 228). This incapacity derives from their specific role in relation to reality. Both types of theoretical structures, critical and specialised, derive their statements on real relationships from basic universal concepts, where the relationships are taken as necessary, and both are alike when it comes to logical necessity. The difference arises when one turns from the logical to the real necessity involved in a factual sequence. Natural scientists are able to prove various causal effects, for example, that certain processes in an organism lead to its destruction. However, this fails to address the question as to whether there are any influences that may act to alter the causal character of such processes or change them in their totality.

Hence, the isolationism of traditional theory is the crucial point of critique for critical theorists. The aim of critical thinking (activity) is not, either in its conscious intention or in its objective significance, to improve any of the elements in the structure; a structure which appears to be "an unchangeable force of nature, a fate beyond man's control"; a structure which only confirms its own rationality (Horkheimer 1972 [1937], p. 204). For Horkheimer, critical thinking is, in contrast, motivated towards transcending and eliminating the opposition between an individual's spontaneity, purposefulness and rationality and those basic principles and relationships upon which society is built. Critical thinking is in opposition to being a function of the isolated individual or the sum-total of individuals; rather, it captures the individual in his/her real, particularly conflicting, web of relationships with others, with social totality[6] and with nature. Categories such as value and profit comprise elements in a conceptual whole where the meaning of the whole is to be sought not in the descriptive preservation practiced by traditional theories, but in its critical transformation into the right kind of society. Traditional theory is thus explanatory and descriptively oriented, whereas critical theory is emancipatory. This is closely related to the resignation of economics with concern to emancipatory ends and the descriptive approach adopted in recent years.

Postone (2006) maintains that *Traditional and Critical Theory* continues to ground critical theory in the contradictory character of capitalist society. Traditional theory assumes the essential immutability of the relationship between subject, object and theory, which results in the inability to think within the unity of theory and practice. Consequently, capitalist society is characterised by blind mechanical necessity, which diverts human powers from the general good. In contrast to traditional theory, the dialectical character of critical theory grasps the intrinsic interrelatedness of subject and object. According to Hrubec (2011), critical theory thus opposes an affirmation to reality, particularly underlined by Adorno (2005 [1951]), with the aim of true cognition, which derives from the detachment of phenomena and the essence or being and appearance.

Horkheimer highlights the fact that the isolated consideration of particular activities requires an accompanying awareness of its limitations concerning its validity. Contemporary economics is partly aware of its theoretical limits. While new branches of economics have validated their theoretical achievements, they have done so almost exclusively via the application of empirical methods. This is the case of both behavioural and experimental economics, whose aims are to confront established economic theories with new data. However, the subchapter on the critique of positivism will demonstrate that this empiricist approach may do more harm than good. A certain awareness of knowledge relativity in terms of the relationship between theoretical thought and facts is not enough to "bring the concept of theory to a new stage of development". The missing element here concerns the radical reconsideration of the knowing individual as such (Horkheimer 1972 [1937], pp. 198–199), especially in contemporary economics. The following subchapter serves to explain the importance of critical theory to the field of economics.

## Critical Theory and Economics

Critical theory has contributed to many fields of the humanities and social sciences. Undoubtedly, economics is the least developed discipline in the social sciences and humanities in terms of the consideration of critical theory. Critical theory has never developed a considerable critique of economic relations; hence, only exiguous fragments of its findings can be directly related to economic disciplines. Nevertheless, its materialistic foundations have given rise to various critical arguments, demonstrated within a number of diverse fields such as literary criticism, culture and sociology, which provide unique perspectives on a range of economic questions. The aim of this chapter is to outline these arguments and to prepare them for contextualisation within contemporary economics. Although the recent works of Pugh (2005), Rockmore (2015), Buzgalin and Kolganov (2016), Prusik (2020) and papers in the 2016 special issue on philosophy and the (political) economy of the Frankfurt School in *History of the Human Sciences 29(2)* vividly pictured a potential bridge between critical theory and the political economy, an extensive unexplored area still exists for theorising on fundamental economic questions.

In general, critical theory sees modern societies as being built upon commodity and exchange relations, which, inspired by Marx and Lukács, constitute reified structures in which humans are degraded to mere things. The capitalist mode of production gradually commodifies not only goods and services but all spheres of human life as well, and appears to be "natural" and beyond human control. Critical theory opposes this ideology of eternal "naturality" and exposes aspects of the modern social order as being both historical and changeable. Horkheimer underlines the role of economic relationships as the fundamental characteristic of this materialistic tradition. Under his leadership, scholars affiliated with the Institute were expected to study theoretical economics and economic history (Kellner 1990). In contrast to the contemporary trends in critical theory (e.g. the afore-mentioned Honneth 1995), this insistence concerns the suggestion that the "[u]derstanding of the present becomes more idealist the more it avoids the economic causes of material need and looks to a psychologically naive elaboration of so-called 'basic elements of human existence'" (1972 [1937], pp. 25–26). Obviously, this statement is in conflict with contemporary psychological trends in economics since truly critical research should also call into question the mechanisms that produce modern subjectivity; do current social institutions, structures and their processes contribute to the psychological development of human individuality?

Critical theory begins with abstract determinations. As Horkheimer writes, "it begins with the characterisation of an economy based on exchange" (1972 [1937], p. 225). When Antonio (1983, p. 325) speaks about the outcomes of critical theorists that consist of constituting "a cultural as well as [an] economic critique", he does not consider any type of developed knowledge apparatus that enables the systematic analysis of the economic order, but rather the general direction of the critique. What, therefore, is the hidden and forgotten political economy in critical theory? Due to its main philosophical, sociological and psychoanalytical orientations, critical theory does not provide a conceptual framework for the political economy (and less so for economics), and the points thereof are somewhat fragmented, obscured, indeterminate and undeveloped. Nonetheless, despite these rare connections to economics, the fragmentation and theoretical underdevelopment of the field provide new standpoints and a new critique, which is invaluable for encapsulated contemporary economics. Nevertheless, economics and critical theory may well have more in common than is evident at first sight. A study by McCloskey attempts to approximate literary criticism and economics, where economic theory is itself a "species of criticism". As with Marxism and psychoanalysis, the "bourgeois economics of the school of Adam Smith is literally a critical theory" (1989, p. 111), which might also be claimed, with respect to the conditions of the 18th and 19th centuries, for liberalism as such. Marxism is then seen as a conscious reaction to all its doctrines, and psychoanalysis as an unconscious reaction to its doctrine of conscious rationality.

Critical theorists are, via their inner struggles for human emancipation, often confronted with questions concerning the form that such an emancipated society should take. In place of general metaphysical claims such as the fulfilment of human potential or the richness of life, Adorno asserts the very elementary consideration "that no-one shall go hungry any more" (2005 [1951], p. 156). This simple but very powerful assertion encompasses two of the three main economic questions: *what* to produce; *how* to produce; and *for whom* to produce. The assertion does not encompass the question "*how*", which, due to its merely processual-practical nature, does not usually belong to the scope of critical theory. The statement also implicitly contains the normative dimension of critical theory. On the basis of Marxian "normative realism", it defines a good society via conditions that ensure that all human beings are able to survive; our judgement of the existing socioeconomic system should be based on whether it secures humane conditions as the highest priority or not. We read that instead of utilising the various technical capacities available to abolish hunger, the economic system utilises and develops these capacities for the aesthetic purposes of mass consumption (Adorno and Horkheimer 2002 [1944], p. 111). Adorno (2005 [1951]) continues that the naïve supposition of unambiguous development towards increased production is the only direction permitted by the contemporary socioeconomic system, which is integrated into a totality dominated by quantification and which is hostile to any qualitative differences. When considering an emancipated society, we must detach emancipation from this totality, which, by now, has little in common with increased production and its human reflections. In simple language, increased production, ruled by quantitative rather than qualitative aspects, does not contribute to elementary natural human needs. Rather than production forces being the deepest substratum of man, they express his adaptation to these forces. Such a society is compelled "under a confused compulsion to the conquest of strange stars" (2005 [1951], p. 156). Adorno continues that a humankind that no longer knows scarcity may soon intuit the delusory nature of the arrangements adopted to abolish scarcity; such arrangements hitherto adopted in order to escape scarcity resulted in both wealth and scarcity at the larger scale. The rich man is the realisation of the general spirit, but "on his own initiative". Such a man results from "the truly irrational predestination of a society held together by brutal economic inequality" supported by "the supreme might of the law by which society reproduces itself" (Adorno 2005 [1951], pp. 185–186). Only a very small minority are privileged "but the structural possibility suffices to preserve the illusion of equal opportunities" (2005 [1951], p. 194). Adorno adds that the powerless individual is unable to calculate his economic fate in advance; the rigidity of class-membership is forgotten. The downfall of the individual is decided by "an opaque hierarchical structure in which no-one, scarcely even those at the very top, can feel secure: an egalitarian threat" (2005 [1951], p. 194).

Unemployment, precarity and economic crises – the broad conditions of the masses – remain a threat; according to Horkheimer (1972 [1937]), this is no longer due to limited technological options, but to the circumstances of production. Modern production is not geared to the life of society as a whole, rather it is geared to the power-backed claims of individuals in line with the "look out for yourself" principle. For critical theorists, the course of history is the necessary product of an economic mechanism, which contains protests generated by the socioeconomic order itself – the idea of a self-determined human race where man's actions are no longer determined by the mechanism of a blind necessity, but – as similarly put by Adorno (2005 [1951]) – by man's own decision. While economic subjects believe that they act according to personal determination, their complicated calculations exemplify the workings of an incalculable mechanism.

The connection between the development of technology and the rapidly increasing concentration and centralisation of capital is obvious even today, which implies that the forces of production and production itself serve in the interest of domination instead of human needs. Scepticism then arises when the development of productivity enhances the potential for emancipation whilst leading to increased repression (Horkheimer 1973). A slightly more optimistic viewpoint was provided by Kalivoda (1968) for whom historical human existence, based on domination, must formulate repression in the dialectical totality with progress, brought about by repression within the conflicting organisation of society. Conflicting societies develop tools of repression that while not aimed at repressing human instincts in general are used by rulers to repress the rest in order to create better conditions for their own reconciliation with nature. Repression is, as Kalivoda puts it, only one side of the process, while the other creates enhanced conditions for the satisfaction of human needs. Another Czech author – Kosík – notes that freedom and the equality of simple exchange are "developed and realised in the production of the capitalist system as inequality and a lack of freedom" (1976, p. 32). His contribution, therefore, strives to expose a formally equal and free system – which, in the language of critical theory, hypostatises phenomenal aspects of reality and thus inevitably leads to apologetics – in the essence of its contradictions.[7]

In addition to his reputation as an aesthetician and cultural criticist, Adorno should be considered, as is frequently emphasised in this book, as someone who expanded upon the Marxian critique of the exchange society, particularly the theory of commodity fetishism. Adorno states that in times of undeveloped material production, it could be reasonably asserted that there is still not enough for all. However, these objective preconditions have changed. In the face of the immediate possibility of surplus, even the most narrow-minded bourgeois must recognise the superfluous restriction. The imperative of the master-morality – he who wants to live must seize the opportunity for himself – has become a miserable lie (2005 [1951]). By the same token, Farr (2008) explains Marcuse's Hegelian statement "This world contradicts itself" in the sense that this contradiction consists of the perpetuation of injustice and inequality. It is manifested in extreme poverty on the one hand and unbridled wealth on the other. The contradiction arises from the fact that society contains resources to overcome scarcity with the potential for liberation. But the more wealth society accumulates, the more oppressive it becomes. Marcuse's views on the eradication of poverty and the biological character of human needs have been further interpreted for instance by Hohoš (2013).

Postone (2006) demonstrates through an immanent critique that critical theory considers the basic social relations of capitalism as contradictory. He argues that its dialectical historical dynamism is intrinsic to society, and it points further "to that realisable 'ought' which is immanent to the 'is' and which serves as the standpoint of its critique". This critique is immanent and is more fundamental than that which attaches to reality over potentialities. The notion of social contradictions thus exceeds the narrow interpretation of the basis of economic crises in capitalism. In addition, social contradictions refer to the very structure of societies, a "self-generating 'non-identity' intrinsic to its structures of social relations", which are not a "stable unitary whole". Social contradictions are, therefore, a precondition of the immanent social critique itself, which allows for theoretical self-reflexivity. Postone (2006) concludes that the fundamental categories of the critique of capitalism must be expressed in its social contradictions.

Returning to Adorno, one of his lectures in his *Introduction to Sociology* (2000 [1968]) captures the general attitude to economics of the critical theorists of his time. Firstly, his thesis concerns the strict division between sociology and economics, accompanied by an effort to marginalise Marxian theory in general, which leads to the conclusion that they should be dismissed since they both fail to assert decisive social questions. By criticising the autonomisation of sociology, Adorno asserts that, restricted mainly to opinions and preferences, sociology alone disregards its raison d'être, that is, to examine the process of the self-preservation of human society. This process is held together by exchange and has no other purpose than to maintain the momentum of and guarantee – principally at the material level – social production and reproduction. According to sociology, relationships between people are free from objectified economic forms and mechanisms. However, as soon as one raises these questions, one is immediately accused of economism. As an opponent of such autonomisation, Adorno even favourably recalls one of his theoretical rivals – Max Weber – concerning his understanding of the importance of the connection between sociology and economics. Conversely, economists do not engage in domains outside the market economy that are not compatible with the mathematised and calculable phenomena of current market economy systems. This automatically excludes historical, sociological and even philosophical insights; hence, economic relationships between people are reduced to their calculable nature. In this sense, Adorno desiderates that which was once behind the term "political economy", which emphasised the decisive questions that have disappeared from both sociology and economics. To be specific, sociology has lost sight of how fundamental social processes maintain themselves, the sacrifices and threats that they employ and their various potentialities. The aim is not to incorporate the mathematised market economy into sociology. Economics, in turn, must translate economic laws back into social processes and human relationships, that is, exactly what has been systematically removed from its scope over the past century.

Critical theory relates to economic questions not only within social sciences but also within aesthetics and the cultural and art critique. Gartman (2012) refers to Bourdieu who presents a social source that inevitably and unconsciously mediates economic and political struggles and reflects them in form. Such reflections are only possible when culture is freed from practical necessities. Kosík (1976) recalls Schelling, Smetana and Dembowski for whom art was a kind of *free* human act that is not subject to outside necessity and is independent of extraneous purposes. Thus, art helps to reveal the noxious antagonisms of present-day society, particularly in the economy. For Adorno, art contributes to defining and remembering the ugliness of a given era. Art should not integrate or mitigate ugliness or reconcile it with its existence through humour that is even more offensive than the ugliness (1997 [1970]). Rather, art exposes ugliness via its form in order to denounce the creative force behind it. Via an aphorism, in which Adorno touches upon Veblen's theory of luxury, it is suggested that the promise of happiness in luxury, which is linked to the non-fungible, necessarily presupposes economic inequality and a society based on fungibility (2005 [1951]).

Despite being classified largely as a cultural theorist, Adorno's support for the political economy is evident both in his sociological theses and in his examination of the cultural aspects of society. The unique connection between the political economy and this prominent figure at the Frankfurt School was elaborated upon by Braunstein (2014), who stresses that, for Adorno, the essence of society is understood in historical and logical terms based upon exchange equivalents and not in the framework of class struggle or the principle of rule. An example of the importance of the role played by the political economy in cultural questions is provided by Bourdieu's discussion with Adorno, as summarised in a review by Gartman (2012). Both the "popular" (Bourdieu) and "mass" (Adorno) culture theories are insightful with concern to several economic aspects. Gartman suggests that both authors share the fundamental idea that the manifestation of culture in modern capitalism, including art, music and consumer goods, is "inextricably linked with the unequal structures of power and wealth". Modern society is seen as "a structure of domination founded on the unequal distribution of material resources". For both authors, economic domination structures create "a system of cultural domination that unintentionally legitimates its material inequalities" (2012, p. 41). Bourdieu and Adorno also share the idea that the defining difference between "high" and "low" cultures comprises autonomy from economic purposefulness, that is, from the force to "make money by pleasing the masses". The high "critical" culture represents the potential of freedom in a world of subjugation to material production. Gorz (1989) shares this view and continues that autonomous activities must not be motivated by exchange, but by general goals such as good, beauty and truth.

Bourdieu's theory of "popular culture" works on the assumption that the scarcity of material resources forces the working class to be concerned with acquiring the necessities of life. They internalise a set of unconscious dispositions, a "habitus", that favours function over the form of appearance. The bourgeoisie, conversely, has sufficient economic capital "to instil a habitus that conditions a taste of freedom" which reveals itself in "distance from necessity by a concern for aesthetic form or appearance" (Gartman 2012, p. 50). Taste comprises an internalised historical relation to domination that derives from a sufficiency of resources, which allows for disinterestedness in the practical value of culture. The aestheticised good distinguishes the consumer from the masses of humanity, whereas aesthetic judgements are based on disinterestedness. According to Kant's aesthetic theory, aesthetic pleasure is neither practical nor useful and is based on the subject's necessity to possess physical existence. This finally results in the inferiority of the rest since a lack of resources dictates that those who live in scarcity be concerned with the pay-off culture. Thus, such cultural superiority not only legitimates economic inequality, but claims general domination due to its superior position.

A problem arises with the reference to "hierarchical and differentiated nature" (Gartman 2012, p. 50), which appears to render some people superior. The dominant class is seen as selfless when dedicating its resources – which it owns over and above the fundamental level for survival – to cultural products that have no immediate use. The dominant class transcends the mere animal pleasures and operates above the heteronomy of nature. Culture, as a realm of autonomous and self-conscious efforts devoid of material interests and necessities, thus legitimates such inequalities by symbolically presenting them as if their unequal rewards are deserved. The former disinterestedness suddenly becomes a tool that acts to secure dominance. With this in mind, Bourdieu in his *Pascalian Meditations* introduces the term "*Realpolitik* of the universal" as a political struggle aimed at defending institutional and intellectual autonomy. He places this struggle in the context of the "unequal distribution of the social conditions of access to the universal" (2000, p. 80). Bourdieu's theory criticises the fact that social inequalities are structurally overlooked, which facilitates the monopoly of universality by those with privileged economic status. One of Bourdieu's later works opines that the state must act as the institutional protector of these interests.

Despite both Adorno and Bourdieu viewing modern society as a "structure of domination founded on the unequal distribution of material resources" (Gartman 2012, p. 41), and autonomous high culture being grasped with the hope of "potential freedom in a world of human subjection to material production" (Gartman 2012, p. 54), Bourdieu's theory does not align itself with Adorno's universalism of interclass human needs. Adorno's universalism lies in his assigning the same needs to workers and the bourgeoisie – to assert that one is a free, self-determining individual. "The repetitive and formulaic character of cultural goods, their utter standardisation, makes them more 'cosy' and predictable and capable of answering an individual's need for security and for meeting the producer's need for predictability in the market" (Witkin 2004, p. 5). Thus, homogeneous mass culture provides the illusion of the individual satisfaction of these needs. Adorno's theory argues that culture is a priori interested and provides consumers with immediate sensual pleasure and "a soporific, a superficial satisfaction for needs that prevents people from taking action to create a more just and equal society" and thus "an interested, commodified culture legitimates the status quo by accommodating the victims to the inequalities of capitalism" (Gartman 2012, p. 43). Culture is commodified and serves as a substitute for the denied needs of consumers such as individuality and freedom due to capitalist production being fixed on the maximisation of profit. This lack of individuality and freedom lead to superficial diversions and easily consumable differences. As Gartman (2012) interprets Adorno's theory, the greater economic freedom of the early bourgeoisie led its members to demand high culture that required the sustained exercise of intellectual abilities cultivated in their leisure time. In sum, Adorno holds that such inauthentic aesthetics are imposed on all of society by the market and serves as the legitimation of inequalities.

Despite its proposed importance in economic issues, critical theory was considered only by the early Frankfurt economists Friedrich Pollock, Henryk Grossman and, partly, Franz Neumann. Without wishing to devalue their contributions, their works did not act to dramatically shape economic thought. Firstly, the focus of these economists can, to some extent and from today's perspective, be considered obsolete. Pollock was mainly concerned with the Soviet planned economy, National Socialism and the social aspects of the introduction of automation. Grossman focused on general Marxian economics, especially the law of accumulation and the theory of economic crises. However, despite Pollock's slight tendency towards progressivity, both can be considered to be somewhat orthodox "old fashioned" Marxists, at least compared to their current counterparts at the Institute.

Pollock contributed significantly to demystifying the Soviet form of economy for which he established the term "state capitalism". In contrast to "private capitalism", state capitalism was defined in two typical forms – democratic and totalitarian[8]. Pollock (1941) adopts the traditional claim that the market is centrally constitutive for social relations under liberal capitalism. As Postone summarises one of Pollock's conclusions, people in the social relationships determined by the market confront one another in the public sphere as "quasi-autonomous agents" since "the market is the source of all non-conscious social structures of necessity; it constitutes the basis of the so-called 'laws of motion'" (2006, pp. 173, 176). Pollock also makes another valuable remark when analysing the role of state capitalism – states with such a form of socioeconomic order are supposed to eliminate the economic causes of, *inter alia*, "cumulative destructive process" (1941, p. 217). Both these features, that is, the cumulative destructive process and the quasi-autonomy of economic agents, play key roles in the following chapters and are further developed as intrinsic attributes of contemporary economics.

Grossman's work (1922) stresses crises caused by the capitalist economic mechanism. In his opinion, such crises occur when merchandise of a definite value cannot be sold within the limits of the mechanism. This is the assumption upon which theories of overproduction and underconsumption are constructed. Grossman addresses established Marxist variables by focusing particularly on the accumulation of capital. In the closing parts of his article, he concludes with the interesting and empirically verifiable assertion that the process of accumulation does not stop even in periods of deep depression (1922). In another work, Grossman (1929) divides his research into two layers: the first approach involves the reconstruction of the method underlying *Capital*, which consequently prepares the ground for a new perspective on Marx's system of theory. Grossman then describes the economic presuppositions of the capitalist breakdown, which via theoretical economic means serve to fill the proclaimed gap between the extensively expounded theory of political revolution and the neglected economic aspects of the Marxist tradition.

Franz Neumann operated on the edges of economics and political theory. His contribution, however, falls mainly into the latter category. Despite confronting central economic questions, the context of Neumann's later works concerns political freedom (1953) and the character of the state (1957). Alfred Sohn-Rethel also contributed to the understanding of economic questions in the early Frankfurt School milieu; his contribution is related to the general economic categories of the Marxian critique of the political economy.[9] The contemporary generation of critical theorists has recently discussed the economic policy of redistribution and proposed, for example, the "principle of the parity of participation" (Fraser 2007); the "tripolar theory of justice"[10] (Fraser and Honneth 2003) and the trichotomy of critique, explanation and normativity with a new grasp of the socioeconomic and politically cultural aspects of recognition (Hrubec 2013). However, all these theoretical concepts are positioned principally in the fields of political and social theory and philosophy. The most direct attempt to connect critical theory and economics was recently made by Bonefeld (2014). His seminal work (which has been reviewed frequently, see, for example, O'Kane 2018 or Moraitis 2018) deals primarily with methodological questions in the context of the classical political economy. The bridge between critical theory and the political economy was constructed not as forward-looking – with reference to current challenges in the political economy – but rather in reverse by reviving the ideas of former political economists such as Adam Smith, David Ricardo and Karl Marx. Certain common denominators with critical theory can also be found in Robinson (2004; as reviewed by van der Pijl 2005), whose "panoramic" analysis of global capitalism provides a useful framework for a number of global issues. Stephen Gill is probably the most famous contemporary political theorist in terms of connecting various aspects of critical theory and the global political economy (e.g. 2008 or Gill and Law 1989). Finally, *Time, Labor, and Social Domination* (Postone 1993) has attracted a great deal of attention, especially due to its unique approach to the category of value in Marxian theory. Postone's book re-interprets the general Marxian politico-economic categories that were developed particularly in *Capital* and *Gründrisse* in an original way while maintaining the typical concern about production not – as can be seen frequently in today's mainstream political economy – merely with concern to distribution. The central point for Postone is to oppose "traditional Marxism" based on the "transhistorical" concept of labour, which continues to remain alienated so that "traditional Marxism" is in the end indistinguishable from state capitalism; a term which he also associates with the former communist states of the Eastern bloc.

Unfortunately, with the exception of the aforementioned authors, links to economics are rare, fragmentary and semi-finished; and all of them favour other social sciences, particularly social philosophy. For instance, Postone (2006) confirms in one of his contributions that the Frankfurt School has replaced the political economy with philosophy. The principal question therefore is: why incorporate a broader scientific and philosophical context into contemporary economics? To answer this question, it is important to understand that the social sciences, particularly contemporary economics, have experienced internal specialisation and emancipation from external influences. Economics has provided several relevant and important insights; however, the interpretation of these insights is restricted by the narrow borders of its dominion. One of the integral elements of scientific knowledge is, necessarily, the exceeding of the authority of specialisation. Philosophy does not serve in this respect as the summation of knowledge, rather it strives to interpret the insights of various specialised sciences in terms of structural relationships, and it grasps tendencies that exceed our immediate empirical world. The bridge between critical theory and economics is, undoubtedly, unstable. However, various directions in critical theory gravitate towards the laws of the production process and confront those intrinsic moments that relate to human non-freedom. The platform for the various questions posed comprises the unequal distribution of resources and material deprivation in general. These questions remain the central pillars of economic thought and play the central role in the following chapters of this book.

## Notes

1 The term "critical theory", as used in this book, is not capitalised since the capitalised form usually refers solely to the Frankfurt School. Despite most of the cited authors having direct links to the Frankfurt School, the intention is also to reflect the findings of related authors inspired (including indirectly) by the Frankfurt School; therefore, the use of the capitalised form would be misleading.

2 Intentionally stated in the plural in order to emphasise the variances in critical theory and to support the idea that not just one single critical theory exists.

3 It appears that there is a terminological inconsistency here – while Kellner refers to the same subject he uses the terms "critical theory" and "Frankfurt School" in the same sense.

4 In order to make the first interlink with economic thought, it is interesting to recall a famous quote from Keynes: "When my information changes, I alter my conclusions. What do you do, sir?".

5 This question will be particularly important in the subsequent chapters when dealing with the current research content of economics.

6 However dominant the concept of totality among critical theorists, it is important to point out the critical poststructuralist attitude to social order.

7 The relationship between freedom and equality was mainly built upon the legacy of the French Revolution. Balibar (2015) therefore uses the term "*egaliberté*" which excludes freedom without equality.

8 The term "state capitalism" was developed particularly in the context of the Trotskyist tradition; one can name, for example, Ante Ciliga, Raya Dunayevskaya and C. L. R. James who, using pseudonyms, introduced the Johnson-Forrest Tendency. It is also important to mention Tony Cliff for whom Soviet bureaucracy played the same role as the bourgeoisie in capitalist countries, employing the same economic policy tools: decreasing wages, increasing the intensity of labour (in Marxian language a higher rate of exploitation) and increasing productivity (see 1974, pp. 79–90).

9 For a deeper contextual insight, see, for example, Prusik (2020).

10 Honneth's theory is based on "recognition", which brings him close to Taylor (1994), for whom the identity of human beings is shaped by recognition, which means that it does not exist in itself, and its ontology is inter-subjective. This approach opposes Fraser's dualism with the claim that any injustice is a matter of the central category – recognition, while redistribution is a derivative category.

## References


Adorno, T.W. (1997 [1970]). *Aesthetic theory*. Minneapolis: University of Minnesota Press.

Adorno, T.W. (2000). *Introduction to sociology*. Gödde, C., ed., Jephcott, E., trans. Cambridge: Polity Press.

Adorno, T.W. (2000 [1968]). Lecture Sixteen, 9 July 1968. In: *Introduction to sociology*. Stanford, CA: Stanford University Press, pp. 136–144.

Adorno, T.W. (2005 [1951]). *Minima Moralia: reflections on a damaged life*. London and New York: Verso.

Adorno, T.W. and Horkheimer, M. (2002 [1944]). *Dialectic of enlightenments: philosophical fragments*. Stanford: Stanford University Press.

Antonio, R.J. (1983). The origin, development, and contemporary status of critical theory. *The Sociological Quarterly*, 24(3), pp. 325–351.

Bonefeld, W. (2014). *Critical theory and the critique of political economy: on subversion and negative reason*. London: Bloomsbury Academic.

Bourdieu, P. (2000). *Pascalian meditations*. Stanford: Stanford University Press.

Braunstein, D. (2014). *Adornos Kritik der politischen Ökonomie*. Bielefeld: Transcript Verlag.

Bronner, S.E. and Kellner, D. (1989). *Critical theory and society: a reader*. New York and London: Routledge.

Buzgalin, A. and Kolganov, A. (2016). Critical political economy: the 'market-centric' model of economic theory must remain in the past-notes of the post-soviet school of critical Marxism. *Cambridge Journal of Economics*, 40(2), pp. 575–598.

Cliff, T. (1974). *State Capitalism in Russia*. London: Pluto Press.

Connerton, P. (1976). *Critical sociology*. Harmondsworth and New York: Penguin.

Dubiel, H. (1985). *Theory and politics: studies in the development of critical theory*. Cambridge: MIT Press.

Farr, A. (2008). *The task of dialectical thinking in the age of one-dimensionality*. Berlin: Springer Science & Business Media B.V.

Fraser, N. (2007). *Rozvíjení radikální imaginace*. Hrubec, M., ed. Praha: Nakladatelství Filosofického ústavu AV ČR.

Fraser, N. and Honneth, A. (2003). *Redistribution or recognition? A political-philosophical exchange*. London and New York: Verso.

Fuchs, C. (2016). Critical theory. *The International Encyclopedia of Communication Theory and Philosophy*, pp. 1–20. doi: 10.1002/9781118766804.wbiect002.

Gartman, D. (2012). Bourdieu and Adorno: converging theories of culture and inequality. *Theory and Society*, 41(1), pp. 41–72.

Geuss, R. (1981). *The idea of critical theory: Habermas and the Frankfurt school*. Cambridge: Cambridge University Press.

Gill, S.R. (2008). *Power and resistance in the new world order*. Basingstoke: Palgrave Macmillan.

Gill, S.R. and Law, D. (1989). Global hegemony and the structural power of capital. *International Studies Quarterly*, 33(4), pp. 475–499.

Gorz, A. (1989). Critique of economic reason. In: *Critique of economic reason*. London and New York: Verso, pp. 107–180.

Gramsci, A. (2003). *Selections from the prison notebooks*. London: Lawrence and Wishart.

Grossman, H. (1922). The theory of economic crisis. In: *Bulletin international de l'académie polonaise des sciences et des lettres. Classe de philologie. Classe d'histoire et de philosophie. I Partie.* Les Années 1919, 1920, 1922. Kraków: Brill, pp. 285–290.

Grossman, H. (1929). *Law of the accumulation and breakdown*. Banaji, J., trans. and abr. from H. Grossmann. *Das Akkumulations- und Zusammenbruchsgesetz des kapitalistischen Systems (Zugleich eine Krisentheorie)*. Leipzig: Verlag von C.L. Hirschfeld.

Habermas, J. (1967). Kritické a konzervativní úkoly sociologie. In: *Dialektika a sociologie*. Praha: Svoboda, pp. 75–89.

Habermas, J. (1981). New social movements. *Telos*, 49, pp. 33–37.

Hohoš, L. (2013). Veda a utópia. In: *Kritická teorie společnosti: Český kontext*. Praha: Nakladatelství Filosofického ústavu AV ČR, pp. 549–573.

Honneth, A. (1995). *The fragmented world of the social*. Albany, NY: State University of New York Press.

Horkheimer, M. (1972 [1937]). *Critical theory*. New York: Herder and Herder.

Horkheimer, M. (1973). The authoritarian state. *Telos*, 15, pp. 3–20.

Horkheimer, M. (2018 [1931]). The state of contemporary social philosophy and the tasks of an institute for social research. *Journal for Cultural Research*, 22(2), pp. 113–121.

Howard, D. (1974). A politics in search of the political. *Theory and Society*, 1, pp. 271–306.

Hrubec, M. (2011). Vývoj kritické teorie. In: *Od zneuznání ke spravedlnosti: Kritická teorie globální společnosti a politiky*. Praha: Nakladatelství Filosofického ústavu AV ČR, pp. 99–167.

Hrubec, M. (2013). Globální ne/spravedlnost. In: *Kritická teorie společnosti: Český kontext*. Praha: Nakladatelství Filosofického ústavu AV ČR, pp. 13–79.

Javůrek, Z., Černý, J., Havelka, M. and Horák, P. (1976). *Filosofie a ideologie Frankfurtské školy: Kritika některých koncepcí*. Praha: Academia.

Jay, M. (1973). *The dialectical imagination*. Boston: Little, Brown and Company.

Kalivoda, R. (1968). *Moderní duchovní skutečnost a marxismus*. Praha: Československý spisovatel.

Kellner, D. (1975). The Frankfurt school revisited: a critique of Martin Jay's the dialectical imagination. *New German Critique*, 4, pp. 131–52.

Kellner, D. (1990). Critical theory and the crisis of social theory. *Sociological Perspectives*, 33(1), pp. 11–33.

Keucheyan, R. (2014). *The left hemisphere: mapping critical theory today*. London and New York: Verso.

Kosík, K. (1976). *Dialectics of the concrete: a study on man and world*. Dondrecht: D. Reidel Publishing Company.

Löwenthal, L. (1981). The origins of critical theory: an interview with Leo Lőwenthal. *Telos*, 49, pp. 141–154.

Marx, K. (1994 [1844]). A contribution to the critique of Hegel's philosophy of right. In: O'Malley, J., ed. *Marx: early political writings*. Cambridge: Cambridge University Press.

McCloskey, D. (1989). The dismal science and Mr. Burke: economics as a critical theory. In: Simons, H.W. and Melia, T., eds. *The legacy of Kenneth Burke*. Madison: University of Wisconsin Press, pp. 99–114.

Moraitis, Y. (2018). A review of 'critical theory and the critique of political economy' by Werner Bonefeld. *Critique*, 46(3), pp. 489–491.

Neumann, F.L. (1953). The concept of political freedom. *Columbia Law Review*, 53(7), pp. 901–935.

Neumann, F.L. (1957). *The democratic and the authoritarian state: essays in political and legal theory*. Washington, DC: Free Press.

Nichols, R. and Allen-Brown, V. (1997). Critical theory and educational technology. In: Jonassen, D., ed. *Handbook of research for educational communications and technology*. New York: Palgrave Macmillan, pp. 226–252.

O'Kane, C. (2018). On the development of the critique of political economy as a critical social theory of economic objectivity: a review of critical theory and the critique of political economy by Werner Bonefeld. *Historical Materialism*, 26(1), pp. 175–193.

Pearson, G. (1974). Book review: the dialectical imagination, aspects of sociology, dialectic of enlightenment. *The British Journal of Sociology*, 25(1), pp. 111–113.

Piccone, P. (1980). The future of critical theory. In: McNall, S.G. and Howe, G.N., eds. *Current perspectives in social theory*. Vol. 1. Greenwich, CT: JAI Press.

Pollock, F. (1941). State capitalism. *Studies in Philosophy and Social Science*, IX(2), pp. 200–225.

Postone, M. (1993). *Time, labor, and social domination: a reinterpretation of Marx's critical theory*. Cambridge: Cambridge University Press.

Postone, M. (2006). Critique, state, and economy. In: Rush, F., ed. *The Cambridge companion to critical theory*. The Cambridge Companion Online. Cambridge: Cambridge University Press, pp. 165–193. doi: 10.1017/CCOL0521816602.

Prusik, C.A. (2020). *Adorno and neoliberalism: the critique of exchange society*. London: Bloomsbury Publishing.

Pugh, M. (2005). The political economy of peacebuilding: a critical theory perspective. *International Journal of Peace Studies*, 10(2), pp. 23–42.

Pullmann, M. (2013). Historický vývoj. In: *Kritická teorie společnosti: Český kontext*. Praha: Nakladatelství Filosofického ústavu AV ČR, pp. 293–323.

Rainko, S. (1976). *Marksizm i jego krytycy*. Warszaw: Ksiazka i Wiedza.

Robinson, W.I. (2004). *A theory of global capitalism: production, class, and state in a transnational world*. Baltimore: Johns Hopkins University Press.

Rockmore, T. (2015). Habermas, critical theory, and political economy. In: Smulewicz-Zucker, G. and Thompson, M.J., eds. *Radical intellectuals and the subversion of progressive politics: political philosophy and public purpose*. New York: Palgrave Macmillan, pp. 191–210.

Smith, J. (1993). *After the demise of empiricism: the problem of judging social and educational inquiry*. New York: Ablex.

Steigerwald, R., ed. (1969). *Herbert Marcuses dritter Weg*. Köln: Pahl-Rugenstein Verlag.

Taylor, C. (1994). *Multiculturalism: examining the politics of recognition*. Princeton: Princeton University Press.

Thompson, M.J. (2017). *The Palgrave handbook of critical theory*. New York: Palgrave Macmillan.

Van der Pijl, K. (2005). Feature review of 'a theory of global capitalism: production, class and state in a transnational world' by W.I. Robinson. *New Political Economy*, 10(2), pp. 273–277.

von Heiseler, H.J. (1970). *Die Frankfurter schule im lichte des marxismus: zur kritik d. philosophie u. Soziologie von Horkheimer, Adorno, Marcuse, Habermas*. Frankfurt am Main: Verlag Marxistische Blätter.

Witkin, R. (2004). *Adorno on popular culture*. London: Routledge.

Zelený, J. (1982). *Pojednání o dialektice*. Praha: Academia.

# 2 Prolegomena to Economic Theory

## Foundations of Contemporary Economics

Lionel Robbins (2007 [1932]) was clear in his statement: "Economics is the science which studies human behaviour as a relationship between ends and scarce means which have alternative uses". It is clear that this widely accepted definition of economics originates from a period in which economics had already separated itself from the classical political economy. Clearly, the statement makes no reference to the ethical dimension, in contrast to the works of classical political economists who pursued a certain normative content. This separation from the political economy on the one hand allowed economists to focus on details that can be mathematically captured and analysed, thus enabling the study of narrowly defined and isolated issues in greater detail than was previously possible. On the other hand, as demonstrated in the previous chapter, such a degree of specialisation in the social sciences suffers from the related lack of a social context. In other words, the translation of social questions to the mathematically analysable form may lead to the failure to consider certain highly important aspects of our world.

Economics has experienced only a small number of dramatic paradigms shifts over its history. Economists today continue to rely on the outcomes of the so-called marginalist revolution, which is widely seen as the single most powerful transformative theoretical shift to affect the field of modern economics. In the second half of the 19th century, marginalists confronted the concept of price formation as espoused by the classical political economists. This "new wave" of economists, including particularly William Stanley Jevons, León Walras and Carl Menger, directed their attention away from the "objectivistic" costs of production (or socially necessary labour) as the sole determinant of value in favour of subjectively perceived values. The value of labour was no longer determined by its subsistence level, but was linked to the value of its product *in relation to others*. Workers sell their labour since they value the level of the accepted wage more than they do leisure. Labour has since ceased to be viewed as a necessity and this issue was subsequently reinterpreted as a *preference* problem between leisure and labour. Even though this shift internalised the threat of starvation into the consideration thereof, it no longer comprised a universal

DOI: 10.4324/9780429273841-3

cause; the threat of starvation became the subject of individualised optimisation. Combining differential calculus with utility theory subsequently allowed for the employment of marginal values for the determination of market prices. According to this shift, wages no longer determine the price of the product; conversely, wages are supposedly determined by the price of the product.

Hence, market prices are not perceived as the result of objective producer costs, but rather as a complex subjective valuation problem. The logic of this shift was quite simple – if the consumer does not value a particular commodity in the market, the market price of this commodity goes down, no matter how high the production costs of the commodity. Menger opined that production became subject to the marginal utility theory, according to which two trading parties exchange what they value less for what they value more. This new approach provided the basis for the determination of the market price which prevails today, and it also helped to formulate a set of axioms from which all economic phenomena can be explained. Economics has, consequently, been narrowed down to the study of the logic of individual choice under scarcity. The combination of subjective value and individual choice with the utility theory has a long history that stretches back to the former supporters of utilitarianism, principally Jeremy Bentham and John Stuart Mill. Since it is not the intention here to provide a comprehensive review of their theoretical legacy, the discussion is reduced to their immediate role in contemporary economic thought.

William Stanley Jevons was an early follower of utilitarianism and a pioneer of modern economics. He is known as one of the first economists to systematically pursue the mathematisation of economic phenomena. Jevons claimed (1888) that a science that deals with quantities, in this particular sense a science that is capable of deciding whether things are greater or less, must be mathematical. Logical sciences deal with phenomena that happen or do not happen, but if phenomena may be greater or less, or the phenomenon happens sooner or later, nearer or farther, then it should be quantitatively analysed via mathematical notions.

Although Bentham does not apply a formal apparatus, his *Introduction to the Principles of Morals and Legislation* (2000 [1781]) is inherently mathematical, and his approach to moral science forms the background for later theories based on human action. A possible interpretation of his work is that he suggests the summation of the values of both pleasures (+) and pains (−) so that they neutralise each other: adding pain decreases pleasure; a decrease in pain increases pleasure. This point is made clear in the first chapter:

> Nature has placed mankind under the governance of two sovereign masters, "pain" and "pleasure". It is for them alone to point out what we ought to do, as well as to determine what we shall do. On the one hand, the standard of right and wrong, on the other the chain of causes and effects, are fastened to their throne. They govern us in all we do, in all we say, in all we think: every effort we can make to throw off our subjection, will

> serve but to demonstrate and confirm it. In words a man may pretend to abjure their empire: but in reality he will remain subject to it all the while. (2000 [1781], p. 14)

The positive balance of these two considerations indicates that the individual will take the action, whereas a negative balance means that the individual will not take the action. The individual perception of pleasure and pain is generally subject to the following circumstances as formulated by Bentham as components of felicific calculus: (a) intensity, (b) duration, (c) certainty or uncertainty, and (d) propinquity or remoteness, all of which should also be contextualised with anticipated feelings as underlined by Jevons (1888), for whom the power of anticipation is of significant importance for economics since it comprises the main incentive for business and saving. Unlike unaware individuals occupied by momentary pleasures and pains, a state of civilisation is built upon those with the most delicate foresight that works for the future. The challenge for economics is to maximise pleasure, that is, to procure the greatest possible amount of what is desired at the expense of the most undesired. In brief, pleasures and pains are the drivers of human action.

Jevons (1888) doubted that humans will ever determine a measurement method for pleasures and pain. However, it is not necessary to have a method that employs measurement units, in connection with which Jevons claims that the effects of experienced pleasure and pain can be estimated. Since the manifestation of the estimation measurement approach is one's actions, the final judge of the quantities of one's feelings comprises the individual measurement of the balance. By following Alexander Brain, "[i]t is only an identical proposition to affirm that the greatest of two pleasures, *or what appears such* (R. M.), sways the resulting action; for it is this resulting action that alone determines which is the greater" (Jevons 1888, p. 33). This means that making a choice, manifesting one's will or taking action is inseparable from an excess of expected pleasure, regardless of the varying estimates of the motives or a natural incapacity to fully grasp the quantities concerned. To provide an example, the pleasure gained by purchasing a commodity is always greater than (or equal to) the pleasure of possessing its money value. Naturally, the subjective aspect is crucial here: the motives in one's mind are always weighed against other motives in the same mind; no means exist via which to compare mentally perceived quantities of pleasure and pain across individuals. Jevons determined no common denominator for individual feelings, even though it is possible to determine general patterns related, for instance, to the satisfaction of basic human needs.

Thus, in economics, the result comprises the aggregate of the feelings of individuals. In addition to the fallacy of aggregability, it remains beyond the analytical power of science (due to the complexity of individual motivation) to investigate, for example, the impacts of the resulting behaviour at the level of the state. On the other hand, it is possible via simple aggregation to approximate general laws such as the decreasing quantity demanded with increasing price: if the price of a commodity in the market increases, it is expected, *ceteris paribus*, that some individuals will reduce the consumption of that commodity, others will not react at all and a small number will increase their consumption; however, on balance, the quantity demanded is likely to decline. Generally, the variation of quantities demanded in relation to variations in prices results from aggregated changes in the market.

In order to clarify the terms used, Jevons, in Chapter III, "Theory of Utility" (1888, p. 46), clearly states that by "commodity" one should understand "any object, substance, action, or service, which can afford pleasure or ward off pain". The term denotes the quality of anything that is capable of serving humans; thus, whatever produces pleasure or prevents pain possesses utility. By utility, Bentham (2000 [1781], pp. 14–15) means

> that property in any object, whereby it tends to produce benefit, advantage, pleasure, good, or happiness, (all this in the present case comes to the same thing) or (what comes again to the same thing) to prevent the happening of mischief, pain, evil, or unhappiness to the party whose interest is considered: if that party be the community in general, then the happiness of the community: if a particular individual, then the happiness of that individual.

In accordance with Jeremy Bentham, William Stanley Jevons and others, Hermann Heinrich Gossen (1983 [1854]) understands economics as a theory of pleasure and pain so that both individuals and society pursue the maximum pleasure with the minimum of painful effort. Gossen was behind one of the most powerful analytical tools applied in economics, that is, the "law of diminishing marginal utility", which states that an additional unit of the same good yields pleasure (*Werth* or utility) at a continuously diminishing rate up to the point of satiety. Marginal utility, therefore, represents the change in the total utility with respect to a change in the quantity of a given commodity. Gossen's second law refers to the optimal situation of an individual when the marginal costs of acquisition (e.g. the price) of an additional unit of a commodity equal the marginal utility across all commodities. The last of Gossen's laws refers to scarcity as the precondition for economic value. Everyone is, therefore, able to distribute his/her resources in a way that each increment of a pleasure-giving commodity is equal to the resources sacrificed for gaining the commodity.

Jules Dupuit (1849) elaborated upon the theory of utility thus: the utility of a certain commodity varies not only among individuals but also for the individual according to the circumstances. Utility, therefore, rather than being an inherent quality of commodities, is "*a circumstance of things* arising out of their relation to man's requirements", so that one cannot claim that a certain object has utility and another does not (Jevons 1888, p. 49). Clearly, there are numerous aspects to the assessment of utility depending on the nature of the need, the character of the commodity, the time frame, the situation and so on. For example, following the first law of diminishing marginal utility, our satisfaction increases with the amount of a consumed commodity at a decreasing rate, which does not necessarily mean that our marginal utility always falls to zero. In contrast to our immediate biological need for food and water that represents the type of satiety for which additional units provide no additional utility, our more sophisticated needs, for example, concerning the arts and sciences, have no such strict limits. Similarly, our utility is driven not only by quantity but also by diversity. Possessing two identical books clearly does not generate twice the utility of possessing only one. A further important feature relates to Banfield's "Law of the Subordination of Wants", which states that scarce resources (commodities) are allocated so as to satisfy the most urgent needs first. It is then deduced that, for instance, a glass of water per day will be consumed to satiate an individual's thirst instead of for watering ornamental plants.

Modern economics treats utility in various ways. In addition to the Benthamite tradition of capturing the mental states of pleasure and pain, utility can be measured in terms of happiness (Sumner 1996) or preference satisfaction (Mongin and d'Aspremont 1998). The concept of utility in the broader context of the social sciences may refer to more objective notions such as the opportunity for welfare (Arneson 1989), resources (Dworkin 1981), capabilities (Sen 1985), access to advantage (Cohen 1989) or, most famously, to primary goods (Rawls 1971). The regular methodological approach involves the definition of an observable proxy for utility and the collection of data related to the proxy. Empirical research, for example, on utility in relation to measuring happiness, includes for instance the works of Easterlin (1974, 1995), Simon (1974), Myers (1993), Veenhoven (1993), Clark and Oswald (2002), Ng (1996), Frank (1997), Kahneman et al. (1997), Oswald (1997), Winkelmann and Winkelmann (1998) and Di Tella et al. (2001). Based on a combination of theoretical and empirical insights, the researcher is able to determine a specific functional form for utility. However, for the purposes of this publication, the author suggests the simplified conclusion that utility theory in economics is grounded in Bentham's felicity calculus of pleasure and pain. Despite plausible arguments that indicate that Bentham did not regard utility as a measure of net pleasure (pleasure minus pain), but rather as an objective property of things (see e.g. Mongin and d'Aspremont 1998), his general idea prepared the ground for the completeness of an individual's preferences. Hence, economic theory, equipped with such a theoretical apparatus, is able to cover all possible situations, thus implying that the individual experiences utility when pleasure exceeds pain (+), disutility when pain exceeds pleasure (−), and inutility when pleasure equals pain (0). The primary attribute of rational behaviour is to maximise utility; in other words, to behave with the aim of creating the greatest possible difference between pleasure and pain. The utility of possessing a commodity is maximised when the utility of the final unit of the commodity (the marginal utility of that commodity for a given quantity) is equal to the pain endured (e.g. price), which means that the rational individual has no utility-enhancing reason to deviate from such a situation. If an additional unit of the commodity provides greater pleasure than pain, the total utility has not yet been maximised, and the rational individual is expected to increase the demanded quantity of the commodity as it increases the individual's total utility. This powerful logic also has an analogy in the theory of the firm. All profit-maximising entities should always equalise marginal revenues with marginal costs. If marginal revenues are greater than marginal costs, the production of an additional unit of a commodity provides a greater positive change in the revenues of the firm than does the increased costs of production of this unit. The firm is then motivated to produce such units in order to maximise its profit in the form of the difference between revenues and costs.

With respect to value, the prevailing point of departure, at least in terms of certain important aspects of contemporary economics, is placed back in the theory of John Stuart Mill (1909 [1848]). Value is understood as a relative term, which means that the value of a commodity is expressed in terms of the quantity of other commodities for which it can be exchanged. Again, as with pleasure and pain, utilities and disutilities, value is not perceived as a feature inherent to the commodity, but as a circumstance of a given object, which implies the ratio at which it can be exchanged for another item. The value is simply understood as the *exchange value*. The difference between modern economics and Mill's approach lies in the fact that the latter defines the ratio based on the costs of production of exchangeable commodities. Conversely, modern economics relies on Jevons for whom "[t]he ratio of exchange of any two commodities will be the reciprocal of the ratio of the final degrees of utility of the quantities of [the] commodity available for consumption after the exchange is completed" (1888, p. 79). Free exchange ensures that all commodities are distributed in a way that produces the highest benefit for all – all individuals are allowed to exchange anything which serves him less for anything that serves him more, and no one is forced to sacrifice what he desires more for what he desires less. In line with John Stuart Mill and John Elliott Cairnes, economics is operationalised as a logical science with a deductive methodology. It starts with general psychological laws, for instance, that a greater gain is preferred over a smaller one. Based upon these laws, economics can draw general conclusions on the effects of such laws, which can be further verified through observed statistical phenomena. It should be noted that, for example, Jevons himself was aware of the difficulty of statistical verification, a factor that represents one of the main counterarguments of critical theory against the empiricalised social sciences – that a statistical examination simply cannot satisfactorily resolve the essence of a thing.

As previously outlined, theorists of the subjective value claim – as opposed to classical political economists – that no matter how high production costs are, if there is no benefit for consumers, no one will be willing to pay for the commodity. The actual market price thus converges to the price that corresponds to the benefit as perceived by consumers. On the other hand, if the aggregate subjective value of consumers is below production costs, no producer will be willing to deliver the commodity to the market. Hence, the final market price must reflect both the subjective values of consumers and the "objective"[1] production costs of producers, which are mutually interdependent – the prices of production factors are dependent on the valuation of consumers of the final product. Specifically, the consumer's ability and willingness to pay for a product is mirrored by the ability and willingness of a firm to pay for the production factors necessary to produce that product, thus explaining in a very simplified way how the mental calculation of pleasure and pain establishes the utility theory. From utility, one can derive the value on the side of consumers, which is reflected by a firm's calculation of the production factors, employing the same logic when comparing the benefits and the costs of the production factors applied.

It is, however, important to note that there is no single economic theory. The various economic theories that have been formulated to date are characterised by a range of mutually conflicting standpoints on price formation, business cycle determinants, drivers of growth, causes of crisis and so on. Simply put, there is no single grammar available to explain society through the economic lens. Moreover, even the latest economics textbooks are unable to clarify what the "correct" or "best" economic theory is. Unlike in the case of the natural sciences, for example biology or astronomy, where the latest research, surely with minor exceptions, represents the highest level of knowledge on a given phenomenon, the latest research in economics is of a different nature. As a branch of the social sciences, economics and the ongoing research thereof provide new perspectives which do not necessarily disprove previous insights. Advanced theories of consumption do not act to delegitimate the general Keynesian consumption function – in some cases, they attempt to explain broader, and in other cases narrower points of view; focusing on various issues – be it with regard to the intertemporal choice or the form of the function and so forth. The original core logic of the consumption function has not been disproved as, similarly, exogenous models of growth have not been rejected under the pressure of endogenous growth theories. The theory may merely be less applicable when explaining a certain phenomenon under various circumstances, that is, in terms of time, place and the specific research question posed by the researcher. In such cases it is difficult to decide on the form the criterion for the theory to be approved as valid should take. Stand-alone empirical evidence or logically consistent translatability into formal language are, quite simply, insufficient for this purpose.

Thus, neoclassical economics, enriched with the Keynesian macroeconomic approach, remains the mainstream position. As noted by Wolff and Resnick (2012), neoclassical economic theory arose from the humanist tradition of the Renaissance and the transition from feudalism to capitalism. The theoretical backbone uses deduction as the prime methodological principle. All neoclassical concepts are deduced from neoclassical entry points concerning human preferences, production and rewards for production factors. This implies that subsequent concepts of supply and demand that imply equilibrium between prices and quantities in the market are comprehensible through the deductive chain between human preferences, the production of firms and rewards for capital and labour. The economy is thus derivable from these three dimensions of human activity. In fact, neoclassical theory interprets these three dimensions as the eternal causes, the "essential determinants", of everything else. Since these entry points determine the whole of the spectrum of global phenomena, the neoclassical logical system displays strong elements of essentialism and determinism.

Keynesian theory follows a similar logic, that is, it also works with essentialist assumptions; however, the propositions and arguments thereof rely on the structuralist tradition. Economic events are not deduced from individual optimising behaviour, as suggested by neoclassical theory, rather the essential entry points relate to mass psychological propensities within a given institutional framework. Keynesian theory therefore prioritises structuralist elements such as social conventions and institutions over individual motivation as the prime driver of economic processes. This may explain why microeconomics is still embedded in neoclassical theory, whereas macroeconomics is explained through the Keynesian viewpoint. Both theories, however, reduce their concepts into simple cause-effect mechanics. To complete the mosaic, Marxian economics also adopted the structuralist understanding of society and its emphasis on individual freedom and the actualisation of human potential (however different this emphasis may be to its liberal tendencies) also places Marxian economics in the tradition of European humanism.

Due to its essentialist nature, which allows for the explanation of all the relevant phenomena from just a small number of principles, economics became highly immune to its own paradigm shifts and the penetration of knowledge from other (social) sciences. In Lakatosian language (1980), a "research programme" as a sequence of theories within a domain of scientific inquiry moves forward under two conditions: it must be progressive both theoretically and empirically. The progress of scientific knowledge (he would term it a "problem shift") occurs when a new theory predicts more than did its predecessor and when, at the same time, current observations fit into the new prediction. "Negative heuristics" thus means that certain principles of the research programme are *not* revisable; they constitute the "hard core" of a particular scientific discipline. Confronting these hard-core elements is beyond the limits of a given discipline. "Positive heuristics" therefore relates to a *revisable* body of beliefs which form a "protective belt" around the hard core. Conversely, research programmes degenerate when new insights only serve to protect the hard core from refutation without providing predictions on new phenomena and/or when these predictions do not correspond to current observations. The problem of economics appears to lie in its axiomatic nature; defining the pillars in the form of unlimitedly deducible basic principles based on formal logic is not suitably falsifiable. This essentialist approach, which absorbs all economic phenomena, renders the economic "hard core" unquestionable. Progress thus occurs only within the "protective belt", and the hard core – the conditions of the capitalist economy – remains untouched.

## Distributional Theories

Economics is broadly recognised as a positivist science. For the present, setting aside the fact that this is something of a normative claim since economists have intentionally shaped economics in such a way over the past century, the positivism of economics does not stem from the metaphysical essence of this field of study, rather it has evolved into a positivist science because this is what economists desired. For instance, the proposition that the allocation of scarce resources *should be* based on a competitive struggle between freely behaving agents is in itself a normative claim since it is also possible to adopt distributive systems that operate upon principles other than free market competition. This example is no coincidence; questions concerning distribution remain unshakably in the forefront of economic thought. And as was indicated in the first chapter, the question of economic distribution was also seen by critical theorists as fertile ground for disputes with economists.

The questions why someone is relatively poor and another relatively rich; whether the final result of distribution is just or unjust; and how politics and the legal system should intervene with respect to economic distribution are inseparable from the constituting of the socioeconomic order. According to Ricardo (2001 [1821]), discovering the laws that lay behind distributive shares comprises the principal problem of the political economy. As expected, different economic theories provide different answers. However, the currently prevailing explanation stems from neoclassical theory. Taking the example of the goods and services market, Wolff and Resnick (2012) begin with individual agents who choose what part of their income they prefer to save and what part they prefer to consume. The saved part of the income is invested in the form of capital that funds the production process. With respect to the production factors market, individuals decide between the number of labour hours supplied and those to be devoted to leisure time. The production process and the reward for the individual in the form of income are thus given by the individual's preference ranking process. Incentives for economic growth stem from the individual preference between sacrificing immediate consumption and leisure on the one hand and the expected rewards in the future on the other. Individual income is, therefore, subject to individual preferences, which finally comprise the determinant of the income. This idea is not limited only to wage-earners; owners of other production factors – capital and land – also decide on an individual basis the amount and the productivity of production factors they provide for use in the production process. These two attributes thus imply the share of the output the owners of the various production factors obtain in return in the form of income. The final output of the neoclassical theory also depends on technology; hence, the final distribution of income between wage-earners, rent-earners and profit-earners depends on and reflects the choices made by individuals, their endowments and technology:

> Neoclassical theory reduces each individual's income to its conceptual entry points. We all receive income in direct relation to how we choose to

> use our time and our endowments of productive resources. The more we sacrifice, the more we can contribute to production, the more we can and should obtain of the fruits of that production. We should therefore look to our individual choices, our self-interested behaviour, to explain our high or low incomes. It follows in neoclassical theory that the relatively affluent do not earn their income at the expense of the poor. The choices of the former to work long and hard and to be thrifty are independent of the latter's opposite choices. Each individual gets rewarded – his or her income – according to his or her choices about contributing to production. No-one's wealth is the result of another's poverty.
>
> (Wolff and Resnick 2012, p. 354)

Wolff and Resnick continue with the assertion that neoclassical theory under capitalism – from the inspiration provided by Adam Smith to Gérard Debreu's formal explanation – establishes two social institutions. Firstly, a free competitive market for all the inputs and outputs with no control by the individual over the prices thereof. Secondly, legally enforced private property and owners' rights which guarantee that they may dispose of their property as they please. Rewards in the market are thus based on the marginal productivity theory where, rather than needs being explicitly stated, they remain an inherent part of the individual's preferences. Productivity thus explains all the variances in terms of production factor rewards and leaves no room for undeserved allocation. The question of distributive justice is thus rendered unnecessary.

The first problem faced when dealing with unequal distribution is to define a benchmark, that is, what do we mean by equal distribution? Naturally, a wide range of normative aspects are in play here. All states of inequality are deviations from a normatively formulated state of equality or the "appropriate" form of distribution. A number of ideas in this respect were formulated by Rein and Miller (1974) and subsequently summarised by Maialeh (2020). The starting point concerns income shares according to the Rawlsian maximin principle that maximises the share of the disadvantaged lowest social strata. Equalising policies inspired by this principle ensure that no-one falls below a given minimum standard of well-being. Conversely, equalisation can be implemented via policies that establish a ceiling on incomes and wealth, thus restricting relatively affluent social groups in terms of the accumulation of additional resources. Inequality can be seen as the result of disproportionate political power, education and a host of other social phenomena, that may finally result in unequal economic distribution. Equalisation may also refer to endeavours to maintain inequality at a certain ratio to another comparable unit (e.g. the national state). Complete horizontal equity means that all equal agents are treated equally. However, this inevitably implies that equal treatment may even increase the inequalities between already unequal agents. If one considers inequality in terms of lifetime income profiles, it is necessary to focus on future economic prospects rather than on the current economic position. Equalising policies may be directed towards eliminating the initial barriers to, or initial advantages of, the occupational groups involved. Other forms of equalising policies may even aim at the eradication of the potential social exclusion caused by differences in the allocation of economic power. Moreover, a further question concerns whether to formulate the approach to a just distribution based on needs or deserts; since the distributive rules thereof are in conflict, it is impossible to accommodate both without striking compromises. In conclusion, inequality can also be formulated in terms of capabilities when more equally distributed elements (not only income, wealth and primary goods but also formal [legally established] opportunities and liberties) are unable to furnish individuals with *real* possibilities. The concept of inequality, however, concerns not only the definition of *what* is meant by equality, bearing in mind the qualitative aspect of the problem, but also to *whom* the concept of equality should be applied. Pioneers of political freedom, who vociferously declared that "all men are created equal", automatically excluded women and black people since white adult men only were considered the subjects of freedom and equality; today, one might consider, for example, the automatic exclusion of refugees who are not equal to regular citizens. It is clear that critical theorists, in their quest for universal human emancipation, must consider this perspective as a highly important factor.

Clearly, the aspect of individual economic distribution is salient. Moreover, the concept of individual utility blurs the difference between wants and needs which, of course, serves to complicate the question of individual welfare functions and the interpersonal comparison thereof. A modest individual with fewer wants may well experience the same level of utility as a profligate individual, but with a significantly lower income. Alternatively, a needy individual who suffers from health issues needs a higher income than a healthy individual in order to attain the same level of utility. In other words, in both cases, the same income produces differing individual utilities. A level of income which, under normal conditions, suffices for a decent life may render another person who lives according to different conditions impoverished, a concept that was emphasised by Rowntree (2010 [1901]) who differentiated between primary poverty, which is connected to low incomes in absolute terms and secondary poverty, which results in the inability to meet one's basic needs for other than income reasons. Bearing in mind the Smithian (1776) notion of "appearing in public without shame", which accentuates the interpersonal dimension of subjectivity in the sense that subjective needs are co-determined by society, Sen (1983, 1985) suggests that the same levels of social functioning and participation in the life of the community require different levels of income in different spaces and times. The conversion of income into capabilities therefore diverts the concept of poverty away from a low level of income towards a general inability to secure one's basic needs. This "poverty line", however, differs from state to state, family to family and even individual to individual. The "weak equity axiom" presented by Sen (1997) suggests that an individual with greater needs should receive a higher share of total income. But what kinds of needs (which are in any case difficult to measure in terms of urgency or intensity) should be considered to provide the relevant argument for compensation? The assessment of relative needs presents an enormous challenge for normative economics. One of the simplest (but, nevertheless, viable) solutions might be to ask oneself whether the one who makes the judgment prefers to be person A, with a given income, or person B with the same level of income. Undoubtedly, if person A has identifiably greater needs than person B, the same level of income provides person A with a lower level of effective income and utility (welfare)[2].

Similar questions concerning economic distribution were scrutinised by Karl Marx. While some of his predictions of economic distribution failed, for instance, the steadily increasing concentration of production capacities and the continuing immiseration of the proletariat, the Marxian point of view still provides a number of valuable insights. According to Marxian theory, the share of wages should decrease with increasing production, while wages can increase only as the result of the increased collective organisation of the working class that aims towards reducing exploitation. Marx expected that this would happen through reducing the length of the working day rather than by increasing wages. Experience from the 20th century, however, proves that both channels can occur side by side. Despite all the evident differences, Marxian theory, which is founded on the theory of labour value, might have more in common with neoclassical theory than first meets the eye. In both cases, economic distribution is deserts-based, but not in the neoclassical sense of marginal productivity. The major distinctive factor comprises the institute of "exploitation" which is interrelated with the concept of "surplus value", as given by the difference between the value added and paid wages. In neoclassical terms, the surplus value stems from the difference between the marginal revenue product of labour and marginal factor (labour) costs. Returning to the classical period of the mid-19th century, even liberal economists such as Mill wondered how it was possible that someone can grow rich when sleeping "without working, risking or economising" (1909 [1848], p. 573). Is such wealth generated by the extracted labour of others?

Assuming labour is the ultimate source of all value, firms continue to increase their profits as long as the value added is greater than the costs of labour up to the point where both variables are equal. Inspired by Joan Robinson (particularly 1933, later discussed in 1956 and 1960), the concept of exploitation can be pushed even closer towards neoclassical economics on the examples of "monopolistic exploitation" and "monopsonistic exploitation". As pointed out in the *Critique of the Gotha Programme* (Marx 1938 [1875]), when outlining the first stages of a socialist society with bourgeoisie residua, the exchange of equivalents would exist at the average rather than at the individual level, and the measurement is performed applying an equal standard – labour. In order to allow for it to act as such a standard of measurement, labour is defined by its duration and intensity. Differences between people's capabilities, regardless of whether they are physical or mental, serve as natural privileges since one person is able to work longer or harder than another. Applying the equal standard to unequal labour, where no class differences play a role, results in the "right of inequality". It is evident that the first stage of the socialist society persists even under the rule of the bourgeois equivalence of commodity exchange (which continues to be based on labour performance) but with one exception – that labour as the sole source of value deserves the whole net product. Overcoming exploitation, which somehow naturally shifts the emphasis from deserts-based to needs-based distributional schemes, allows society to inscribe on its banners: "From each according to his ability, to each according to his needs!" The role of the free market is, therefore, perceived from a completely different perspective: while pro-capitalist thinkers fight against taxation that acts to restrict the motivation of capitalists to innovate and inhibits them from enjoying all the fruits of their work, the Marxian concept of exploitation argues that workers are also unable to enjoy all the fruits of their work since a part of their work is appropriated by capitalists in the form of surplus value.

Thus the salient question concerns the distributional scheme that should be applied; whether the emphasis should be on needs or on performance in the market (and the subsequent flow of deserts). Neoclassical economic theory, which arose from the marginalist tradition, is quite clear on this issue: the dominating theoretical background supports the competitive market form of distribution, which is based on marginal productivity which, in turn, is associated with deserts-based distributions. The outcomes associated with such a distributional scheme are Pareto-optimal since a competitive equilibrium of this kind implies that the prices of production factors are equal to their marginal productivities. John B. Clark (1891) explicitly argued that distribution based on marginal productivity is both fair and unavoidable. For Clark, "fairness" is represented by simple equivalency, and so markets ensure fair distribution when the agent receives the equivalent of what the agent contributed to the output. The argument behind its "unavoidability" is that competitive markets ensure that if the agent is paid less than his/her marginal productivity, other producers will bid his/her wage upwards since it will still be beneficial up to the point at which marginal productivity matches the wage.

This clearly fails to provide an all-embracing answer to the stated problem – what about the rent received from a piece of land? Should it be considered distribution based on the desired market performance? Would the argument that the land was purchased from "productively" earned money be valid? And what about naturally talented individuals? Is it justifiable to reward them for their innate abilities? What if a less talented person produces the same outcome, should the reward be the same? And should innate abilities have the same weight in economic distribution as derived competencies gained through education or training? It is easy to prove that alternative concepts of deserts may be in sharp conflict. In this sense, is needs-based distribution more straightforward? Which needs should be included? In any case, concerning the aforementioned distributional dilemmas, neoclassical theory posits that as long as it is mirrored in enhanced market performance, we *should* reward talent; that we *should not* differentiate between innate and derived competencies as far as they do not matter to market performance; or, for the same reason, that the less talented, who must exert greater efforts than others in order to produce the same outcome as others, *should not* be better rewarded. Despite this fixation on rewards concerning objective, measurable and, supposedly, value-neutral market outcomes, it is easy to decipher certain hidden normative market distribution aspects. This particular position of neoclassical theory simply cannot claim to be seen as the ultimate and universal distributional authority.

However, it is also tempting to formulate a distributional theory based on diminishing marginal utility, as was the case of early welfare economists such as Arthur C. Pigou and Abba P. Lerner. They pursued the Benthamite tradition in the sense that comparing *A*'s and *B*'s utilities is a factual rather than a prescriptive proposition. Their assertions arose from the assumption that subjective utility from commodities is evenly distributed throughout the population. As noted by Fleurbaey and Hammond (2004), it is not clear whether this was meant as a factual assumption or as a convenient ethical principle formulated for egalitarian purposes. Be it as it may, the same strictly concave utility function of income allows for the equalisation of income without any deeper elaboration of the notion of utility and the measurement thereof. Hence, applying diminishing marginal utility to money implies that obtaining an additional unit of money when one is wealthy results in a lower increase in utility than does obtaining the same unit of money when less wealthy. Such a theory would necessarily lead to redistribution from the rich to the poor since an additional "five bucks" is assumed to be, in terms of utility, insignificant to a billionaire, but important to a homeless individual. However, this presumes controversial interpersonal comparisons of utility (see e.g. Fleurbaey and Hammond 2004; Hammond 1991; Suzumura 1996). As pioneered by Bentham, and followed, for example, by Alfred Marshall and Vilfredo Pareto, the early utilitarian concept, with comparable individual cardinal utility functions and the maximisation of social welfare as the sum of individual utilities, requires the final distribution to follow the equality of individual marginal utilities. Thus, assuming homogeneous individuals automatically implies equating total utilities; in other words, such circumstances lead to absolute equality.

Still, utilitarianism is not as strictly egalitarian as it might seem from the aforementioned description, despite several accusations to the contrary. We may remind at this point Sen (1997) who illustrates the problem of dividing a given amount of income between two agents *A* and *B*. The share of *A* is measured by the distance *AB*, and, symmetrically, *B*'s share is measured by the distance *BA*. The maximised total utility is given by *C*, where *AC*=*BC*. Nevertheless, when assuming the case in which *B*'s marginal utility is exactly half that of *A*, *B* becomes worse-off and the egalitarian approach would suggest a redistribution from *A* to *B*. But what does utilitarianism recommend in this situation? Exactly the opposite, that is, a transfer from *B* to *A* (for more see details see Sen 1997, pp. 16–18).

However, it is, perhaps, unrealistic to assume identical individual tastes. Moreover, it is hard to accept the fact that even if all individuals are endowed with the same tastes, their utility functions of income should be viewed as identical without having a more detailed and specific definition of utility. This issue was famously addressed by Jevons who strictly individualised the issue of utility. He saw "no means whereby such a comparison can be accomplished. Every mind is inscrutable to every other mind and no common denominator of feeling is possible" (1888, p. 33). Robbins (2007 [1932]) concluded that the interpersonal comparison of utility is unscientific since individual mental states are inscrutable and, hence, comparing interpersonal utilities is necessarily normative. This question was also scrutinised, inter alia, by Rosenbaum (1995) and Blaug (1992). The claims of, particularly, Jevons and Robbins shook the foundations of the classical utilitarian theory for which a common unit for the measurement of individual pleasures and pains was considered perfectly adequate for interpersonal comparison purposes.

If one considers modern demand theory as proposed by Pareto, Allen, Hicks and Samuelson, utility is understood simply as an individual's revealed preference. Such an approach involves a shift in terms of its conceptual framework towards an ordinal rather than a cardinal scaling. This suggests that real individual behaviour is preferable to other alternative forms of behaviour, without being armed with a deeper knowledge of utility value differences across given alternatives. It is no longer necessary to have a common unit via which to measure and compare individual utility differences. Here one can identify two main strands of argument against interpersonal utility comparisons: firstly, that the same commodity generates a different utility depending on the environment and conditions; and, that individuals have inherently different tastes and preferences, which means that even under the same conditions, two individuals may value a commodity differently. In the light of the aforementioned passages, the argument against an interpersonal utility comparison, which primarily serves for the evaluation of the situations of different individuals under different conditions, sounds plausible.

As the applicability of the interpersonal comparison of utility weakened, other distributional schemes began to dominate. Perhaps the most common distributional criterion in economics concerns Pareto-optimality, which refers to a situation in which no individual (or preference criterion) can be better-off without rendering another worse-off. While so-called weak Pareto-optimality means that at least one individual is better-off and others are at least as well-off, "strong Pareto-optimality" requires that all individuals must be better-off. Interpersonal comparisons thus play a role only when deciding *between* the alternative Pareto-optimal allocations, and not when deciding on the allocation as such. On the other hand, the Pareto optimisation also has a number of weaknesses. Firstly, one should bear in mind that, as with other distributional criteria, Pareto-optimal allocations contain strong normative aspects. The economic literature sometimes presents such allocations almost as being the only thinkable distributional criterion, which, nevertheless, is rarely contextualised with the normative purposes thereof. The claim that economic distribution *should* follow the rule that no allocation happens at someone else's costs is not a natural law that independently governs the distribution of scarce resources, but a socially constructed criterion. Welfare theorems prove that competitive market allocation leads to Pareto-optimal states. If the economy produces a certain amount of wealth and all individuals prefer to have more of that wealth rather than less of it, then, naturally, every distribution must be Pareto-optimal since no one can become better-off without making another worse-off. If all the resources in a competitive market are assigned to one agent and the rest of the agents have no resources, the situation is Pareto-optimal since any alternative distribution would happen at the expense of the dominant agent. Literature inspired by Barone (1908) and Kaldor (1939), which posits that if those who are becoming better-off can slightly compensate those who are negatively affected by the change, neither solves the problem: in such a situation, everyone becomes better-off compared to the former situation; however, compensating those who would otherwise be worse-off means that those who are supposed to benefit from the change must be less better-off than if no compensation had been applied. Therefore, and despite its wide acceptance, Pareto-optimality continues to generate considerable controversy in terms of welfare economics applications.

Conversely, it should be noted that several concepts concerning social choice theory, for instance Sen's (1970) contribution to social welfare modelling or the numerous works of John Harsanyi, are still capable of – fully or partly – accommodating interpersonal comparisons. The general idea is that, on the one hand, individuals do not share the same tastes, but, on the other, they share a robust common background. It is not necessary to investigate whether one desires to eat, drink or sleep, and it is similarly naïve to claim the strict incomparability of interpersonal utilities due to individuals having differing tastes, as well as to follow the early utilitarian (and principally essentialist) assumption that a commodity provides the same utility to all individuals. Most distributional questions can, however, be answered through simple alternative principles (Sen 1997): for instance, to judge that $U_j(x) > U_k(y)$ is the same thing as preferring to be individual $j$ in state $x$ rather than individual $k$ in state $y$.

## The Impotence of the Behavioural "Critique"

Previous subchapters have outlined the foundations of modern economic thought in connection with distributional rules. As was alluded to in the first chapter, economics raises important questions which are hard to separate from the broader social context. On the other hand, mainstream economics, rather ambitiously, dares to explain a vast range of social phenomena which are usually considered as being beyond the realm of economics. Nonetheless, in addition to mainstream economics, it is necessary to consider the mainstream critique thereof, which involves, principally, behavioural approaches to economic phenomena. The unfortunate aspect of this critique, however, is that many behavioural economists have succumbed to the misconception that economic models must be identified with a degree of observable reality. Therefore, the behavioural approach supplements sober neoclassical models with various psychological aspects surrounding the decision-making process aimed at more accurately describing the immediate reality. However, in contrast to the natural sciences, the social sciences focus on variance-based phenomena and, thus, researchers face a trade-off between theoretical objectiveness and empirical particularity. Behavioural insights are, therefore, at risk of comprising mere fragmented empirical "evidence" of psychological descriptivism. Moreover, as a reaction to a further aspect of the behavioural critique, this subchapter provides a progressive interpretation of rationality through the mainstream neoclassical viewpoint. This is important since it both outlines the blind approach of the economics critique and underlines the essential features and theoretical strengths of mainstream economics. The subchapter is closely based on Maialeh (2019).

A large body of research over the past few decades indicates that neoclassical models may not provide the most reliable tool for the description of economic reality, not to mention economic predictions or public policy measures. Starting with Allais (1953), Simon (1955), Kahneman and Tversky (1979) and Thaler (1980), various insights from the field of psychology were incorporated into economics, which significantly influenced the way economists related to their discipline. In addition, the behavioural approach has already affected various public policies; one might recall, for example, Benartzi and Thaler (2004) and their policy tools aimed at increasing retirement savings. Interestingly, a range of new policy tools and prediction options (see particularly Chetty et al. 2013) generated by behavioural economics have been suggested by Thaler and Sunstein (2008), Congdon et al. (2011), Keller-Allen and Li (2013) and Madrian (2014). Undoubtedly, behavioural insights – such as framing incentives or changing default options – have the potential to considerably influence the outcomes of an individual's behaviour. Nevertheless, a number of fundamental methodological questions related to the behavioural approach remain, at least partly, unanswered. This subchapter is, therefore, structured in the form of three sections that address (i) empirical analysis in the social sciences, (ii) the behavioural confrontation of central neoclassical arguments and, finally, (iii) the application of the behavioural approach in social practice. The aim of each part is to highlight the substantial limits of the behavioural approach.

Firstly, the author focuses on the generalisation of variance-based results in empirical social sciences. The main point of this section is that despite applying similar research methods, the nature of phenomena in the social sciences differs substantially from the phenomena researched in the natural sciences. Empirical social scientists thus face an enormous challenge – how should one generalise empirical results in view of the fact that the researched phenomena are difficult to isolate and immanently vary in terms of space and time? And can such variance-based socioeconomic phenomena be repeatedly verifiable through the observed data?

Starting with general methodological questions, the purpose of any model is to grasp the decisive factors that explain the *systematic movement* of the researched phenomena. The natural sciences have been relatively successful when applying this approach – they have clarified various causal relationships and established law-abiding motions. One example in this respect concerns the gravity of the Earth. Acceleration due to gravity ranges from 9.76 to 9.83 $m/s^2$ (N/kg), depending on the altitude and latitude, and the standard is considered to be 9.81 $m/s^2$. The nominal gravitational acceleration of an object is, however, based on the surface of the Earth and, more unrealistically, in a vacuum. Despite the unrealistic assumption of vacuum conditions (aimed at eliminating air resistance), the natural sciences are equipped with an accumulation of knowledge that allowed for the proposal of this particular law of mass motion. Economics applies similar quantitative modelling tools as does physics, with similar purposes and, regrettably, employing a similar approach to the interpretation of the results. Whereas neoclassical economics also adopted "unrealistic" assumptions on the researched phenomena, the crucial distinction comprises the phenomena itself. As demonstrated, neglecting a number of frictions that exist in reality can lead to the detection of law-based regularities that are, in fact, objective since the phenomena researched in the natural sciences are invariance-based. Such invariancy is linked to a situation where the subject of the research reacts/behaves consistently under given conditions, that is, where any empirical test under the given conditions necessarily produces identical results. Established objective laws can then be smoothly extrapolated to an unlimited number of repetitions, which serve to test the researched relationship, for example, when carbon dioxide reacts with water, all the empirical testing of this combination will result in the same weak acid provided the original conditions hold. Theories formulated in the natural sciences, for example, theories on the chemical reactions between gases and liquids, in general correspond to the respective empirical verifications since theories in the natural sciences are derived from observed phenomena, and the respective theory is only valid when it aligns with empirical reality. Thus, the generalisation of the results of a random (but controlled) empirical verification contributes to a theory, insomuch as the generalised results are repeatedly verifiable and finally verified. The external validity of any experimental test is thus secured, and the empirical results take the form of general laws.[3]

Modern economic methodology has been widely inspired by that of the natural sciences in the sense that theory should be based on observed data. The increasing influence of empirical evidence in economics has been documented by Hamermesh (2013), whose results revealed that the percentage of empirical papers increased from 38% to 72% between 1980 and 2010. The aim here, rather than attempting to reverse this trend, is to consider the most controversial aspects of this turn of events, aspects that are closely linked to the nature of the researched phenomena, bearing in mind that, unlike the natural sciences, economics as a branch of the social sciences deals with variance-based phenomena. This factor must inevitably lead to a different approach to economic theory represented by mathematical models and the interpretation of empirical results. This issue has already been developed by numerous researchers, for example, Gechter (2015) focused specifically on experimental data on Mexican micro-entrepreneurs and concluded that standard methods may lead to an over-reliance on generalisability; however, Druckman and Kam (2011), for example, are more optimistic concerning the generalisability of experimental results.

With respect to the formal structure of the debate, empirical findings in economics can be split into two main subfields according to the source of the empirical results. Firstly, we can consider empirical findings based on experiments. One of the most intriguing recent publications concerns Leigh (2018) who persuasively advocates the use of randomised controlled trials (RCTs) throughout various fields of the social sciences. The second subfield of empirical analysis is based on observations from the real world, an approach to analysis that is still dominating the mainstream. Both subfields emphasise the idea that only factual evidence can form the criterion of theoretical correctness. Without going into too much detail on his methodological foundations, it is easy to recognise Friedman's influence here: in his *Essays*, we read that predictive power should form the prime benchmark for theory. This means that the only test of the validity of a model lies in the comparison of its predictions with experience. Such predictions, however, do not need to be compared to phenomena that have not yet occurred, that is, they do not necessarily need to forecast future events. On the other hand, as a lesson for contemporary economists, Friedman was fully aware of the fact that factual evidence cannot prove a hypothesis, it might only fail to disprove it (1953, pp. 8–9). Thus, the decisive challenge remains the verification of empirical predictions in the social sciences.

These methodological comments are strongly related to the behavioural critique of neoclassical economics. The standpoint from which behavioural economists confront neoclassical theory is linked directly to the relationship between behavioural empirical evidence and mainstream models. The aforementioned argumentation indicates that the behavioural critique supposedly "hit the spot": it requires, in the tradition of Friedman, that predictions of economic models be as accurate as the observed reality. This critique is supplemented by behavioural insights that may act to enrich the oversimplified abstraction of economic phenomena in order to form predictions that are closer to the observed reality. The fact that the social sciences work with variance-based phenomena, however, significantly complicates such methodological questions. The fluidity and complexity of economic events result in, for instance, the role of values in an individual's behaviour becoming a non-isolable factor; thus, empirical conclusions tend to be reduced to merely the directly observed phenomenon. In addition, it would be too naïve to assume that human cognition is always able to grasp phenomena in their "totality" in the sense of all the relations, processes and properties involved; in brief, all the aspects of reality. This question was famously raised by Hayek:

> The object of scientific study is never the totality of all the phenomena observable at a given time and place, but always only certain selected aspects. . . . The human mind indeed can never grasp a "whole" in the sense of all the different aspects of a real situation.
>
> (1943, p. 55)

It is necessary to note here that the simplicity of Hayek's position is based on the rationalist-empiricist idea that cognition proceeds via the analytic-summative method. As pointed out by Kosík (1976), this approach will never overcome the atomist idea of cognition as a mere summation of things. Despite the underlying objectivity of relations, facts and processes, it does not provide tools for the demystification of their genesis or structure. Nevertheless, it is probably sufficient for the purposes of this chapter to work with Hayek's standpoint that man is unable to grasp all the aspects of reality. Be that as it may, intricate relations between complexity and empirical analysis are approached in a more sophisticated manner by current research, but on a less fundamental basis (see e.g. Durlauf 2005). In simple terms, current economic research tends to make use of advanced scientific methods which themselves become the criterion for economic research – their applicability decides what can be researched, whether it be applied to subjects of banal curiosity or themes with a high degree of social urgency.

The difference between empirical evidence in the social and natural sciences thus lies in the relevance of the generalised results – although empirical results in the natural sciences establish general laws, similar results in the social sciences merely provide information on a particular phenomenon under highly selective conditions which, due to the non-isolability of social phenomena, may never occur again. This question was raised as early as during the formation period of modern economics by Robbins (Chapters III and IV 2007 [1932]) and Marshall (2013 [1890]). The latter argues that all sciences (i.e. physical) that aim at exactness precipitate "the result of a multitude of observations into provisional statements, which are sufficiently definite to be brought under test by other observations of nature". Marshall continues:

> [T]hese statements, when first put forth, seldom claim a high authority. But after they have been tested by many independent observations, and especially after they have been applied successfully in the prediction of coming events, or of the results of new experiments, they graduate as laws.
>
> (2013 [1890], p. 25)

Economics in modern times continues to strive to establish similar laws as those outlined by Marshall. Empirical evidence in the social sciences (economics), as opposed to the natural sciences, assigns a lower level of "lawfulness" to researched relationships due to the complexity of factors that affect the results; these factors, for example, the situational context, values, the history of the subject or the mental state are always present and can never be fully isolated (for a deeper discussion see Rosenberg 1995; Mäki 1992, or Hanzel 2010). The social sciences therefore face the following trade-off: the more accurate the model is, that is, the more accurate are the predictions of empirical reality it generates, the more difficult it is to generalise the results. Hence, the nature of economic events complicates efforts to establish a theory from particularised empirical insights. Briefly, social science theories cannot simply be established based on the mere summation of particular facts due to the inconsistency (variance) of the researched phenomena. The lawfulness of economic insights is thus of a different character. If a central bank lowers interest rates, it will always generate universal incentives for consumption and investment. The final empirical moment – whether falling interest rates really led to increasing consumption and investment – is simply unable to either validate or disprove general economic theory. What is important for economic theory at this point is the general law that lower interest rates render present consumption and investment cheaper and, therefore, stimulate economic agents, who are in principle under economic scarcity, to behave in a certain way (this might represent an equivalent to gravity in physics). Whether what economic theory assumes happens or not relates to narrowly defined empirical research, which is hardly likely to disprove the general tendency following a fall in interest rates. The degree of lawfulness therefore concerns the underlying forces that operate within the economic system rather than the final empirical result. It is simply a delusion that economics should strive for the empirical demonstration of its results with the accuracy and generalisability possible in the natural sciences. In summary, variance-based phenomena are characterised by the fact that the empirical verification conditions are too difficult to control and, therefore, empirical verification necessarily provides incoherent results. Thus, regularities detected via empirical verification, based merely on statistical inference, cannot be considered to be objective laws since they cannot be extrapolated to an unlimited number of repetitions as opposed to invariance-based phenomena in the natural sciences.

Economic theory cannot be based *exclusively* on empirical evidence as can natural science theory since the evidence varies in terms of a multitude of human and social aspects. And conversely, it is hard to imagine that neoclassical theory could be disproved by random (or supposedly systematic) empirical evidence: for instance, if lower interest rates, at a certain place and time, do not lead to increases in consumption and investment. Such empirical evidence would not disprove the fact that lower interest rates generate positive incentives for consumption and investment. Due to such limitations to the generalisation of empirical results, economic models should serve as a tool merely for the clarification of the direction, tendencies and principles of changes at a highly general theoretical level. Predictive power, in the sense of its corresponding with empirical reality, cannot comprise the only criterion for the validity of economic theory. However, this does not suggest that social scientists should completely abandon empirical analysis, rather they should be aware of the fact that their empirical results are burdened with selectivity, particularity and subjectivity due simply to the unavoidable variance-based nature of the phenomena investigated in the social sciences. Moreover, it does not mean that the empirical testing of theoretical predictions is of no importance; in this sense, it is possible to recall a number of ground-breaking examples, for example, the issue of the minimum wage, which shows that empirical evidence is capable of activating a fruitful debate. However, if one goes back to Deaton and

Cartwright (2016) and slightly modify his theses, it is also necessary to appreciate that such an approach can contribute to scientific knowledge only by adding to the conceptual and theoretical background, since the aim of scientific knowledge is to discover not only "what is" but also "why it is". Thus, while empirical findings are able to enhance our interpretation of selected frictions of reality, they cannot serve as the prime source for a theory and nor can they serve as the sole and reliable criterion for the validity of a theory.

The following section discusses the rationality of economic agents. It is widely acknowledged by behavioural economists, among others, that the foundational assumptions of neoclassical economics that operates with rational agents should be challenged. Contributors to the contentious debate on the rationality of individuals from the behavioural perspective include for example Levitt and List (2007), Lee et al. (2009) and DellaVigna (2009). Current research points towards context-dependence; idiosyncratic mistakes can be cancelled out via arbitrage, experience effects or aggregation (see e.g. List 2004 or Farber 2014). Some decisions, however, continue to include behavioural phenomena due to the limits of arbitrage (Shleifer and Vishny 1997), and problems with debiasing consumers (Gabaix and Laibson 2006) may lead to persisting anomalies in the decision-making of economic agents. Here, the author adds to this discussion by providing an approach to reading neoclassical economics in the context of behavioural analysis and critically reflecting on the behavioural approach from a new perspective. According to Sen (1991), rationality is assessed based on the maximisation of utility and the consistency of choice. This section, therefore, presents the main behavioural arguments against the neoclassical concepts of utility and the consistency of choice and, subsequently, responds to these arguments from the neoclassical position. The aim of this section is to clarify the reasons for the maximisability of the utility function even with unselfish motives and satisficing behaviour, and to demonstrate the reasons behind the fact that behavioural findings do not disprove neoclassical rationality.

Neoclassical economics is often the subject of critique from various standpoints, for which, admittedly, there are a number of serious reasons. The behavioural critique frequently highlights the supposedly irrational, or at least non-rational (Selten 1999), behaviour of economic agents. Consequently, economic models that assume fully rational agents allegedly do not correspond to the observed data. Behavioural economics, therefore, strives to establish descriptively accurate findings with implications for economic behaviour. In doing so, the behavioural approach investigates market situations in which some of the agents display human limitations which are linked to various cognitive biases and bounded rationality in general. This also relates to the central point of the behavioural critique of neoclassical economics – the assumed rationality of economic agents.

A rational agent is characterised by self-interested motives which lead to utility-maximising behaviour. Sen[4] (1991) splits neoclassical rationality into (i) the maximisation of self-interest and (ii) the consistency of choice. As a critic of the neoclassical concept of rationality, Sen (1991), supported, for example, by Becker (1962), warns that any deviation from self-interested behaviour is qualified as irrational by economic theory. He provides an example from Japan where economic agents allegedly do not blindly follow the self-interest imperative. The argument suggests that such agents report high levels of loyalty and goodwill as the key to success. However, if such behaviour is the key to success, is not it a rational way in which to fulfil self-interested goals related to personal success?

Behavioural economists are not alone in disputing the assertion that rational economic agents exist. Following the line of Marxian scholars, Wolff (1990) uses the critique of self-interestedness to attack methodological individualism. He claims that such a presumption remains firmly in the centre of classical and neoclassical economics despite its not being compatible with basic human experience; it is not universal to human history, nor does it grasp the logic of collective action. He names analytical schemes such as the "Prisoner's dilemma" or "Free riders" as inappropriate since they assume only egoistic preferences. On the other hand, behavioural economists believe that the behaviour of economic agents is full of biases related to other aspects of irrational or at least non-rational behaviour, which consequently lead economic agents to suboptimal outcomes. It must be noted here that without normative and universal value-judgements, it is not clear what is meant by utility maximisation and, hence, what is meant by rational behaviour. We read in Jevons (1888), who supposedly relied on the narrower view of individual motivation, that the quantity of utility or pleasure is derived from goods delivered to its consumer. For now, let us leave homogeneous pleasure aside. This redirects the debate towards decision-making situations in which an individual decides, for example, between altruistic sacrifice and self-interested gain. Is such a decision-making process beyond the utility calculus as Mandler (2001) claims? Does neoclassical theory posit that satisfaction delivered through goods and services is the only source of utility/pleasure as interpreted by Goodwin et al. (2013)?

It is important to understand that utility theory was incorporated into economics with a very astute purpose, that is, to express an individual's pleasures and pains via a common scale, a point that was captured by Kosík (1976). Although Kosík is mercilessly critical of the neoclassical concept of *homo oeconomicus*, he understands that *homo oeconomicus* is a systemic connecting element which transforms empirical chaotic multiplicity into lawfulness. However, neoclassical economists from time to time tend to forget that they are pursuing a positivist social science when they incorporate the normativity of something that might be termed "vulgar hedonism". For the purpose of this book, this term is used in order to designate the difference between self-interest and selfishness. The point of the following examples is not to show how often this misunderstanding leads to systematic error in "want-to-be" neoclassical models, but to show that the behavioural critique of vulgar hedonism in neoclassical economics is false. For instance, we assume certainty when facing the decision whether to (i) lose 5 USD but still have good family relationships or (ii) whether to gain 5 USD but suddenly have bad family relationships. The typical misinterpretation of self-interested utility that assumes purely economic values will conclude that the latter is preferable. Utility, however, must be understood in its fundamental sense, that is, as a subjective amount of net pleasure delivered through the decision of an individual. When utility is understood in this way, economists elegantly circumvent the normative ethical dimension necessary for such decision-making. The mental calculation of potential utility changes is thus intuitive since the net effects of both options are negative, but, presumably, the negative effect of bad family relationships outweighs the negative effect of the loss of 5 USD – the utility is maximised via monetised loss. Such a maximisation of the difference between one's own costs and benefits comprises one of the central ideas of economic thought; see, for example, Friedman (1953, pp. 15, 21, 31). The crucial misunderstanding thus concerns the narrow view of a small number of economists (whether behavioural or neoclassical) of what costs and benefits, disutility and utility represent in neoclassical theory.

Such misunderstandings stem principally from the definition of self-interest (subjectively perceived costs and benefits) and the related utility derivation. The utility function of an individual is constructed according to states of the world that provide the individual with the greatest amount of pleasure. Admittedly, neoclassical economists have contributed significantly to the egoist subversion of utility – self-interest has been substituted with the aforementioned vulgar hedonism. This is, however, very distant from (indeed, in contradiction with) the former understanding of utilitarianism, in which altruism, compassion and sympathy also serve to motivate humans as mentioned by Mill (2007 [1861]). Persky (1995) confirmed the fact that a "monomaniacal economic man" is far from Mill's thinking; conversely, Persky presents Mill's rather colourful psychology in terms of the broader spheres of human motives, from free time to sexual relationships. We must also remember that all these motives are highly subjective: what one person finds pleasing may be painful for another – a gym visit accompanied with its objective physical suffering results in completely different emotional outcomes depending on the individual. Such a general and complex understanding of utility overcomes misinterpretations of man as a greedy cold-rational subject. According to Mill, the social sciences must work with well-defined and simple abstraction, for instance, with strictly selfish behaviour. On the other hand, it would be a huge mistake to take these human behaviour attributes as an exhaustive list of human motivational elements, in a similar way to Jevons' fixation that utility from consumption does not mean that utility is determined exclusively by the consumption of monetised goods and services.

Nevertheless, such a viewpoint is not restricted to neoclassical and behavioural economists; at this point, one might, again, recall Wolff (1990) who presents the typical anti-neoclassical argumentation that human action is not based on self-interest, it is not universal to human history, and it is not compatible with basic human experience, nor can it grasp the logic of collective action. The point is that every human action, even the most altruistic action, is explainable from the position of self-centred preferences, that is, through neoclassical utility theories. The behavioural answer, however, does not theoretically eliminate the widespread fallacy of vulgar hedonism in neoclassical utility theory. Conversely, the behavioural critique follows up on the perverted part of neoclassical misinterpretation – the fetishised abstraction of egoist behaviour – and empirically disproves the obvious consequence of such fetishisation. It serves merely the very self-evident assertion that individuals are not vulgar hedonists with narrow motivations. However, the problem with utility is much more fundamental. This subchapter is aimed at clearly demonstrating that only subjective individual preferences[5] establish the utility function of a given agent. The objects of the agent's desires may vary according to the agent, the place and the time. Since these desires and motivations are assumed to be strictly subjective, the accusation of non-maximising utility appears ridiculous, the reason being that every step an agent takes is explainable from the perspective of utility maximisation since no reliable means exist for verifying such individual human actions. It must be understood that utility maximisation is *assumed* rather than *explained* in economics. This fact serves to problematise the second part of the issue, that is, specifically, that economics strives to explain various real-world phenomena via the utility concept. While it may appear to be a tautology and give the impression of unscientificity, it certainly cannot be confronted from such a misinterpreted perspective, that is, one from which the observer defines behaviour that goes against observed individual utility.

A cost-benefit analysis based on Bentham's utility calculus of pleasure and pain is applicable to various examples of the behavioural critique of neoclassical theory. Modern literature on social preferences and fairness, for example, by Rabin (1993), Levine (1998), Fehr and Schmidt (1999), Bolton and Ockenfels (2000) or Gul and Pesendorfer (2004), attempts to capture the idea that under certain circumstances, individuals are altruistic and under others egoistic. An example is provided by the Dictator "game" (Kahneman et al. 1986), which has been replicated several times accompanied by suggested results (see e.g. Forsythe et al. 1994). This experimental paradigm supposedly refutes the notion of the rationally self-interested individual in neoclassical theory. Basically, the dictator decides how to split endowments between himself and a second recipient, while the recipient has no influence over the outcome of the dictator's decision. Neoclassical theory would supposedly conclude that in such a situation, the dictator will take all. The rewriting of the dictator's decision-making process in the form of simple constraint optimisation applying the Cobb-Douglas utility function provides the following:

$$u_D\left(x_D, x_2\right) = x_D^{\alpha} x_2^{\beta}$$

$$\text{s.t. } x_D + x_2 = 1$$

where $x_D$ denotes the part of the endowment for the dictator himself and $x_2$ denotes the part of the endowment the dictator has determined for the second player. Further, $\alpha$ is the dictator's "selfish coefficient" and $\beta$ is the "altruistic coefficient", while $\alpha, \beta \in \mathbb{R}^+$. The dictator will always choose the most preferred bundle from the set of affordable alternatives and the final split of the endowment depends on the dictator's marginal utilities $u_{D}\cdot(x_{D})$, $u_{D}\cdot(x_{2})$. If $\alpha > \beta$, then selfish motives dominate over altruistic motives and vice versa. Since altruistic motives are inseparable from an individual's happiness, let us assume that the second player is the dictator's own child. Such a situation represents the parent-child relationship where the parent has full control over economic distribution; hence, it is easy to understand that the wellbeing of the dictator's child comprises a significant component of the dictator's own utility function. Thus, we approach a situation where potentially $(\beta > \alpha)$. A simple calculation yields $x_2 = \frac{\beta}{\alpha} x_D$; after substituting into the budget constraint, we obtain $x_D = \frac{\alpha}{\alpha + \beta}$. By assuming that altruistic motives prevail over selfish motives when the dictator's child is the second player $x_2 > x_D$, we obtain $\beta = \alpha \rightarrow x_2 = x_D$. Even a typical neoclassical analytical tool such as constraint optimisation with the Cobb-Douglas utility thus allows the capture of the dictator maximising his utility through distributing the endowment in various ways – for example, $\beta = \alpha \rightarrow x_2 = x_D$ when the second player is a friend; $\beta < \alpha \rightarrow x_2 < x_D$ when the second player is an unknown individual or $\beta = 0 \rightarrow x_2 = 0$ when the second player is a hated individual.

It is also possible to further manipulate the dictator's conditions: for instance, it is to be expected that when the decision-maker is exposed to competitive pressure his/her altruistic motives decline, as documented, for example, by Houser and Schunk (2009) or in a meta-study on the dictator game by Engel (2010). Nevertheless, the example presented earlier illustrates that if utility is comprehended fundamentally in its pure sense, then the utility function can be maximised without the undue totalisation of selfish motives. Finally, this does not suggest that self-interest is not the prime motive. On the contrary, the example demonstrates self-interest as the justification for any human action. It is not necessary to return to Aristotle's *Nicomanchean Ethics* to appreciate the point; for instance, care for others as presented earlier is an inseparable part of self-interest. In other words, it may well be in one's own interests to enjoy good relationships or not to seem too greedy and so forth. The fundamental understanding of utility thus allows for the agent's own interests potentially including, for example, the aforementioned wellbeing of a child, which serves to connect the topic, for example, with the bequest motive (see Bernheim et al. 1985). This legitimate form of pursuing one's own interests is thus in contradiction to vulgar hedonism which has contaminated economic thought with the ruthless and perverse obsession with one's own material wellbeing at any costs. Obviously, such behaviour can never be supported by any relevant empirical evidence since it contradicts the very essence of most human motivations. To summarise, based on experimental and empirical evidence, the behavioural critique argues that economic agents do not adopt the selfish behaviour presumed in neoclassical theory. The fallacy of such a critique is thus that (i) in contrast to regularly assumed self-interestedness, neoclassical theory never assumed such a kind of selfishness; and that (ii) behavioural results simply report what is self-evident – that economic agents do not appropriate all the available resources just for themselves all the time and everywhere, that is, the conclusion that can be derived from the neoclassical understanding of utility.

The behavioural critique discourse includes a further point of view that relates to utility maximisation, and which is worthy of discussion. It is often claimed (e.g. Sen 1993 and especially, in terms of its influence, Simon 1956) that, for various reasons, economic agents are not maximisers in terms of their utility. The utility function is not maximised because (i) the agent does not fulfil self-interested objectives or (ii) the agent ends up with a suboptimal outcome. It is also important to emphasise that as long as we operate with mere preferences, we do not problematise economic questions – the transition to economics requires a constraint. This obvious fact is, however, not always considered. One of the most profound arguments relies on satisficing behaviour (Simon 1955, 1956). Simon's contribution concludes that satisficing behaviour differs from maximising behaviour or, alternatively, that agents satisfice rather than optimise in terms of maximisation. Thus, agents decide on a satisfactory level that is "good enough" for each objective. Such a form of decision-making supposedly generates a suboptimal outcome since the outcome does not correspond to the maximum level of satisfaction but to a sufficient level of satisfaction. Satisficing behaviour is, thus, most likely the most acknowledged *monistic* cognitive strategy confronting the mainstream maximising behaviour if one considers its inspiration to a number of partial "save-time" heuristics, for example, "fast and frugal heuristics" (Gigerenzer and Goldstein 1996; Goldstein and Gigerenzer 2002). Such heuristics are labelled "partial" since they form just a part of the decision maker's repertoire of cognitive strategies, as opposed to the monistic strategy (satisficing versus maximising) which supposes that the agent decides based on one strategy alone.

At this point, let us employ constraints in order to outline the similarity between satisficing and maximising behaviour. One of the similarities between these two cognitive strategies has already been discussed by van Witteloostuijn (1988) who claimed that if choice theoretic models are well-designed, which means that they introduce goal-setting procedures, uncertainty, group decision-making or computational disabilities, they might produce the same results. This is rather a laborious way of proving that these two cognitive strategies posit the same thing in two different languages – here we show that satisficing and maximising must be the same *in principle*. Hence, we investigate whether satisficing behaviour, a sequential process that ceases its search once a predefined threshold has been reached, is in contradiction with the neoclassical assumption that agents generally try to achieve the best possible outcome from the decision-making process. A simple example is possible employing the neoclassical apparatus. Assume Doucouliagos' (1994) student who has the capacity to attain better grades but chooses not to do so. The utility function of the student naturally contains the potential to attain the best possible grades; however, the student's constraint takes into account the time and effort (price or disutility) that have to be sacrificed in order to attain the desired grades. The intuitive calculation is as follows: if the marginal subjectively perceived utility from attaining better grades exceeds the marginal subjectively perceived disutility from the sacrificed time and effort, then the student continues to improve his/her grades. Conversely, if the marginal subjectively perceived disutility exceeds the marginal subjectively perceived utility, then continuing to improve his/her grades decreases the student's net utility. At a certain *subjectively defined point*, pursuing better grades ceases to be the best alternative since the net utility, as the difference between the gained utility and the experienced disutility, decreases. It follows that the student can maximise his/her utility (comprising the best possible grades) with grades that are not objectively the best. Nevertheless, utility is based on subjective perceptions. Alternatively, when the agent expects a fixed level of utility for which he/she minimises expenditure, it is possible to apply a further neoclassical textbook tool – Hicksian demand – which latently corresponds to Simon's (1956, p. 136) claim concerning a satisficing path "that will permit satisfaction at some specified level of all of its needs". To conclude, satisficing behaviour signifies a "good enough" situation in which the agent's marginal utility equals his/her marginal disutility, that is, when the agent has no utility-increasing reason to deviate. However, if the agent has no reason to deviate, then he/she has reached the optimum point, thus maximising his/her utility.

Further, it is also necessary to consider the second pillar of rationality as postulated by Sen (1991) – rationality as the consistency of choice. At least since Robbins (2007 [1932]), consistency has played a serious role in economic rationality. Behavioural economics has robust empirical evidence at its disposal that the consistency of choice is violated and, hence, economic agents cannot be considered rational; here one can mention, for example, the crossing indifference curves in Knetsch (1990) and other violations of the axiom of transitivity in the work of Lee et al. (2009). Maialeh (2019) in this respect provides a formal explanation which, for the purpose of this book, can be summarised as follows. Firstly, the agent's choice inconsistency is usually attacked as a violation of the transitivity axiom, which states that if a decision-maker prefers choice $x$ to $y$, and at the same time choice $y$ to $z$, then $x$ must necessarily be preferable to $z$. Naturally, one can examine the consistency of choice through the axiom of transitivity, but what if the conditions of choice change? This is secured by the independence axiom which, in the context of the Chernoff condition, states that if a decision-maker prefers $x$ to $y$ from the bundle $\{x, y\}$, then adding an independent alternative $z$ cannot change the former preferential ranking, that is, the decision-maker still prefers $x$ to $y$ from the bundle $\{x, y, z\}$. But who decides which alternative is truly independent of the choice? Let us assume that an individual prefers salad to pasta in summer but pasta to salad in winter. Another individual may prefer pasta to salad regardless of the season, so that the season plays the role of an independent alternative since it does not affect the decision-maker's choice in terms of utility, whereas others may prefer these meals according to the season in the opposite way. In simple words, even objectively given variables such as the time or place may influence the chosen alternative without harming the rationality concept. The problem is that only a subjectively formed utility function defines what the independent alternative is. Understanding this concept requires a return to Jevons who posits that utility is not an inherent quality of a commodity but rather "*a circumstance of things* arising out of their relation to man's requirements" (1888, p. 49; emphasis is original).

Based upon its axiomatic background, neoclassical economics constructed a much stronger argumentative position than is usually observed – as shown previously, consistency as an element of rational behaviour in neoclassical theory is violated when transitivity and independent alternative axioms no longer hold. Inconsistency means that an agent who repeatedly and with a strict preference faces the same choice from the bundle $\{x, y\}$ changes his/her mind and picks both $x$ and $y$ on an irregular basis. The *ceteris paribus* requirement naturally also applies to the axiom of transitivity – if the conditions of choice change, then it loses its purpose in a similar way to the independence axiom becoming nonsensical if an added alternative is able to influence the agent's utility. In other words, it is rational for the decision-maker to switch from one commodity to another if the change serves to enhance the agent's utility. On the other hand, it might be irrational to insist on a certain choice even though the conditions of the choice are changing. The fact that changing conditions lead to changes in the decision-making process may, conversely, be a sign of rational behaviour – the agent adapts to new conditions that may affect his/her utility and rationally pursues his/her own goals through flexible changes in the decision-making process. Consistency under changing conditions should, therefore, be understood as a mental procedure via which the agent makes decisions that do not deviate from the maximisation of utility rather than openly rigid decisions that may be in conflict with one's utility – such rigid decisions undoubtedly cannot form a part of rational behaviour. The behavioural critique should, therefore, avoid the risk of setting observable rigidity as a proxy for consistency, which is non-controllable without being aware of the utility function.

If the conditions of choice only *seem* to change[6] yet *de facto* remain unaffected, then we involve cognitive limitations, a factor that belongs in the domain of the behavioural approach, whereby consistency is challenged through both of the stated axioms. Such an approach, however, is unable to distinguish whether the agent follows a rational-choice *procedure* based on the stated axioms or whether the suboptimal outcome stems from the agent's cognitive limitations. Without such a distinction, the behavioural results may indicate non-rational behaviour despite the fact that the agent intentionally follows a rational decision-making process, but where his/her cognitive limitations result in suboptimal or inconsistent decisions. This is because the agent is simply unable to fully control the environment (due to the agent's objective limitations), while the environment finally serves to co-produce the outcome of the agent's decisions. The typical definition of rationality as instrumental is especially important in economics – the agent is rational insofar as he adopts suitable means to his/her ends. Such agents optimise based on current beliefs, while the previously outlined outcome-based assessment of rationality concerns *ex-post* rationality, which is in contradiction with the *ex-ante* approach of the Bayesian agent in neoclassical economics.

For the moment, let us consider an example based on retirement policies: current research (e.g. Poterba 2014) has demonstrated that many people are unlikely to reach a sufficient level of savings to cover their retirement, which has led policymakers to stimulate the household savings rate (Thaler and Benartzi 2004). The following example challenges the behavioural idea that cognitive biases, which may result in suboptimal outcomes, signify that an agent's utility is not maximised and, hence, such an agent necessarily acts non-rationally. To put it simply, we have an agent who is equipped with certain information on his health. The agent maximises the utility function based on consumption which suggests consumption-smoothing preferences over the whole period of his expected life. Given the consumption-smoothing preference and our assumption that the agent's income in retirement will not be sufficient to cover consumption demands in retirement and his labour income exceeds consumption when working, the rational solution is to enrol in, for example, the "Save More Tomorrow" programme. Since the agent works as an actuary, the decision is supported by advanced computational methods which use all the disposable data to determine all the risks of death and the time spent in retirement, which indicates that the risk of premature death is low and the expected period in retirement is substantial. However, after decades of participating in the programme, the agent dies in a car accident just before retirement. Was the agent's decision to enter the "Save More Tomorrow" programme rational? If such a situation is assessed on outcome-based criteria (*ex-post*), that is, whether the agent maximised his utility from consumption when alive, the agent can never be labelled rational. The reason is very simple – the agent adapted to his current consumption in favour of consumption in retirement, but the consumption in retirement was lost due to an unlikely event. In other words, the agent chose inappropriate means to meet his long-term goal (to maximise utility from consumption over his whole lifetime), which is seen by behavioural economists as a sign of non-rational behaviour. On the other hand, enrolment in the programme took place at a given time and with the information available, that is, *ex-ante*, and it was the most rational act regardless of the unlucky and unlikely outcome. This example shows that by applying outcome-based criteria to rationality concepts, we face the risk that someone who *procedurally* behaves rationally but has bad luck might be assessed as being less rational than someone else who may procedurally behave irrationally but have good luck. This example outlines that even though the agent uses the best available means to his ends, it was not guaranteed that the agent's utility would be maximised in the expected way. Therefore, behavioural attempts to prove systematic irrational behaviour, which is supposedly based on the discrepancy between preestablished ends and appropriate means, methodologically suffers from a certain variant of the "outcome bias". Outcome-based criteria, which inevitably entail both cognitive limitations (e.g. in the computation probability in Baron et al. 1993 or Rottenstreich and Hsee 2001) and pure randomness and unpredictability; simply put, all uncontrollable factors affecting all outcome-based criteria are, thus, highly problematic with concern to the assessment of rational behaviour.

The final question related to the behavioural critique is related to public policy. Based on the previous sections of this chapter, it is argued that a combination of the uncertainties linked to an agent's utility and the problematic generalisation of the behavioural results may result in serious challenges with respect to real-life applications. Undoubtedly, there are several reasons for incorporating behavioural insights into public policy, as recently shown in, for example, Munro (2009), Chytilova (2017) and Oliver (2017). With respect to rational behaviour, it should be understood that not every deviation from a desired outcome that empirically provides an impression of systematic deviation is necessarily a result of non-rational behaviour. Value-neutral economic analysis has necessarily failed to provide a coherent idea of the specific aims pursued by agents in the context of utility-maximising behaviour. Despite the discussion on the position of normativity in behavioural economics (e.g. Berg 2003; Bernheim 2009; Mullainathan et al. 2012), the inevitable conclusion is that no all-embracing normative background exists related to the aims of an individual.

We observe significant empirically evident impacts when considering loss aversion or automatic enrolment based on the behavioural models of passive choice. Moreover, Benartzi and Thaler (2004) prove that such "nudges" may be of a more permanent nature due to the low opt-out rate. Nevertheless, the risk of the decontextualisation and depoliticisation of such questions is both high and dangerous – without normative value-judgements, specific socioeconomic conditions and political responsibility, it is almost impossible for policymakers to determine whether to act to increase the amount of resources people save for retirement or to set an optimal default savings rate. From the neoclassical perspective, it is necessary – due to the plurality of the aims of individuals – to abandon the idea that individual self-interest postulates unambiguously defined normativity; this implies that within the value-neutral economic framework, it is not simple to decide which type of behaviour is desired and which is not. Hence, the utility functions and rationality of differing individuals are – at least according to neoclassical theory – difficult to analyse in terms of a single normative base. Sen fittingly claims that without knowing what the agent is aiming for, that is, without "knowing something external to the choice itself" (1993, p. 501), we cannot determine whether the agent is failing or not; whether the agent rationally chooses the appropriate means to his/her ends. An external knowledge of values, goals and motivations, which are all united under the utility function, is essential with concern to designing public policy that supposedly helps to maximise utility.

As already outlined earlier in this subchapter, a number of other problem issues surround behavioural methodology that may act to complicate its application in public policy. In order to demonstrate how the application of behavioural concepts might be confronted, it is worth considering one of the common declarations of behavioural economics based on prospect theory, which states that people tend to overweight small probabilities and underweight large probabilities, which inevitably contradicts traditional utility theory with its expectation of balanced probability weightings. A number of examples of the potential application of public policies based on prospect theory can be considered from, for example, insurance policy (e.g. Schmidt 2012) to taxation (Dhami and al-Nowaihi 2007). If we assume two types of individuals (optimists and pessimists) and two types of potential events (positive and negative) with the same probability of occurrence, we approach the following:

If a positive possible event (e.g. winning the lottery) has the same probability as a negative possible event (e.g. becoming ill), the optimist and the pessimist will tend to assess the two situations differently. Further, when assuming (very intuitively) the normal distribution of pessimists and optimists in society, as well as the normal distribution of positive and negative potential events, what does this imply for policymakers? And what if we consider, for example, Harbaugh et al. (2002) who claim that young individuals tend to underweight low probabilities and overweight high probabilities? A further example concerns Bruhin et al. (2010) who conducted an experimental study which uncovered a robust percentage of traditional utility maximisers, with, moreover, considerable differences evident between men and women and Swiss and Chinese. The expected utility hypothesis, which works with the von Neumann – Morgenstern utility function, simply adopts a general (linear) probability weighting, in a similar way to that via which we generally assume a certain elasticity of demand and supply. Thus, just as elasticities vary according to the countless states of the world, probability weighting functions also vary considerably. Hence, just as Giffen goods do not disprove the general law of demand, varying probability weightings do not disprove the general idea of expected utility theory. In conclusion, it appears that under the proposed settings, these over/under/estimations will offset each other, which implies that the probability weighting can be simply averaged as linear. The example provided shows that there may be numerous viewpoints from which the adoption of linear weighting probabilities might be justified in general economic theory and public policy issues. It further shows just how easily a respected empirical result (but lacking theoretical background) can be refuted not only via simple reasoning, but also by competing empirical evidence which leads to completely opposite conclusions. Kahneman and

*Table 2.1* Hypothetical probability weightings by optimists and pessimists

| | *Positive event* | *Negative event* |
|---|---|---|
| **Optimist** | Overweights probability | Underweights probability |
| **Pessimist** | Underweights probability | Overweights probability |

Source: Maialeh (2019)

Tversky were keenly aware of the problematic aspects of the validity of the method and the generalisability of their results (1979, p. 265), thus indicating that their followers should carefully consider these concerns.

According to variance-based phenomena in the social sciences, similar counter-examples can also be provided of other behavioural insights. Let us assume, for instance, the status quo bias (e.g. Samuelson and Zeckhauser 1988) as the preference for the current state of affairs. Intuitively, if the current situation is sufficiently satisfying, individuals are not motivated to change.[7] However, does the status quo bias apply if the experimental group is composed of war refugees accommodated in a refugee camp? Would behavioural scientists identify a preference for the current situation? In fact, do we not witness the exact opposite, that is, that refugees would do anything to change their situation, despite the risk of being even worse-off? Should we be inspired by the status quo bias in public policies when targeting a subgroup of those who have nothing to lose? A further example is provided by Tversky (1969) who reported that individuals systematically violate the transitivity of preference. Birnbaum and Gutierrez (2007) applied a new statistical technique to the same situations studied by Tversky, and arrived at the opposite conclusion, that is, that only very few individuals repeat intransitive patterns. And what about the decoy effect famously detected by Ariely (2009)? Can experimental results based on a sample of 100 students at the prestigious MIT Sloan School of Management be extrapolated to the whole population always and everywhere as challenged in the first part of this subchapter? Examples can be further expanded more directly to public policy: for example, Chetty et al. (2014) analysed the Danish pension system which is similar to that of the United States. However, could the outcomes of such a study possibly be realistically inspirational for US policymakers? Do the remarkable differences in social systems between Denmark and the United States, for example, having to pay high college fees (US) versus being paid to attend college (DEN) play a role in behavioural (active/passive) responses? And what if policymakers face biases, at least the blind-point bias (Pronin and Kugler 2007), when deciding on the biases of others? And what if a large number of behavioural factors are in play? In sum, the implementation of behavioural insights into public policy generates a wide range of questions. Of course, neoclassical theory operates with "unrealistic"[8] assumptions, for instance that all individuals are fully informed. However, a number of famous examples, for example, Akerlof (1970), Rothschild and Stiglitz (1976) and Stiglitz and Weiss (1981) have demonstrated that information asymmetry can be relatively smoothly accommodated without behavioural impulses. And previous examples show that this is not only the case of information asymmetry. Thus, the generalisation of variance-based results is extremely problematic.

The aim of this subchapter was to highlight the limits of the behavioural critique. It was argued that the rationality of the typical Bayesian decision-maker is immune to most of the behavioural critique. Various examples served to demonstrate that central behavioural concepts such as satisficing behaviour and prospect theory are unable to fundamentally challenge the pillars of the neoclassical framework. To recap the main points: firstly, the generalisation of the variance-based results of behavioural research appears to be highly problematic. It is argued that the behavioural approach is unable to cope with the very essential question: "If the effect worked here, will it work elsewhere?" Despite behavioural insights allowing us to more closely approach selected aspects of reality, the inherent uncertainty means that the results of behavioural research have no lawful character and, hence, such research cannot serve as the prime source for the formulation of theories; neither can it reliably determine whether a theory is valid or not.

Further, we discussed the question of rationality. The behavioural approach frequently challenges the neoclassical assumption that economic agents are principally rational: the first main argument is that economic agents do not maximise their utility; second, their decision-making is inconsistent. As regards the first class of reasoning, concerning primarily satisficing behaviour, cognitive biases and unselfish behaviour, it is shown that none of these arguments are able to fundamentally disprove the neoclassical concept of utility maximisation. In other words, the examples provided clarify the reasons why utility can be maximised even though unselfish behaviour, cognitive biases and satisficing behaviour are in play.

The second pillar of an agent's rationality comprises consistency of choice. Applying the example of the Chernoff condition, which provided methodical inspiration for the behavioural critique, it is demonstrated that the violation of this condition does not necessarily contradict neoclassical axiomatisation. This misunderstanding stems from the fact that the neoclassical consistency of choice is assumed strictly *ceteris paribus*, while the behavioural approach relies on changing conditions of choice, no matter how ostensible or fabricated these changes might be. After considering both of the major dimensions of rationality in economics (maximisation and consistency), it is not claimed that economic agents always behave rationally, only that the behavioural approach is unable to prove that economic agents behave non-rationally or even irrationally.

With regard to the behavioural approach and its praxis, despite the undisputable fact that incorporating behavioural factors into economic models may substantially positively impact certain policy questions, with the related potential to subsequently induce new welfare implications, noticeable methodological difficulties exist based on previous findings. Applying widely acknowledged examples of behavioural research (e.g. prospect theory or the status quo bias), it is illustrated to what extent their application in public policy can be controversial; specifically, that the probability weighting may vary enormously or that the preference for current conditions may be highly selective.

In conclusion, behavioural models based on psychologically inspired methodology focus on particular dysfunctions and successfully explain narrowly defined phenomena for a certain time and space. Conversely, neoclassical axiomatic models focus on general patterns of behaviour and provide relevant results over a broad range of social settings. Thus, the aims of the two approaches are very different. The most negative aspect of the behavioural critique is that it has created a straw man of neoclassical economics that postulates fabricated theses with concern to the agent's selfishness, full rationality and so forth, and processes them through selective empirical verification. This has never formed a part of genuine neoclassical theory. The question is for whom is behavioural research useful? As has been demonstrated, mainstream economic models should explain general interrelationships; they are not designed for the prediction of particular occasions. The systemisation of behavioural patterns or the detection of cognitive biases are, undoubtedly, useful for business purposes, from the sale of every-day consumer goods to the analysis of financial markets. But does this push forward the frontiers of science? Mainstream economics remains, to a certain extent, grounded in medieval scholasticism (see e.g. Beveridge 1937). As has been demonstrated, we cannot disprove the existence of utility maximising individuals just as we cannot disprove the existence of God. The suggested impotence of the behavioural critique explicitly represents the inability to penetrate the essence; thus, it is difficult to decide what causes more harm, mainstream economics or the poor critique thereof. The aim of the following chapters, therefore, is to provide a more comprehensive and detailed explanation of the issues involved.

## Notes

1 Since producers on competitive markets have no power to influence these prices, they act as objectively given.
2 The notions of utility and welfare are used interchangeably following the traditional practice in welfare economics.
3 For the sake of simplicity, the author neglects the quantum branches of selected natural sciences.
4 The reason for basing the following argumentation on Sen, despite the fact that he is not a behavioural economist, is that he is one of the few prominent economists who confronts the neoclassical concept of rationality *theoretically* rather than empirically. Sen's contribution therefore represents a unique theoretical base and inspiration for the behavioural approach.
5 No matter how they are formed for the present purpose.
6 For instance, when the designer of the experiment wishes to cause cognitive noise and to bring cognitive biases into play.
7 See the argumentation on satisficing behaviour earlier in this subchapter.
8 Naturally, assumptions can never be realistic – every assumption reduces the level of reality and thus acts against reality.

## References

Akerlof, G.A. (1970). The market for 'lemons': quality uncertainty and the market mechanism. *Quarterly Journal of Economics*, 84(3), pp. 488–500.

Allais, M. (1953). Le comportement de l'homme rationnel devant le risque: critique des postulats et axiomes de l'ecole Americaine. *Econometrica*, 21(4), pp. 503–546.

Ariely, D. (2009). *Predictably irrational: the hidden forces that shape our decisions*. New York: Harper Collins Publishers.

Arneson, R. (1989). Equality and equal opportunity for welfare. *Philosophical Studies*, 56, pp. 77–93.

Baron, J., Granato, L., Spranca, M. and Teubal, E. (1993). Decision making biases in children and early adolescents: exploratory studies. *Merrill Palmer Quarterly*, 39, pp. 23–47.

Barone, E. (1908). Il ministero della produzione nello stato collettivista. *Giornale degli Economisti*, 37, pp. 267–293, 391–414. Translated as "The ministry of production in the collectivist state". In Hayek, F.A., ed. (1935). *Collectivist economic planning*. London: Routledge & Kegan Paul, pp. 310–334. Reprinted in Newman, P., ed. *Readings in mathematical economics. Vol. I: value theory*. Baltimore: The Johns Hopkins Press.

Becker, G.S. (1962). Irrational behavior and economic theory. *Journal of Political Economy*, 70(1), pp. 1–13.

Benartzi, S. and Thaler, R. (2004). Save more tomorrow: using behavioral economics to increase employee saving. *Journal of Political Economy*, 112(1), pp. 164–187.

Bentham, J. (2000 [1781]). *An introduction to the principles of morals and legislation*. Kitchener, ON: Batoche.

Berg, N. (2003). Normative behavioral economics. *The Journal of Socio-Economics*, 32(4), pp. 411–427.

Bernheim, D. (2009). Behavioral welfare economics. *Journal of the European Economic Association*, 7(2–3), pp. 267–319.

Bernheim, D., Shleifer, A. and Summers, L.H. (1985). The strategic bequest motive. *Journal of Political Economy*, 93(6), pp. 1045–1076.

Beveridge, W. (1937). The place of the social sciences in human knowledge. *Politica*, 2(9), pp. 459–479.

Birnbaum, M.H. and Gutierrez, R.J. (2007). Testing for intransitivity of preferences predicted by a lexicographic semi-order. *Organizational Behavior and Human Decision Processes*, 104, pp. 96–112.

Blaug, M. (1992). *The methodology of economics*. Cambridge: Cambridge University Press.

Bolton, G.E. and Ockenfels, A. (2000). ERC: a theory of equity, reciprocity, and competition. *American Economic Review*, 90(1), pp. 166–193.

Bruhin, A., Fehr-Duda, H. and Epper, T. (2010). Risk and rationality: uncovering heterogeneity in probability distortion. *Econometrica*, 78(4), pp. 1375–1412.

Chetty, R., Friedman, J., Leth-Peterson, S., Heien Nielsen, T. and Olsen, T. (2014). Active vs. passive decisions and crowd-out in retirement savings accounts: evidence from Denmark. *Quarterly Journal of Economics*, 129(3), pp. 1141–1219.

Chetty, R., Friedman, J. and Saez, E. (2013). Using differences in knowledge across neighborhoods to uncover the impacts of the EITC on earnings. *American Economic Review*, 107(7), pp. 2683–2721.

Chytilova, H. (2017). *Economic literacy and money illusion: an experimental perspective*. London: Routledge, Taylor & Francis Group.

Clark, A. and Oswald, A.J. (2002). A simple statistical method for measuring how life events affect happiness. *International Journal of Epidemiology*, 31, pp. 1139–1144.

Clark, J.B. (1891). Distribution as determined by a law of rent. *Quarterly Journal of Economics*, 5, pp. 289–318.

Cohen, G.A. (1989). On the currency of equal justice. *Ethics*, 99, pp. 906–944.

Congdon, W., Kling, J. and Mullainathan, S. (2011). *Policy and choice: public finance through the lens of behavioral economics*. Washington, DC: Brookings Institution Press.

Deaton, A. and Cartwright, N. (2016). Understanding and misunderstanding randomized controlled trials [online]. NBER Working Paper No. 22595. Available from: www.nber.org/system/files/working_papers/w22595/w22595.pdf.

DellaVigna, S. (2009). Psychology of economics: evidence from the field. *Journal of Economic Literature*, 47(2), pp. 315–372.

Dhami, S. and al-Nowaihi, A. (2007). Why do people pay taxes? Prospect theory versus expected utility theory. *Journal of Economic Behavior & Organization*, 64(1), pp. 171–192.

Di Tella, R., MacCulloch, R.J. and Oswald, A.J. (2001). Preferences over inflation and unemployment: evidence from surveys of happiness. *American Economic Review*, 91, pp. 335–341.

Doucouliagos, C. (1994). A note on the evolution of homo economicus. *Journal of Economic Issues*, 28(3), pp. 877–883.

Druckman, J.N. and Kam, C.D. (2011). Students as experimental participants: a defense of the 'narrow data base'. In: Druckman, J.N., Green, D.P., Kuklinski, J.H. and Lupia, A., eds. *Cambridge handbook of experimental political science*. Cambridge: Cambridge University Press, pp. 41–57. doi: 10.1017/CBO9780511921452.004.

Dupuit, J. (1849). De l'influence des péages sur l'utilité des voies de communication. *Annales des Ponts et Chaussées*, 8(207), pp. 170–248.

Durlauf, S.N. (2005). Complexity and empirical economics. *The Economic Journal*, 115(504), pp. 225–243.

Dworkin, R. (1981). What is equality? Part 2: equality of resources. *Philosophy & Public Affairs*, 10, pp. 283–345.

Easterlin, R. (1974). Does economic growth improve the human lot? Some empirical evidence. In: David, P.A. and Reder, M.W., eds. *Nations and households in economic growth: essays in honour of Moses Abramowitz*. New York: Academic Press, pp. 89–125.

Easterlin, R. (1995). Will raising the income of all increase the happiness of all? *Journal of Economic Behavior and Organization*, 27, pp. 35–48.

Engel, C. (2010). *Dictator games: a meta study*. Bonn: Preprints of the Max Planck Institute for Research on Collective Goods.

Farber, H. (2014). Why you can't find a taxi in the rain and other labor supply lessons from cab drivers [online]. NBER Working Paper No. 20604. Available from: www.nber.org/system/files/working_papers/w20604/w20604.pdf.

Fehr, E. and Schmidt, K.M. (1999). A theory of fairness, competition, and cooperation. *Quarterly Journal of Economics*, 114(3), pp. 817–868.

Fleurbaey, M. and Hammond, P.J. (2004). Interpersonally comparable utility. In: Barbera, S., Hammond, P.J. and Seidl, C., eds. *Handbook of utility theory*. Boston: Springer.

Forsythe, R., Horowitz, J.L., Savin, N.E. and Sefton, M. (1994). Fairness in simple bargaining experiments. *Games and Economic Behavior*, 6(3), pp. 347–369.

Frank, R.H. (1997). The frame of reference as a public good. *Economic Journal*, 107, pp. 1832–1847.

Friedman, M. (1953). *Essays in positive economics*. Chicago: University of Chicago Press.

Gabaix, X. and Laibson, D. (2006). Shrouded attributes, consumer myopia, and information suppression in competitive markets. *Quarterly Journal of Economics*, 121(5), pp. 505–540.

Gechter, M. (2015). *Generalizing the results from social experiments: theory and evidence from Mexico and India* [online]. Working Paper. Available from: www.bu.edu/econ/files/2015/05/Gechter_Generalizing_Social_Experiments.pdf.

Gigerenzer, G. and Goldstein, D.G. (1996). Reasoning the fast and frugal way: models of bounded rationality. *Psychological Review*, 103(4), pp. 650–669.

Goldstein, D.G. and Gigerenzer, G. (2002). Models of ecological rationality: the recognition heuristic. *Psychological Review*, 109(1), pp. 75–90.

Goodwin, N., Harris, J.M., Nelson, J.A., Roach, B. and Torras, M. (2013). *Microeconomics in context*. New York: Routledge.

Gossen, H.H. (1983 [1854]). *The laws of human relations and the rules of human action derived therefrom*. Cambridge: MIT Press.

Gul, F. and Pesendorfer, W. (2004). *The canonical type space for interdependent preferences* [online]. Working Paper. Princeton Economics. Available from: http://adres.ens.fr/IMG/pdf/14032005.pdf.

Hamermesh, D. (2013). Six decades of top economics publishing: who and how? *Journal of Economic Literature*, 51(1), pp. 162–172.

Hammond, P.J. (1991). Interpersonal comparisons of utility: why and how they are and should be made. In: Elster, J. and Roemer, J.E., eds. *Interpersonal comparisons of well-being*. Cambridge: Cambridge University Press, pp. 200–254.

Hanzel, I. (2010). *Studies in the methodology of natural and social sciences*. Frankfurt am Main: Peter Lang.

Harbaugh, W.T., Krause, K. and Vesterlund, L. (2002). Risk attitudes of children and adults: choices over small and large probability gains and losses. *Experimental Economics*, 5(1), pp. 53–84.

Hayek, F.A. (1943). Scientism and the study of society: part II. *Economica*, 10(37), pp. 34–63.

Houser, D. and Schunk, D. (2009). Social environments with competitive pressure: gender effects in the decisions of German schoolchildren. *Journal of Economic Psychology*, 30, pp. 634–641.

Jevons, W.S. (1888). *The theory of political economy*. London: Palgrave Macmillan.

Kahneman, D., Knetsch, J.L. and Thaler, R.H. (1986). Fairness and the assumptions of economics. *Journal of Business*, 59(4), pp. 285–300.

Kahneman, D. and Tversky, A. (1979). Prospect theory: an analysis of decision under risk. *Econometrica*, 47(2), pp. 263–292.

Kahneman, D., Wakker, P.P. and Sarin, R. (1997). Back to Bentham? Explorations of experienced utility. *Quarterly Journal of Economics*, 112, pp. 375–406.

Kaldor, N. (1939). Welfare propositions of economics and interpersonal comparisons of utility. *Economic Journal*, 49, pp. 549–552.

Keller-Allen, C. and Li, R.M. (2013). Psychological science and behavioral economics in the service of public policy. Meeting Summary, National Institute of Health, National Institute on Aging, Washington, DC.

Knetsch, J.L. (1990). *Derived indifference curves*. Working Paper. Vancouver, Burnaby: Simon Fraser University.

Kosík, K. (1976). *Dialectics of the concrete: a study on man and world*. Dondrecht: D. Reidel Publishing Company.

Lakatos, I. (1980). *The methodology of scientific research programmes. Vol. 1: philosophical papers*. Cambridge: Cambridge University Press.

Lee, L., Amir, O. and Ariely, D. (2009). Search of homo economicus: cognitive noise and the role of emotion in preference consistency. *Journal of Consumer Research*, 36(2), pp. 173–187.

Leigh, A. (2018). *Randomistas: how radical researchers are changing our world*. New Haven: Yale University Press.

Levine, D.K. (1998). Modeling altruism and spitefulness in experiments. *Review of Economic Dynamics*, 1(3), pp. 593–622.

Levitt, S. and List, J. (2007). What do laboratory experiments measuring social preferences reveal about the real world? *Journal of Economic Perspectives*, 21(2), pp. 153–174.

List, J. (2004). Neoclassical theory versus prospect theory: evidence from the market-place. *Econometrica*, 72(2), pp. 615–625.

Madrian, B. (2014). Applying insights from behavioral economics to policy design. *Annual Review of Economics*, 6(1), pp. 663–688.

Maialeh, R. (2019). Generalization of results and neoclassical rationality: unresolved controversies of behavioural economics methodology. *Quantity & Quality*, 53(4), pp. 1743–1761.

Maialeh, R. (2020). *Dynamic models and inequality: the role of the market mechanism in economic distribution*. Cham, Switzerland: Springer Nature.

Mäki, U. (1992). On the method of isolation in economics. *Poznan Studies in the Philosophy of the Sciences and the Humanities* (special issue *Idealization IV: Intelligibility in Science*. Dilworth, C., ed.), 26, pp. 319–354.

Mandler, M. (2001). A difficult choice in preference theory: rationality implies completeness or transitivity but not both. In: Milgram, E., ed. *Varieties of practical reasoning*. Cambridge: MIT Press, pp. 373–402.

Marshall, A. (2013 [1890]). *Principles of economics*. Houndmills: Palgrave Macmillan.

Marx, K. (1938 [1875]). *Critique of the Gotha program*. English translation in Marx, K. and Engels, F. *Selected works*. Vol. II. Moscow: Foreign Language Publishing House; New York: International Publishers.

Mill, J.S. (1909 [1848]). *Principles of political economy: with some of their applications to social philosophy*. London: Longmans, Green and Co.

Mill, J.S. (2007 [1861]). *Utilitarianism*. New York: Dover Publications Inc.

Mongin, P. and d'Aspremont, C. (1998). Utility theory and ethics. In: Barbera, S., Hammond, P.J. and Seidl, C., eds. *Handbook of utility theory*. Vol. I. Dordrecht: Kluwer Academic Publishers, pp. 371–482.

Mullainathan, S., Schwartzstein, J. and Congdon, W. (2012). A reduced-form approach to behavioral public finance. *The Annual Review of Economics*, 4(17), pp. 1–30.

Munro, A. (2009). *Bounded rationality and public policy: a perspective from behavioural economics*. Dordrecht, Netherlands: Springer Science & Business Media.

Myers, D.G. (1993). *The pursuit of happiness: who is happy and why?* New York: Avon.

Ng, Y.K. (1996). Happiness surveys: some comparability issues and an exploratory survey based on just perceivable increments. *Social Indicators Research*, 38, pp. 1–27.

Oliver, A. (2017). *The origins of behavioural public policy*. Cambridge: Cambridge University Press.

Oswald, A.J. (1997). Happiness and economic performance. *Economic Journal*, 107, pp. 1815–1831.

Persky, J. (1995). The ethology of homo economicus. *Journal of Economic Perspectives*, 9(2), pp. 221–231.

Poterba, J. (2014). Retirement security in an aging population. *American Economic Association*, 104(5), pp. 1–30.

Pronin, E. and Kugler, M.B. (2007). Valuing thoughts, ignoring behavior: the introspection illusion as a source of the bias blind spot. *Journal of Experimental Social Psychology*, 43(4), pp. 565–578.

Rabin, M. (1993). Incorporating fairness into game theory and economics. *American Economic Review*, 83(5), pp. 1281–1302.

Rawls, J. (1971). *A theory of justice*. Cambridge: Harvard University Press.

Rein, M. and Miller, S.M. (1974). Standards of income redistribution. *Challenge*, 17(3), pp. 20–26.

Ricardo, D. (2001 [1821]). *On the principles of political economy and taxation*. Kitchener, ON: Batoche.

Robbins, L. (2007 [1932]). *An essay on the nature and significance of economic science*. Auburn: Ludwig von Mises Institute.

Robinson, J. (1933). *Economics of imperfect competition*. London: Palgrave Macmillan.

Robinson, J. (1956). *The accumulation of capital*. London: Palgrave Macmillan.
Robinson, J. (1960). *Collected economic papers-II*. Oxford: Blackwell.
Rosenbaum, E.F. (1995). Interpersonal comparisons of utility: positive, normative or value-laden? *Journal of Economic Methodology*, 2, pp. 239–257.
Rosenberg, A. (1995). Laws, damn laws, and ceteris paribus clauses. *The Southern Journal of Philosophy*, 34(1), pp. 183–204.
Rothschild, M. and Stiglitz, J.E. (1976). Equilibrium in competitive insurance markets: an essay on the economics of imperfect information. *Quarterly Journal of Economics*, 90(4), pp. 629–649.
Rottenstreich, Y. and Hsee, C.K. (2001). Money, kisses, and electric shocks: on the affective psychology of risk. *Psychological Science*, 12, pp. 185–190.
Rowntree, S.B. (2010 [1901]). *Poverty: a study of town life*. Bristol: The Policy Press.
Samuelson, W. and Zeckhauser, R.J. (1988). Status quo bias in decision making. *Journal of Risk and Uncertainty*, 1, pp. 7–59.
Schmidt, U. (2012). *Insurance demand and prospect theory*. Kiel: Kiel Institute for the World.
Selten, R. (1999). What is bounded rationality? [online]. SFB Discussion Paper B-454. Available from: www.wiwi.uni-bonn.de/sfb303/papers/1999/b/bonnsfb454.pdf.
Sen, A. (1970). *Collective choice and social welfare*. San Francisco: Holden-Day.
Sen, A. (1983). Poor, relatively speaking. *Oxford Economic Papers*, 35(2), pp. 153–169.
Sen, A. (1985). *Commodities and capabilities*. Amsterdam: North-Holland.
Sen, A. (1991). *On ethics and economics*. New York: Wiley-Blackwell.
Sen, A. (1993). Internal consistency of choice. *Econometrica*, 61(3), pp. 495–521.
Sen, A. (1997). *On economic inequality*. Oxford: Clarendon Press.
Shleifer, A. and Vishny, R.V. (1997). The limits of arbitrage. *The Journal of Finance*, 52(1), pp. 35–55.
Simon, H.A. (1955). Behavioral model of rational choice. *Quarterly Journal of Economics*, 69(1), pp. 98–118.
Simon, H.A. (1956). Rational choice and the structure of the environment. *Psychological Review*, 63(2), pp. 129–138.
Simon, J.L. (1974). Interpersonal welfare comparisons can be made – and used for redistribution decisions. *Kyklos*, 27, pp. 63–98.
Smith, A. (1776). An inquiry into the nature and causes of the wealth of nations. In: *History of economic thought books from McMaster university archive for the history of economic thought*.
Stiglitz, J.E. and Weiss, A. (1981). Credit rationing in markets with imperfect information. *American Economic Review*, 71(3), pp. 393–410.
Sumner, L.W. (1996). *Welfare, happiness and ethics*. Oxford: Clarendon Press.
Suzumura, K. (1996). Interpersonal comparisons of the extended sympathy type and the possibility of social choice. In: Arrow, K.J., Sen, A.K. and Suzumura, K., eds. *Social choice re-examined*. Vol. 2. London: Macmillan. IEA Conference Volume, no. 117, pp. 202–229.
Thaler, R. (1980). Toward a positive theory of consumer choice. *Journal of Economic Behaviour and Organization*, 1, pp. 39–60.
Thaler, R. and Sunstein, C. (2008). *Nudge: improving decisions about health, wealth and happiness*. New Haven: Yale University Press.
Thaler, R.H. and Benartzi, S. (2004). Save more tomorrow: using behavioral economics to increase employee saving. *Journal of Political Economy*, 112(S1), pp. 164–187.
Tversky, A. (1969). Intransitivity of preferences. *Psychological Review*, 76(1), pp. 31–48.
Veenhoven, R. (1993). *Happiness in nations: subjective appreciation of life in 56 nations 1946–1992*. Rotterdam: Erasmus University RISBO.

Winkelmann, L. and Winkelmann, R. (1998). Why are the unemployed so unhappy? Evidence from panel data. *Economica*, 65, pp. 1–15.

Witteloostuijn, A. (1988). Maximising and satisficing opposite or equivalent concepts? *Journal of Economic Psychology*, 9(3), pp. 289–313.

Wolff, R.D. and Resnick, S.A. (2012). *Contending economic theories: neoclassical, Keynesian, and Marxian*. Cambridge: MIT Press.

Wolff, R.P. (1990). Methodological individualism and Marx – some remarks on Jon Elster, game theory and other things. *Canadian Journal of Philosophy*, 20(4), pp. 469–486.

# 3 Dialectical-Critical Reflection

## A Critique of Positivism: From Metaphysical Ontologism to Mathematical Formalism

A wide range of questions on economic distribution has been addressed over the past few decades. Thanks to huge advances in terms of data availability and technical processability, most of these contributions have been of an empirical nature.[1] Empirical research undoubtedly brings us closer to understanding economic phenomena and the demystification of economic fallacies. Empirical studies on inequality present valuable background material accompanied by robust data analysis that provides for a general, and in a certain sense even an advanced, picture of our immediate world. Prior to this empirical turn of events, economics, as inspired by William Stanley Jevons and, later, by Paul Samuelson, attempted to more accurately define economic relationships through mathematical language. Mainstream economics, therefore, relies predominantly on a combination of mathematical formalisation and empirical evidence. Despite all the undisputable advantages, the positivist nature of mainstream economics, however, also raises a number of serious questions. Critical theory requires more than just "superficial" correlations and summations since its methodological critique is supposed to reveal an intuitive logic behind the empirical façade. Horkheimer (1972 [1937]) states that facts presented to us through our senses are socially performed: firstly, through the historical character of the object and secondly, through the historical character of the perceiving organ. The following text aims to place contemporary economic research in the methodological context of critical theory and concerns not only that-which-is, as does the positivist imperative of modern economics, but also that-which-is-not; in other words, this subchapter confronts the observable with that-which-is excluded from our formal analytical sight.

"In the science of Economics we treat men not as they ought to be, but as they are" (Jevons 1888, p. 46); it would be difficult to find more straightforward proof than this statement of the positivist methodology in the early formative stages of economics. Critical theory, when dealing with positivism, advances its Marxian heritage. With reference to Dirk Braunstein and Theodor Adorno, Marx never criticised positive sciences. This is, perhaps, not surprising

DOI: 10.4324/9780429273841-4

in the light of his admiration for Charles Darwin; while critical theorists were inspired by Marx, paradoxically they criticised that element that Marx did not fight against, that is, positivist methodology. On the other hand, Marx's theory of scientific knowledge is based on the materialist idea that the object itself defines the approach towards the comprehension thereof, which means, in other words, that the matter of the object precedes the consciousness of the investigator. Murray understands the Marxian point of view as follows:

> This entails necessity in that the relation between the "facts" and the logic that is to draw them together into the shape of a science sheds its arbitrariness. The object under study determines the science now *in second intension*; it determines the *logic* of the "facts". Marx's critique of empiricism is immanent in calling empiricism to submit the question of the relation of "facts" and their logical reconstruction itself to empirical scrutiny. This critical approach to concepts and their logical interconnections is one of the features that sets Marx's theory of scientific knowledge apart from positivist understandings of science.
>
> (1988, p. 41)

A number of articles and book reviews which critically approached the positivist nature of economics were published in *Zeitschrift für Sozialforschung*, one of which comprises a review of Bernardelli's *Die Grundlagen der ökonomischen Theorie* by Georg Rusche (1934) which debates general questions of economic methodology. While Bernardelli tries to provide proof that economics can be a mathematical science, Rusche criticises the psychologising form of the *homo oeconomicus* of the Manchester school which he proposes is built upon outdated ideas of liberal thought. Concerning the example of marginal utility, Rusche endeavours to demonstrate that it cannot be captured by mathematical methods as can psychical phenomena, that is, phenomena related to basic needs cannot be reduced to mathematical expressions. While this type of reproach is typical of the widespread criticism of mainstream economics, it is difficult to accept such claims in the light of the findings of the previous chapter, since all behaviour, as understood in economics, can be accommodated under mathematised marginal theory. Nevertheless, the critical theory perspective provides numerous remarkable critical insights into the positivist methodology.

Simply put, for positivism (which has assumed the judicial office of reason), every trial is prejudged. When the unknown in mathematics becomes the unknown quantity in an equation, it is already known before any value has been assigned. The equation of the mind and the world, Adorno and Horkheimer (2002 [1944]) claim, is resolved as a reduction which condemns the world to be its own measure. Value judgements are mere chatter that cannot be verified and which are subjected to instrumental control. Economic methodology therefore operates with unknown variables as if they were controlled instruments, while perverted scientisation in its positivist way suggests rather that they are instruments of control. The scientific method should comprise an approach which reveals the objective content and meaning of facts. The ideal method is scientific to the degree to which it exposes, interprets and substantiates the richness of reality that is *objectively* (K. K.) contained in the particular researched fact. The "scientific method is a means for decoding facts" (Kosík 1976, p. 26). Fact is a non-transparent coded reality. As Habermas (1967) put it, if analytically empirical science does not step out of its positivist limits, it does not produce ideas of social goals, priorities or programmes, and the misery of its theory lies in the fact that it is supposed to be *ad hoc* derived from and limited to particularities that are practically given and technically solvable. By the same token, Michňák (1965) posits that positivist reduction deprives science of its human substance since it excludes the question of meaning and existence. Put simply, if positivism does not apply the proper scientific methods for examining the essence and related purposes (happiness, good, beauty, justice etc.), both will be transformed into metaphysics.

Positivism basically comprises an element of ideology that advocates the *status quo*: the ideology "exploits the cult of fact by describing bad existence with utmost exactitude in order to elevate it into the realm of facts. Through such elevation existence itself becomes a surrogate of meaning and justice" (Adorno and Horkheimer 2002 [1944], p. 119). Ideological aspects are not merely meaningful and justiciable; that which fits into the context of social utility is also regarded as natural. The fixation on the *status quo* via the alleged triumph of subjectivity – "the subjection of all existing things to logical formalism" – is paid for by the obedient subordination of reason to what immediately exists. Knowledge, on the other hand, does consist not only of mere perception, classification and calculation but also of the negation of what immediately exists. Mathematical formalism therefore arrests thought at mere immediacy (Adorno and Horkheimer 2002 [1944]). Even the insoluble and irrational are formalised so as to protect the world from the return of the mythical. Any deviation of thought from the actual, touching the outside of the jurisdiction of existence, is no less self-destructive "than it would be for the magician to step outside the magic circle drawn for his incantation" (Adorno and Horkheimer 2002 [1944], p. 19).[2] The subject is free from all romanticism. The subject's positivist sublimation into a transcendental and logical sublimation forms the new reference point of reason – the legislating authority of any action. A world reduced to symbols and formulas is then easily manipulable, but only within the given circumstances of a quantifiable formalised sub-world.

In the preface to the *Dialectic of Enlightenment*, it is stated that the positivist focus on the observation of facts and the calculation of probabilities is aimed at protecting the cognitive mind from charlatanism and superstition; simultaneously, however, such a focus provides arid ground for the acceptance of charlatanism and superstition. This leads to the fall of the technologically educated masses into despotism and, based on uncomprehended senselessness, it demonstrates the weakness of the contemporary theoretical understanding. Despotism triumphs when these educated masses arrange the facts in such a way "that they can be grasped as quickly and easily as possible. Wrenched from all context, detached from thought, they are made instantly accessible to an infantile grasp" (Adorno 1991, p. 85).

Empiricism insists that our senses reflect reality in the same way for all individuals. Our senses are supposed to mediate the "real" world in an undistorted way, and mainstream economics follows the exact same path, that is, it processes empirical findings as the accurate and reliable report of real phenomena around which theory should be established. For Marcus (1975), empiricism is a form of reductionism that depends on the fallacious assumption of formal logic. Hence, the universe can be explained via discrete points that are interconnected by formal relations. He opines that the acceptance of the fallacious postulate that the price and utility of commodities are in formal correspondence is implicit to contemporary economics. However, the traditional Marxian view is that these two factors are qualitatively so distinct that no mathematical solution is able to interconnect them; in other words, price and utility cannot be systematised via formal mathematical interpretation. Economics follows the third Descartes maxim (2003 [1637]) – to start with the simplest objects that are easiest to understand in order to gradually grasp complex phenomena.[3] Such a derivation can be applied to all sciences, not only mathematics. The world can thus be captured as a deductive chain of thought.

Such a deductive chain requires the collection of facts in all disciplines – to gather great masses of details in connection with empirical inquiries. This creates a pattern which is – much like the rest of life in society – dominated by industrial production techniques. As with early 20th-century sociology, contemporary economics is based on laborious ascents from the description of social phenomena to detailed comparisons. Only then is the formation of general concepts permitted. True empiricism depends upon complete inductions which supply the primary propositions for a theory, although empiricists remain all too distant from such inductions (Horkheimer 1972 [1937]). Weber discusses this issue in "Objectivity" chapter of *Social Science and Social Policy*. In brief, historians or experts in criminal law (examples provided by Weber himself) do not rest on the fullest possible enumeration of all circumstances, but on the establishment of connections between isolated elements (1949 [1903–1917]).

Continuing with Max Weber, it was he who made the distinction between facts and values central to the foundation of the modern social sciences (1963). Weber posits that no empirical science is able to provide binding norms and ideals upon which practical activities can be grounded. Empirical sciences lack normative aspects and they cannot distinguish what *ought* to be done, only what *can* be done under given circumstances. Applying the original terms, the factual *Sein* ("is") and value-based *Sollen* ("ought") refer to different types of knowledge. Empirical science seeks to explain causal relationships – the thing *is* (exists) in causal relationships with external forces, while causality plays no role in questions of what *ought* to be. In line with the neo-Kantian legacy in Weber's work, values behind our judgements have only subjective qualities. Concepts in social sciences should, therefore, follow phenomena that are pliable to empirically detectable causality.

Critical theory, however, problematises this separation. Firstly, the critical approach naturally operates with a certain normative set which criticises existing states of affairs and outlines a horizon for the alternative organisation of society. Secondly, we cannot rely solely on an empirical description mediated by our senses since it fails to refer to how these empirical facts are constituted. Social facts are produced with normative features which – in contrast to the description of facts or reference to their mere existence – mediates the processual essence, that is, how the facts and objective reality are constituted. Inductive statistics in economics, however, classifies social facts as objectively given. Searle (2010) speaks of "deontic powers" which force individuals to behave in a certain way. Bluntly speaking, empirical science does not explain the forces behind individual behaviour, which, as a consequence, are presented as a type of natural force. Empiricist methodology is merely about capturing the resulting behaviour since it neglects these deontic powers; for the purpose of addressing inequality, the final distribution of resources cannot be understood without considering the broader social conditions and norms which determine the overall system of economic distribution via property relations.

As will be shown in the following subchapter, critical theory addresses this question by applying dialectical approaches which deal with the researched object in terms of the dynamic and processual relationships thereof. Social reality is understood as the product of systemic contexts, relations and causes. Economics is, however, confined to an analytical framework that statically decomposes observable reality into isolated particles. Its aim is, therefore, to accumulate as many empirical facts as possible, which are then processed by means of inductive-statistical methods. Each object of investigation includes a normative layer since the system expects it to perform in a certain way in order to achieve systematicity. The cognitive grasp of the object thus "implicitly contains a normative-evaluative claim in that knowing what *X* is entails knowing the things that ought to occur for *X* to be what it is", and to know "not only what that thing does or is but also have a knowledge, to a greater or lesser extent, of what it *ought to do*, what a properly functioning *X* is supposed to accomplish, achieve and so on". The example provided here concerns a liver. To know what a liver is includes both a knowledge of the empirical mechanics of the object and that of the general normative aspect, which entails the proper functioning of the object and which is related to what the object should achieve. We understand livers only within their context and their purpose, that is, *what* they *ought* to do and *how* they *ought* to operate within the functional system of the body. Without this knowledge, we would not be able to evaluate the object at all, that is, not be able to provide a *diagnosis* of the object. Normative judgements, which are "immanent within the processual structure of the object" are, therefore, difficult to exclude from the knowledge of the object of investigation (Thompson 2017, pp. 237–238). "This does not mean", Thompson adds,

> that all phenomena should be seen as related to all other in some perfect totality. Rather, we can distinguish between first- and second-order

> relations which delineate direct causes and indirect or constitutive causes. In the first case, direct relations would be those that have a direct causal connection to any event. The second-order relations, or constitutive causations, are those things that are indirectly related in the sense that they serve as preconditions for the first-order relations.
>
> (Thompson 2017, p. 244)

As posited by Ross (2008), neither does this mean that the empirical mechanics of the object are of lower importance, rather that empirical insights are sublated into a higher form of knowledge from which we understand the object as a whole. Interrelatedness between the factual (descriptive) and normative aspects in terms of understanding the inspected object has become the pillar for any form of critical epistemology.

Adorno and Horkheimer (2002 [1944]) claim that positivism brings us to the point at which all the possible facts have been gathered and nothing is now unknown. It is important to note here that this is only partially true, in fact positivism presupposes a gap between what has already been gathered and what is *gatherable*, accompanied by the assumption that all the relevant facts can be gathered. What remains is that the fear of the unknown has determined a path towards the demythologisation of enlightenment in a mythical sense – enlightenment is a radicalised mythical fear, the pure immanence of positivism in which nothing remains outside, while the mere idea of the "outside" – the *non-gatherable* – is the source of fear. Positivism then strives to embrace all phenomena not in their dialectical totality, but as a mere summation of facts. The inability to gather all the facts, however, means that positivism has become trapped:

> It takes abstraction and thematization, a project (K. K.), to select out of this full and inexhaustible world of reality certain areas, aspects and spheres, which naïve naturalism and positivism would then consider to be the only (K. K.) true ones and the only reality, while suppressing the "rest" as sheer subjectivity.

Kosík adds that the "physicalist image presented by positivism impoverishes the human world, and its absolute exclusiveness deforms reality, because it reduces the real world to but *one* (K. K.) dimension and aspect, to the dimension of extensity and of quantitative relations". The physical world, a "thematised mode of cognition of the physical reality" (1976, p. 11), provides only one of the various possible images and emphasises only particular aspects of objective reality, however essential they might be.

Adorno accuses positivism of reducing the detachment of thought to reality. Thought hesitates to be more than a "mere provisional abbreviation for the factual matter" (2005 [1951], p. 126). The idea of penetrating the empirical world is possible only from this detachment, which comprises a safety zone for positivists, but a field of tension for critical thinkers. To operate with terms without distance is "childish" – thought must aim beyond its object since it never attains it. Positivism is thus the more childish the more it believes that the object can be attained. In such cases, a transcending thought "takes its own inadequacy more thoroughly into account than does one guided by the control mechanism of science" (2005 [1951], p. 127). The task of science is reduced to the accumulation of facts and to establishing functional, easily surveyed connections between observed fragments. The division of labour in science must enable the location of the desired intellectual commodity in the required variety. Such compilations are already often made with regard to particular industrial administrative interests. The role of philosophy, however, is supposed to be different; it is not a synthesis or a basic science but "an effort to resist suggestion, a determination to protect intellectual and actual freedom". Philosophy is the voice of contradiction "which otherwise would not be heard, but would triumph silently". But even philosophy today serves science in the form of a kind of "intellectual Taylorism": to improve scientific production methods and to rationalise the accumulation of knowledge while preventing the waste of mental energy. Just as Machiavelli wrote for the rulers of his time, today's scientists pander to economic and political committees (Adorno and Horkheimer 2002 [1944], pp. 201–203).

For Kosík (1976), positivist physicalism substitutes a certain image of reality for reality itself and promotes a certain mode of appropriating the world as the only true mode. Positivism denies the inexhaustibility of the objective world and its irreducibility to knowledge (countering materialism) and, secondly, it reduces the wealth of human subjectivity – formed *historically* (K. K.) through objective conditions – to one single mode of reality. Consciousness investigates both the theoretical-predicative form of substantiated rational and theoretical cognition and the pre-predicative, holistically intuitive form. Denying the first leads to irrationalism and to forms of "vegetative thinking", while denying the latter results in rationalism, positivism and scientism with the inevitable irrationality as their own complement.

Finally, this is also mirrored in the scientific categories of subjectivity and objectivity, which positivism perceives inversely. Science aims to distinguish the essential and the peripheral as the intrinsic objective sense of facts. For traditional theory, "[o]bjectivity means the non-controversial aspect of things, their unquestioned impression, the façade made up of classified data" which is preçisely what Adorno assigns to the subjective (Adorno 2005 [1951], p. 69). Such objectively valid data concerns, rather, objective statements on how subjects perceive reality and themselves. The perversion of science therefore lies in the fact that instead of the quality of the subject matter, criteria focus on the objectivity of the results. Scientific exactness, imposed so as to eradicate the dishonesty of scholasticism, thus faces precisely the same dishonesty while extrapolating the results thereof. It is impossible to research partial data on social phenomena and present it with a general validity; at least not at the scale at which the specificities of a piece of *plumbum* refer to the specificities of all *plumbum*, simply due to the fact that human beings do not have the same character as do physical-chemical *materia*. The eradication of totality, which stands beyond strictly scientised methodology, renders isolated social research untruthful. The question of the essence becomes taboo and science clings to a mere phenomenon (Adorno 1967). Objective reality is then transformed into objectual reality – a reality of objects (Kosík 1976). In sum, research on a partial phenomenon has no general relevance and, therefore, must be extrapolated with low external validity. The dishonesty of scientisation then consists of the alleged objectivity of its results, in contrast to the invariant objective results obtained in the natural sciences, as was discussed in the previous chapter.

Despite this critique, critical theorists also occasionally assign credit to positivism. Antonio (1983) stresses that emancipation must be rethought in the context of objective ideological, material and social constraints. Hence, he sees the extreme anti-positivism of certain critical theorists as unfortunate which, from time to time, results in their ignoring techniques and ideas of sociology that have the potential to contribute to the empirical dimension of their research. The techniques and ideas of sociology can, in this sense, easily be exchanged with techniques and ideas in the field of economics. According to Kilminster (1979), the aim is not to uncritically embrace positivist methods but to selectively harmonise them with the dialectical method, which is essential for the empirical moment of an immanent critique. Antonio adds that some of the inaccuracies in *Dialectics of Enlightenment* could have been avoided if its empirical moment had been enlarged. In sum, it indicates that the injection of economics into critical theory and *vice versa* could be beneficial for both disciplines.

Despite all the accusations, Kosík also understands the contribution made by positivism to the destruction of the pseudoconcrete.[4] In so doing, positivism was in opposition to metaphysical concepts with its understanding of *materia* as objects and processes rather than something transcending that lies behind phenomena. Positivism has served to purify philosophy from the theological concepts of reality but, on the other hand, has one-sidedly reduced all reality to physical reality. The credible destructive and demystifying role of positivism was, however, corrupted with the scientism thereof (1976). Economics has the potential to play exactly this role, that is, to destroy the pseudoconcrete world, to which, incidentally, economics contributed. The problem of mainstream economics is that it fails to fulfil the unfulfillable positivist requirement thereof, that is, the correspondence of theory and empirical reality.

To conclude, anything that exceeds correlation under positivist domination is rejected as unclear and as verbal metaphysics. The purified word in its rationalised form has become a straitjacket of positivism, which reduces the world to registering blind and mute data. Language itself has become impenetrable and mirrors its extreme antithesis – spells (Adorno and Horkheimer 2002 [1944]). Positivism is, thus, not immune to the extreme dualism of mathematical formalism and metaphysical ontologism. In this sense, the dialectical conception of the ontological and gnoseological aspects of the structure and the system must play the key role in economic research. The concept of the relationship between ontology and gnoseology "allows one to detect the disparity . . . between the logical structure (model), used to interpret reality, . . ., and the structure of this reality itself". Kosík (1976, p. 21) follows that the model is, by definition, of a lower order than the described area of reality, and that it interprets this complex reality only approximatively. The interpretation of a model beyond the limits of this approximation is false. This depends on the subject matter – the aim is to exhaust the essence of the phenomenon, not only several of its facets. As we will see in subsequent chapters, the emphasis on quantity has also led to the decay of subjectivity, and qualitative being has been declared to be non-existent. This provides a warning against the ontologisation of positivist methods and it demarcates the possible role thereof in the dialectical approach.

## Dialectics as a Reaction to Positivism

The Marxian concept of dialectics operates with the central features of capitalism, for example, the existence of classes, private property and alienation as a product of the division of labour, in their potentiality. Their definition arises from the critical assessment of what exists, which immanently contains the potential (which Marx sees as the necessity) for them to be overcome. The analysed object is, therefore, viewed in its contradictions, and the contradictory character of any analysable object lies behind its dynamic nature. The dynamic nature of the object gives rise to a new quality, which stems from the contradictory powers. In certain aspects, especially in line with the traditional Marxian view, antagonist tendencies such as the relationship between capitalists and workers are sublated via the overcoming of capitalism, while capitalism itself is endowed with both cooperative and dominant forms of organisation and with productive and destructive forces.

As was shown in the previous subchapter and aptly articulated by Lazarsfeld (1941), contemporary social sciences face several epistemic constraints, principally in terms of induction from statistical patterns and the strict division between factual and normative contents. Such epistemological issues call for differentiation between analytical and dialectical reasoning, which, at the same time, serves to separate the mainstream and critical approaches to social sciences. Whereas the former breaks down phenomena into constitutive parts and formulates hypotheses and concepts for the further empirical examination and induction thereof, dialectics considers, as put by Thompson (2017), the empirical-inductive part only as a moment within the greater systemic process of reality to which it seeks to relate the various parts of the phenomena. Critical social science makes use of dialectics to overcome mere inductive-statistical reasoning for the sake of the inherently dynamic and processual nature of social reality. Dialectics, therefore, relates to the division between factual and normative aspects such that it sees social facts as a product of normative or deontic forces, which, together, lead to a distinction between the essence and the appearance. The hidden aspect of normativity raises a question of purpose: what is the end-goal of a given social process? What does the social process seek to achieve? To provide answers, we need not only knowledge on the empirical moment but also a normatively articulated objective with elaborated forms of relationality, which, together, serve to synthetise cognitive and evaluative claims. Dialectics, as a method of investigation, connects particularities with the totality of the researched object.

Thompson (2017) in this sense recalls Hegel's "disjunctive syllogism" as a form of objective rationality. As a part of this logical procedure, we are asked to "connect the subject and predicate through the mediation of the universal" (Thompson 2017, pp. 247–248). The Hegelian understanding of an object requires the inclusion of its inherent dynamic nature, that is, the object is understood as a *process* with its own immanent features, which is, however, also subject to the greater processual whole. The "truth" of an object lies in its interrelatedness rather than in statistical regularities. It acts against positivist methodology since it fails to isolate the object in question but, conversely, explains the object from the network of the relationships thereof. The aim is not to merely inspect the surface appearance of the object, for which inductive-statistical modes of inquiry are sufficient, but to discover the essence which is behind it, and which affects this appearance. Applying this procedure, it is possible to overcome the static cognitive categories that lie behind reified thought and to comprehend the substance of existing relationships in a more objective way. In the context considered herein, the aim is to grasp the higher necessity behind empirical phenomena and to confront the economic supremacy of reified sensible facts; to question the appropriateness and reasonableness thereof. In doing so, philosophy plays the central role. As Kosík states, "naive consciousness finds philosophy to be a world turned upside down" (1976, p. 133). Contemporary economics, full of the certainties of ordinary consciousness and fetishised reality, and accentuating superficially free human actions, should be subjected to this examination.

From an alternative perspective, dialectics aims to abolish the division of reality into two ontological spheres: rational and irrational. For the purposes of this book, dialectics is tasked, in a similar way to that considered by Bonefeld (2014), with subverting economic categories by revealing their broader social bases. It teaches us to discover the admission of falseness. For Adorno, dialectics was always "the principle of constantly and successfully turning the tables" (2005 [1951], p. 244). Critical theory conceives dialectics "non-dogmatically", that is, inter alia, that it does not follow Engels's (1947 [1878]) traditional idea of dialectics as a science of the general laws of nature, human society and thought. Nevertheless, our understanding follows both Hegelian and Marxian dialectics, which correspond closely to those of classical economics, according to which totality is produced and reproduced via the antagonistic relationships[5] between its agents. Profit interests and antagonist relationships make up the objective motor of the production process "which the life of all men hangs by, and the primacy of which has its vanishing point in the death of all" (Adorno 2004 [1966], p. 320). Society, therefore, survives not despite its antagonism but by means of it. The movement of society is antagonistic from the outset; the essence of society is contradiction; society exists by virtue of its contradictions. On the other hand, critical theorists have further developed the dialectical concept, positing that not only individual interaction constitutes society but also that society is in the substance of the individual: "Just as objectivity without the subject is nonsense, subjectivity detached from its object is fictitious" (Bonefeld 2014, p. 63). The interwovenness of subject and object was questioned by Horkheimer who did not see their relationship as an accurately describable and transparent picture of two fixed realities. Accordingly, subjective factors are in play when facing objective facts, and objective factors play a role in the assessment of subjective behaviour. To be specific, the dialectical materialism of critical theory sees the subject as being constituted by objective conditions, while, simultaneously, the subject forms the objective material and historical conditions. Thought and human action are, therefore, always fixed on a particular man within a particular time and space, which together questions the idealistic idea of autonomous thought. This is especially important for economic agent-based models:

> A dialectical process is negatively characterised by the fact that it is not to be conceived as the result of individual unchanging factors. To put it positively, its elements continuously change in relation to each other within the process, so that they are not even to be radically distinguished from each other. Thus the development of human character, for example, is conditioned both by the economic situation and by the individual powers of the person in question. But both these elements determine each other continuously, so that in the total development neither of them is to be presented as an effective factor without giving the other its role.
>
> (Horkheimer 1972 [1937], p. 28)

A further leading representative of critical theory, Herbert Marcuse, explains dialectical thought as grasping all the facts as stages of a single process in which subject and object are joined – that truth can be determined only within the subject-object totality. All facts thus partly embody subjectivity (1960 [1941], pp. vii–xvi), in contrast to the Cartesian tradition, according to which the subject and object are defined separately. Dialectics and totality also go hand-in-hand when applied to economic phenomena. As Mandel claims, such phenomena "are [thus] not viewed separately from each other, by bits and pieces, but in their inner connection as an integrated totality, structured around, and by, a basic predominant mode of production" (1976, p. 18). Any genuinely critical explanation signifies not only a logical process but also a specific historical process. In this context, the social structure as a whole and the relationship between the theoretician and society are transformed. Therefore, both the subject and the role of thought are changed. The acceptance of an "essential unchangeableness between subject, theory, and object thus distinguishes the Cartesian conception from every kind of dialectical logic" (Horkheimer 1972 [1937], p. 190).

Arthur (2004) explains dialectics as a method that addresses a given whole which demonstrates how the whole systematically, and in its interconnectedness, reproduces itself. Bonefeld nevertheless opposes Arthur's systemic dialectics in a sense that dialectics should not be understood as a closed logical system, which more rigorously follows the tradition of critical theory. Dialectics is seen as a method (of course, much less for Hegel) of presenting social categories in a way which unfolds "the social genesis of the whole system of real economic abstractions" (2014, pp. 5–6). Dialectics does not pacify the contradiction, nor does it reconcile the antagonism, but rather presents economic categories on a social basis. The aim remains Marxian – to show relations in their perverted form of economic objectification. The bridge to economics is based precisely on this contradiction – that the producer and the consumer have exactly opposite interests concerning the prices and quantities of goods and services, as do employers and employees in the case of wages and the amount of work performed.

Adorno develops the idea that dialectical thought refuses to affirm particular things in their isolation and separateness since it designates isolation as a product of the universal. He continues that dialectical mediation is not "a recourse to the more abstract, but a process of resolution of the concrete in itself" (2005 [1951], p. 74). The subject as broken down into infinitely complex relationships and the decentralisation of the subject, by which the subject consequently valorises its objective cognition, led Adorno to his concept of "negative dialectics" (2004 [1966]), which was subsequently adopted and interpreted by Honneth (2009). Adorno's distaste for perfect consistency shaped his negative dialectics so as to form a concept of "apparently contradictory statements, which both reflects and resists the reality it tries critically to analyse" (Jay 1984, p. 266). Such an understanding of dialectics is, naturally, the most alienated form of dialectical thought with concern to economics, where rationality is conditioned by infinitely strict consistency, and where the methodology is based exclusively on logical validation or empirical verification. The subject should be simply viewed both within and outside things – a viewpoint that is supposed to react to the isolationism of positivists. According to Kosík, "[a]ll activity is one-sided because it pursues a *particular* goal, and therefore isolates some moments of reality as essential while leaving others aside" (1976, p. 5). In this context, that is, the confronting of romanticist wholeness with practical one-sidedness, one can identify Goethe, Hegel, Marx and others as contemporary economists.[6]

Critical theory opposes the requirement of theoretical systems that all the parts of the system should intermesh thoroughly and without friction. Critical theory does not seek harmony; conversely, contradictions exist in its very core. In Farr's (2008) review of Marcuse's dialectics, the famous statement "This world contradicts itself" is interpreted as the problem of modern society, which is becoming more oppressive despite its accumulation of wealth and, hence, the potential for liberation. Marcuse's understanding of dialectics was influenced predominantly by Hegel for whom dialectics was not a method that is simply applied to phenomena since things in themselves are dialectical. The aim of dialectics is to expose outlined contradictions and, thus, see things as they are, meaning that things should not be understood only within the given framework of established facts, but rather in their unactualised potential. Hence, dialectical thinking is *negative* thinking since it negates the given framework of established facts. In a society that focuses on facts, the potential for liberation, however great the potential may be, remains unrealised – Marcuse's theory is dialectical to the extent that it identifies the coexistence of oppressive and liberating mechanisms in advanced industrial societies. The dialectical analysis therefore emphasises future possibilities, which distinguishes it from positivism – "what was" and "what is" are moments in the analysis of "what is coming to be" and "what can be", which renders the dialectical analysis immune to the positivist reification of existing social arrangements (Antonio 1983). However, the values that define possible social structures are in immanent contradiction in terms of ideology and social reality. Hence, future possibilities are mediated by the analysis of existing material, cultural, social and political constraints. The historical nature of dialectics thus differs from arbitrariness, abstractness, idealism and ahistorical utopianism (Wellmer 1974).

Potentialities are also considered in one of the most significant chapters on the dialectics of critical theory. *A Note on Dialectics* by Marcuse (1960 [1941]) refers to concepts that disregard the fatal contradictions which constitute reality and which, at the same time, neglect the process of reality. Dialectical thought grasps reality by comprehending its contradictory structure. Marcuse describes the dialectic method as exceeding pure philosophy – it does not suffice to comprehend reality by defining what things really are, but their mere factuality should also be rejected. Dialectical thought thus becomes negative in itself. It should serve to break down the self-assurance and self-contentment of common sense and to undermine confidence in the language of facts. Dialectics helps to demonstrate that unfreedom is embedded at the core of things and the contradictory forces thereof necessarily lead to qualitative change. The dialectical contradiction goes to the basic factors and forces of destructiveness, as well as of possible alternatives beyond the status quo. Dialectics does not furnish theorists with certain extrarational standards but drives Reason to recognise the extent to which it is unreasonable and the victim of unmastered forces which act to increase wealth and the productive apparatus on the one hand, but keep man enslaved to prevailing conditions on the other. The dialectic negation is a critique of conformist logic, which denies the reality of contradictions. Dialectical logic is critical in the sense that

> it reveals modes and contents of thought which transcends the codified patterns. . . . Dialectical analysis merely assembles and reactivates these modes and contents; it recovers tabooed meanings and thus appears almost as a return, or rather a conscious liberation of the repressed
>
> (1960 [1941], pp. vii–xvi)

As Marcuse points out, dialectical thought begins with the experience that the world is unfree. It is seen in the perspective of the Hegelian ontological category: "not being a mere object, but the subject of one's existence, not succumbing to external conditions, but transforming factuality into realisation" (1960 [1941], pp. vii–xvi). This renders dialectical thought necessarily destructive with the potential for theoretical liberation and the liberation of thought. For Marcuse, the divorce of thought from action, and theory from practice, forms a part of the unfree world. The aim is to prepare the ground for the potential reunion thereof, which calls for an ability to develop a logic and language as a prerequisite. *Reality* is the "constantly renewed results of the process of existence" where "that-which-is" becomes "other than itself". This implies that identity is the negation of inadequate existence – the subject maintains itself in being other than itself. Reality is thus a *realisation* – a development of subjectivity. In explaining why reality is other, and more, than that codified in the logic and language of facts, Marcuse considers avant-garde literature as the inner link to dialectical thought: "The effort to break the power of facts over word, and to speak a language which is not the language of those who establish, enforce, and benefit from the facts" (1960 [1941], pp. vii–xvi).

According to Kosík (1976), dialectics pursues the "thing itself" and systematically searches for a way to grasp reality. Nevertheless, the "thing itself" does not reveal itself to man immediately. In order to understand the thing, we need not only a certain effort but also a detour. The detour is the *only* (K. K.) path to truth, despite mankind's attempt to shorten the path to truth and to seek to intuit the essence of things directly.[7] As Kosík puts it, dialectics helps to distinguish between the idea of a thing and the concept of a thing. The real existence and the phenomenal form of reality are diverse and often contradict the *law* (K. K.) of the phenomenon, its structure and hence its *essential* (K. K.) inner kernel and the corresponding concept.

Reductionism should also be avoided. Reduction in this context would mean a rigid substance with irreducible elements – the phenomenon is explained when reduced to its essence, to an abstract principle and general laws. As Kosík explains, the critical materialist approach dynamises an immutable substance; the dynamics themselves and the dialectics of being are posited as the substance. The substance therefore does not amount to reducing the phenomenon to a dynamised substance, rather it relies on a "cognition of the laws of movement of the thing itself". It suggests that the "substance" is the very movement of the thing and the thing in motion is the substance. Alternatively, focusing on human agents, "the substance of man is objective activity (praxis), not some dynamised substance in man" (1976, p. 13). In simpler terms, Kosík understands dialectics as a materialist method for the scientific clarification of socio-human reality, as a method for the intellectual reproduction of society and the explication of social phenomena based on the objective activity of the *historically conditioned man* (K. K.).

To conclude, Thompson (2017) meaningfully summarises the differences between the analytical-descriptive (A-D) logic type, which can easily be connected to contemporary economics, and the dialectical-critical (D-C) logic type, which is represented by critical theory. The diachronic level of differentiation concerns the object in terms of developing over time. Whereas the A-D method is *static*, the D-C method places the object in a *dynamic* framework. In terms of the synchronic level of analysis, D-C focuses on the *process* in order to mediate the connection to higher forms of totality, while A-D focuses on mere *mechanisms*. The ontological sphere is *relational* in the case of the D-C method, whereas the A-D method concerns isolated particulars and, hence, it follows *atomistic* ontology. This is all related to the foundation for an explanation that concerns the isolated occurrence (the *empirical* moment) of the object in the case of A-D, whereas the D-C logic type seeks to explain the *essence* of the object in relation to other objects and the relevant objective contexts, that is, beyond the object itself and beneath its mere appearance. The final level of analysis relates to causality. Whereas the A-D method sees causation as simply *directional*, the D-C method classifies causation as *reciprocal* in the sense that any effect is related to its cause and vice versa, that is, causes and effects are mutually self-determined.

## Dialectical Totality and the Pseudoconcrete

As discussed in previous sections of this book, critical theory searches for the essence of the researched object. The essence is observed in terms of mutually interwoven and dynamic relationships with other relevant objects, that is, the essence is not necessarily internal to the object in hand, but it is context-dependent. Critical thinkers therefore introduce the concept of totality with the aim of articulating "the dialectical non-identity of subjects, which were at once individual and collective, empirical and transcendental" (Jay 1984, p. 260). Kellner (1990) reminds us that critical theory does not identify "totality" as a harmonising metaphysical mode of thought which seeks holistic harmony as a normative value. The dialectical method of critical theory exposes contradictions but opposes their superficial reconciliation. With respect to the Marxian critique, critical theory perceives totality in the sense of structuring society that constitutes many social facts. The economic structure of society forms the point of departure since it plays a constitutive role in all areas of social life. Economic categories are inherently social categories; economic relations are also social relations. Critical theory therefore builds on totalising categories such as commodities, exchange relations and values in order to investigate the social aspects of the capitalist system. Since capitalist society is totalising and is organised as a system, a totalising systemic theory is required. Since capitalist logic penetrates all domains of social reality, such a theory provides knowledge on how phenomena within particular domains of social reality are related to such systemic forces. The term "totality" is therefore neither metaphysical nor static. On the contrary, it utilises dynamic and historical modes of totalising thought.

This also naturally applies to individuals who are seen as parts of this systemic social totality. Critical theory has determined no way to isolate the dynamics of individual behaviour, motivation or rationality from social totality:

> Personality is not . . . to be hypostatised as an ultimate determinant. Far from being something which is given in the beginning, which remains fixed and acts upon the surrounding world, personality evolves under the impact of the social environment and can never be isolated from the social totality within which is occurs.
>
> (Adorno et al. 1950, p. 5)

Individual behaviour is, therefore, both the co-product of systemic relations and a co-former of such relations. The analytical-descriptive method of economics, however, treats economic agents as isolated particular points from which it infers the universal. The concept of human reason is hypostasised with no linkages to either the realm of the agent's particular position or the structures and processes that constitute social reality.

Totality is undoubtedly one of the most important terms in the lexicon of Western Marxism. Moreover, in his memorandum to the curator of the University of Frankfurt, Felix Weil proposed the creation of the *Institute für Sozialforshung* with the aim of forming an understanding of the social life in its *totality* (R. M.) (Kluke 1972). As a form of "Marxist holism", the category of totality was reinstated in its central position (as it was in Marx) in Lukács' *History and Class Consciousness* (2000 [1923]). Horkheimer, Marcuse, and Adorno subsequently also considered totality as central but each in different ways. Despite the various differences, the authors of the Frankfurt School, in contrast to other Marxist scholars, did not establish the concept of totality predominantly in the form of class comprising both the subject and the object of history. Lukácsian thinking considered the proletariat a universal class which actively achieved true totality through the dereification of objective social structures, and thus it was aimed at the future (see e.g. Jay 1984, p. 228). A further specific aspect concerns the scepticism that led to the disappearance of the normative aspects of totality, for example, the idea of a true community of fulfilled subjects in a free society, especially among the first generation of adherents of critical theory. Rather, totality became, in their view, a descriptive concept that denoted, almost exclusively, the oppressive integration of society and an "administered world" of one-dimensional homogeneity. However, particularly with respect to Adorno's legacy, totality should not be understood as an affirmative but rather as a critical category:

> Dialectical critique seeks to salvage or help to establish what does not obey totality, what opposes it or what first forms itself as the potential of a not yet existent individualization. . . . A liberated mankind would by no means be a totality.
>
> (Adorno 1977, p. 12)

In order to provide a coherent concept of "totality" in contraposition to the earlier analysed "pseudoconcreteness", we return to Karel Kosík (1976), whose concept of totality is also grounded in materialist dialectics. Kosík's concept of totality represents a version of Hegelian Marxism that was fashionable in the 1960s and that was not particularly typical of critical theory. It is characterised by a more positive dialectical thinking than, for example, Adorno's dialectics, as mentioned previously. The Hegelian legacy is, however, also present in Marcuse's view of totality, where the principal distinction between the Hegelian and Marxist views on totality was that "the latter historicised the metaphysical view point of the former, substituting class struggle for the clash of ideas" (Jay 1984, p. 222). Aside from the issue of history and metaphysics, the two concepts were, at least in *Reason and Revolution*, almost identical. The reason for adopting Kosík's approach is, however, that it more accurately relates to economic thought. The same applies when addressing dialectics as such – some of the more established concepts of the dialectics of critical theory may be too difficult to be absorbed by regular reasoning in economics. In addition, we must also determine the factors that distinguish Kosík's conception of totality, absorbing materialism and dialectics, and the structuralist conception of totality. Concerning the latter, totality arises from the interaction of an autonomous series of structures. The dialectical character, conversely, emphasises the relationship between contradictions and totality, contradictions within totality and the totality of contradictions – a totality that is formed by contradictions and the lawful character of contradictions that constitutes totality. Materialistically conceived totality arises from man's social reproduction. Totality "grasps reality in its internal laws and uncovers necessary internal connections under superficial and haphazard phenomena". It is "juxtaposed against the standpoint of empiricism that dwells on such haphazard phenomena and cannot arrive at a comprehension of the development of reality" (1976, p. 17). Kosík's totality thus derives from the materialist dialectics of lawfulness and randomness, parts and the whole.

Nevertheless, one should not be hoodwinked into blindly believing that totality is merely a methodological precept for the investigation of reality. The concept has degenerated into two ultimate trivialities: that everything is connected with everything else, and that the whole is more than the sum of its parts. It would be too naïve to think that human cognition is able to grasp phenomena in their "totality" in the sense of all the relations, processes and properties involved; briefly, of all the aspects of reality. As was demonstrated previously, this question was also raised by Hayek, who approached it from the simplistic positivist position, which is attacked by Kosík – opinions as to whether the cognition of all facts is relevant or not are based on the rationalist-empiricist idea that cognition proceeds via the analytical-summative method. In contrast, dialectics overcomes the atomist idea of cognition as a summation of things by depicting social reality not only in terms of the objectivity of its relations, facts and processes, but also as the very "*process of forming them* (K. K.), their structure and their genesis" (1976, pp. 23–24). This thesis is close to that of Adorno who claims that society is not a summation of all its parts – no social atlas is able to represent society (1967), as well as to that of Parsons (1950) who sees the irreducibility of social systems into the mere resultant of individual activities. Simply put, totality is not the sum of all the facts and does not signify all the facts. Dialectically understood totality represents the viable, intellectually reproductive (in contrast to positivist immanent reductionism) alternative for grasping – in our case – socio*economic* reality, where facts are comprehensible only in the context of the whole. False totality is based on synthetisation, which leaves aside its contradictory character and works with facts that correspond to the abstract principle of faux totalisation and synthetisation – to an empty static totality without contradictions. Outside totality, the contradictions are formal and arbitrary. The result is that the richness of reality is treated as an irrational residue beyond comprehension; the whole picture of reality is distorted, and it neglects the details thereof. This does not mean that details are not registered, but they are not understood since it fails to grasp their significance: "Instead of uncovering the objective sense of facts (details), it obfuscates it" (Kosík 1976, p. 28). The wholeness of the investigated phenomenon is decomposed into two autonomous parts: that which goes along with the principle and that which contradicts the principle and which, therefore, is an outlier as the rationally unexplained residue of the phenomenon.

Totality, in its genetically dynamic conception, seeks to explain reality as a "structured dialectical whole within which and from which *any particular* (K. K.) fact (or any group or set of facts) can be rationally comprehended" (Kosík 1976, p. 19). Facts serve as the cognition of reality only if they are understood as being the facts of a dialectical whole, that is, not as immutable, further irreducible atoms which, agglomerated, compose reality. Isolated facts are "abstractions, artificially uprooted moments of a whole which become concrete and true only when set in the respective whole" (1976, p. 22). The dialectical concept of totality claims that the parts not only internally interact both among themselves and with the whole but also that the whole cannot be reducible in an abstraction above the facts "because precisely in the interaction of its parts does the whole *form* (K. K.) itself as a whole" (1976, p. 23). This is the origin of the unity of the parts and the whole.[8]

Empiricism, therefore, often slides into mysticism because without setting facts within the structure of meanings, it tends to omit the question of what they actually signify. Inspired by von Bertalanffy (1968), one can argue as follows: it is apparently not sufficient to study parts and processes in their isolation; conversely, it is necessary to solve the decisive problems within the whole that unifies them, to be concerned with the results of the dynamic interaction of the parts and drives which cause the various parts to behave differently when studied in isolation or within the whole. The structural similarities to which von Bertalanffy refers assist – according to Kosík – in the more profound investigation of the *specificity* (K. K.) of phenomena. The construction of economic models should allow for the dynamic interaction of the various agents based on their preferences within systemic structures and processes; and, on the other hand, the behaviour of the agents should also be co-determined by the objective conditions imposed by the capitalist economy.

The inappropriate understanding of totality led Kosík to the concept of the "pseudoconcrete". For him, economic categories must be dialectically analysed so as to capture their internal organisation within a given economic structure. Only then can economic categories acquire their own real sense. The goal should comprise the destruction of the pseudoconcrete. For the purposes of this book, we develop a new approach which deviates from Kosík's original idea. This approach is based on the "reduction" of man to the level of utilitarian praxis, which helps to stabilise the unstable bridge between critical theory and economics.

The concept of the pseudoconcrete has been described as the collection of phenomena from the everyday environment and the routine atmosphere that "penetrate the consciousness of acting individuals with a regularity, immediacy and self-evidence" that, Kosík continues, "lend them a semblance of autonomy and naturalness" (1976, p. 2). The world of the pseudoconcrete, according to Kosík, includes the following: external phenomena which are played out on the surface of essential processes; procurement and manipulation within fetishised praxis; routine ideas (external phenomena) projected into man's consciousness through fetishised praxis that constitutes the ideological form of the movement of this praxis; and fixed objects that give the impression of being natural conditions, that is, not immediately recognisable as the result of man's activities. It recalls a passage from the *Dialectics of Enlightenment* (Adorno and Horkheimer 2002 [1944]) whose authors point to the doctrine that action equals reaction, which maintains the power of repetition over existence, and which revives the old illusion that – by repetition – humankind can identify itself with repeated existence and so escape its power. However, the more the illusion disappears, the more the repetition and regularity imprison human beings in the cycle of the objectified laws of nature to which they are devoted for subsistence reasons as formally free subjects. The autonomously objectified subject decays and positivistically registers the given; subjugated to a power which hands him over to the operations of many purposes.

The pseudoconcrete proclaims that the essence manifests itself in the phenomenon, but only to a certain extent. The essence is *partially mediated* (K. K.) by the phenomenon and the phenomenon indicates something other than itself. The essence, unlike phenomena, does not manifest itself to man directly. On the other hand, if the essence did not appear in the phenomenal world at all, then the world of reality would be "the other world", distinct from that of phenomena, which would have no internal relation to the essence. Such a phenomenal world can be described and exposed via the structures thereof, but not necessarily via the relationship between the phenomenal world and the essence. In order to capture the phenomenon, Kosík writes, we need to investigate and describe how the thing manifests itself in the phenomenon and how it hides within it, that is, grasping the phenomenon mediates *access* (K. K.) to the essence. Without grasping the phenomenon, the essence would be beyond reach. The real world (in its opposition to that of the pseudoconcrete) is neither a world of transcendence that opposes a subjective illusion, nor is it the real opposing the unreal. As Kosík puts it, it is a comprehension of reality as the "unity of production and products, of subject and object, of genesis and structure" (1976, p. 7). Subject-object dialectical unity thus follows the leading direction of critical theory as developed in Kosík's era particularly by Marcuse (1960 [1941]).

In the world of the pseudoconcrete, the phenomenal aspect of the thing is recognised as the essence, and the crucial distinction between the phenomenon and the essence *disappears* (K. K.). According to Kosík's understanding of reality as the unity of the phenomenon and the essence, the latter could be equally as unreal as the phenomenon and *vice versa* due to their isolation, which assigns the one or the other the status of the only "authentic" reality. Since the essence is not manifested to us directly and is partially mediated by the phenomenon, we need science and philosophy in order to grasp the essence: "If the phenomenal form and the essence of things were conterminous, science and philosophy would be superfluous" (1976, p. 4). Philosophy is thus a "systematic and critical effort directed at capturing the thing itself, at uncovering the structure of things, at exposing the being of existents" (1976, p. 4). Dialectical abstraction is the distance of science from things and events which are seen in an undistorted way, and it is thus the only way to grasp the structure of the thing, that is, to understand the thing in its totality. Nonetheless, the regular economic agent's action incites "routine thinking", which finally takes the form of ideology.[9]

As noted previously, dialectics comprises critical thinking that strives to grasp reality and the "thing itself". Dialectics thus cannot relate to the doctrinaire systematisation or romanticisation of the routine. Conversely, dialectics confronts the apparent autonomy of immediate everyday interaction – the world of the pseudoconcrete. Such thinking exposes the "real world under the world of appearances; the law of the phenomenon behind the appearance of the phenomenon; real internal movement behind the visible movement; the essence behind the phenomenon" (Kosík 1976, p. 6). This is close to the aforementioned Lazarsfeld (1941) who distinguishes between "administrative" and "critical" social research. The former deals with empirical trends, variations and the behaviour of an object within *given* social conditions. Administrative thinking disregards broader social relations and focuses on the descriptively empirical aspects of the object itself. Critical thinking, on the other hand, sees the truth of the object in the processual whole for which it presents social totality as related to the systemic conditions of the object's existence.[10] The essence is not limited to the mere appearance of the object and, hence, it is not fully capturable through empirical investigation. As put by Rosen, "[e]ssence is not some part of being, not the 'essential' part, but all of being at a higher level of development" (Rosen 2014, p. 236). This does not mean that the empirical world is false, it is merely insufficient to form a full understanding of the object.

For Kosík, the prime aim is to abolish the world of the pseudoconcrete. In doing so, dialectics dissolves fetishised material and immaterial artefacts in order to penetrate their reality. At the same time, dialectics does not deny the existence or the objective character of phenomena, but rather refutes the fictitious independence through their mediatedness and abolishes their fictitious independence while proving their derivative character.

## Notes

1 For a recent summary thereof, see Maialeh (2020).
2 Compare with Husserl (1972).
3 See, for example, Menger for whom the aim of theoretical research is to "ascertain the *simplest elements* (C. M.) of everything real, elements which must be thought of as strictly typical just because they are the simplest" (1985 [1883], p. 60)
4 More details on the term "pseudoconcrete" are provided in the following subchapters.
5 For instance, interestingly, Michňák (1965) emphasises not only the disharmony of particular interests but also the progressive fact – however mediated by force – that the satisfaction of one's needs has become the subject of the effort of others, which goes back to the thoughts of Adam Smith.
6 Kosík's concrete totality has nothing to do with the non-dialectical neoromantic concepts of wholeness which hypostatise the whole over its parts and mythologise it; see Kosík (1976, pp. 28–29).
7 One of these "shortcuts" is empiricism – everyone understands more than is sensually perceived – individuals are historical agents who automatically rely on both rational and sensual cognition.
8 This dialectical approach of the interaction of parts led analytical Marxists in the 1980s to examine the micro-foundations of social motion.
9 The ideological form can also be approximated by the *Real* and the *Symbolic*. These terms are borrowed from the Žižek-Lacanian treatment (e.g. Žižek 2000). The Real refers to the sphere prior to any categorisation and classification, which is not accessible to us. The Symbolic is the instance commonly referred to as "reality", which symbolises the Real. However, the Real cannot be wholly reflected by the Symbolic; discrepancies between what the Real is and what the Symbolic mediates remain; hence, the Real and the Symbolic stand in conflict. In order to preserve the Symbolic, the mediated remain must be veiled, for which ideology takes the lead.
10 This whole idea of essence goes back to Hegel's Phenomenology: "But here knowledge of the thing is not yet complete: it must become known not only through the immediacy of its being and its determinateness, but also as *essence* (*Wesen*) or *inner reality* (*Inneres*)" (Hegel 1970 [1807], p. 578).

## References

Adorno, T.W. (1967). Sociologie a empirický výzkum. In: *Dialektika a sociologie*. Praha: Svoboda, pp. 19–35.

Adorno, T.W. (1977). Introduction. In: *The positivist dispute in German sociology*. London: Heinemann Educational Books.

Adorno, T.W. (1991). *The culture industry: selected essays on mass culture*. London and New York: Routledge.

Adorno, T.W. (2004 [1966]). *Negative dialectics*. London and New York: Routledge.

Adorno, T.W. (2005 [1951]). *Minima Moralia: reflections on a damaged life*. London and New York: Verso.

Adorno, T.W. and Horkheimer, M. (2002 [1944]). *Dialectic of enlightenments: philosophical fragments*. Stanford: Stanford University Press.

Adorno, T.W., Frenkel-Brunswik, E., Levinson, D.J. and Sanford, N. (1950). *The authoritarian personality*. New York: Harper.

Antonio, R.J. (1983). The origin, development, and contemporary status of critical theory. *The Sociological Quarterly*, 24(3), pp. 325–351.

Arthur, C.J. (2004). *The new dialectic and Marx's capital*. Leiden, The Netherlands: Brill.

Bonefeld, W. (2014). *Critical theory and the critique of political economy: on subversion and negative reason*. London: Bloomsbury Academic.

Descartes, R. (2003 [1637]). *Discourse on method and meditations*. New York: Dover Publications.

Engels, F. (1947 [1878]). *Anti-Dühring: Herr Eugen Dühring's revolution in science*. Moscow: Progress Publishers.

Farr, A. (2008). *The task of dialectical thinking in the age of one-dimensionality*. Berlin: Springer Science & Business Media B.V.

Habermas, J. (1967). Kritické a konzervativní úkoly sociologie. In: *Dialektika a sociologie*. Praha: Svoboda, pp. 75–89.

Hegel, G.W.F. (1970 [1807]). *Phänomenologie des Geistes*. Frankfurt: Suhrkamp.

Honneth, A. (2009). *Pathologies of reason: on the legacy of critical theory*. New York: Columbia University Press.

Horkheimer, M. (1972 [1937]). *Critical theory*. New York: Herder and Herder.

Husserl, E. (1972). *Krize evropských věd a transcendentální fenomenologie*. Praha: Academia.

Jay, M. (1984). *Marxism and totality: the adventures of a concept from Lukács to Habermas*. Berkeley: University of California Press.

Jevons, W.S. (1888). *The theory of political economy*. London: Palgrave Macmillan.

Kellner, D. (1990). Critical theory and the crisis of social theory. *Sociological Perspectives*, 33(1), pp. 11–33.

Kilminster, R. (1979). *Praxis and method: a sociological dialogue with Lukács, Gramsci and the early Frankfurt school*. London: Routledge & Kegan Paul.

Kluke, P. (1972). *Die Stiftungsuniversität Frankfurt am Main 1914–1932*. Frankfurt: Waldemar Kramer.

Kosík, K. (1976). *Dialectics of the concrete: a study on man and world*. Dondrecht: D. Reidel Publishing Company.

Lazarsfeld, P. (1941). Remarks on administrative and critical communications research. *Studies in Philosophy and Social Science*, 9, pp. 2–16.

Lukács, G. (2000 [1923]). *History and class consciousness: studies in Marxist dialectics*. Cambridge: MIT Press.

Maialeh, R. (2020). *Dynamic models and inequality: the role of the market mechanism in economic distribution*. Cham, Switzerland: Springer Nature.

Mandel, E. (1976). *Introduction to Karl Marx: capital*. Vol. I. Harmondsworth: Penguin.

Marcus, L. (1975). *Dialectical economics: an introduction to Marxist political economy*. Lexington: DC Heath and Company.

Marcuse, H. (1960 [1941]). *Reason and revolution: Hegel and the rise of social theory*. Boston: Beacon Press.

Menger, C. (1985 [1883]). In: *Investigations into the method of the social sciences with special reference to economics*, edited by Louis Schneider with an introduction by Lawrence H. White. Translated by Francis J. Nock. New York: New York University Press.

Michňák, K. (1965). Fetiš 'zákona', 'přírody' a 'čísla'. In: *Ekonomie a fetišismus*. Praha: Svobodné slovo, pp. 207–255.

Murray, P. (1988). *Marx's theory of scientific knowledge*. Atlantic Highlands: Humanities Press.

Parsons, T. (1950). Psychoanalysis and the social structure. *The Psychoanalytic Quarterly*, 19(3), pp. 371–384.

Rosen, S. (2014). *The idea of Hegel's science of logic*. Chicago: University of Chicago Press.

Ross, N. (2008). *On mechanism in Hegel's social and political philosophy*. New York: Routledge.

Rusche, G. (1934). Review: Bernardelli, H. 'Die Grundlagen der ökonomischen Theorie', Illinois University, 1933. *Zeitschrift für Sozialforschung*, 3(1).

Searle, J. (2010). *Making the social world: the structure of human civilization*. Economy. Working Paper, No. 1750. New York: Oxford University Press.

Thompson, M.J. (2017). *The Palgrave handbook of critical theory*. New York: Palgrave Macmillan.

von Bertalanffy, L. (1968). *General system theory: foundations, development, applications*. New York: George Braziller.

Weber, M. (1949 [1903–1917]). *The methodology of the social sciences*. Glencoe, IL: The Free Press.

Weber, M. (1963). 'Objectivity' in social science and social policy. In: Natanson, M., ed. *Philosophy of the social sciences*. New York: Random House.

Wellmer, A. (1974). *Critical theory of society*. New York: Seabury Press.

Žižek, S. (2000). *The ticklish subject: the absent centre of political ontology*. London and New York: Verso.

# 4 Subject and Reason

## Instrumental Reason and Contemporary Economics

What is the role of reason in contemporary economics? From Descartes to Spinoza, we see that reason becomes a means to avoid darkness and obscurantism. By this, it is automatically thought about reason in terms of *means* which leads to reason's instrumentalisation. Contemporary economics is not an exception and internalisation of the logic of reason as means is likely the most developed among social sciences. Purely scientific reason however cannot distinguish whether justice is better than injustice or whether protect people against tyranny, slavery and poverty. The intuition brought into light by the critical theory even says that value-neutrality, immanent to instrumentalised scientific reason, prevents people from fighting an oppression. Despite Habermas (1987) fruitfully reconceptualised critical understanding of reason into an intersubjective (communicative) paradigm which differs from the subject-centred one posited by Adorno and Horkheimer, instrumental reason became one of the central subject matters for critical theorists.

The rational action rooted in instrumental reasoning has been already described by Max Weber as "being determined by expectations as to the behaviour of objects in the environment and of other human beings; these expectations are used as 'conditions' or 'means' for the attainment of the actor's own rationality pursued and calculated ends" (1978, pp. 24–25). In addition to instrumentally rational behaviour, agents also follow value-rational, affectual, and traditional behaviour. Critical theory on this account primarily distinguishes subjective (instrumental) and objective reason.[1] The latter recognises purpose and end – reasoning challenges the end and becomes its criterion. It operates with concepts and scrutinises the very nature and meaning of the subject under inspection. Hence, it cannot be neutral. Subjective or instrumental reason works with purpose and end as well. The difference is that it focuses on means – the role of reason is to challenge means so that it functions as the neutral factor in the decision-making process. It operates with probabilities rather than with concepts in order to reach pre-established ends. Both dimensions of reason have always been present; however, the dominance of the subjective one is nowhere clearer than in contemporary economics. This view on reason

DOI: 10.4324/9780429273841-5

is tied to Horkheimer's view on the struggle between materialism and idealism (e.g. 1972 [1937], 1947). While the first aims to *explain* material conditions under specific historical situations, the latter merely *justifies* affirmation to ruling forces. In Horkheimer's later essay, we read that instrumental reason explores not to understand, but in order to reign (2012 [1949–67]). From a Marxian perspective, the dominance of the subjective reason may lead to suppression of class consciousness. The atomised agent in economics follows its own subjective goals which are not generalisable. Economics does not know social goals which finally leads to relativism of any spoken social end, ranging from cultural, through political and economic, to moral sphere. Boldly speaking, the instrumental reason in economics is not the product of enlightenment, but the contrary – emancipated instrumentality stands against enlightenment fundamentals. Economics' hegemony advocates the supremacy of purposes dictated by the relations of production – for this dominant mode of reason, Adorno says (2005 [1951]), dialectical reason is unreason. Dialectical thought, which seeks reason in cancelation the dominance, is thus an attempt to confront the coercion of logic by its own means. The existing can be overstepped only by means of a universal derived from the existing itself.

Not only capitalist mode of production but also orthodox Marxists are accused of domination of instrumental rationality. For Gartman, they supposedly instrumentalise natural world as a mere material means to human ends. Natural world is conceptualised as a set of means to achieve externally imposed human ends and becomes a victim of human oppression. *Dialectic of Enlightenment* is then interpreted as follows: in order to dominate nature, humans must also dominate themselves by "renouncing their own natural needs so as to muster the self-denying labour to appropriate nature". The crucial conclusion is that supposedly enlightened instrumental reason is about to free humans from natural necessity but it also "ultimately enslaves nature and humans to a logic alien to both". In the capitalist mode of production, it eliminates the material basis for an opposition by "producing a perverted consciousness that reduces human needs for individuality and freedom to the consumption of superficially differentiated, standardised goods" which reproduce the system (Gartman 2012, p. 59).

Further, the importance of Simmel as an inspirator for critical theorists increases with the continual "monetisation" of society. He considers money to be the clearest form of instrument that blurs the difference between means and goals and which becomes the goal in itself. Money as an instrument in fact does not provide for definite satisfaction. The danger for men[2] of being "liberated" by money, Simmel claims, is

> part of the general pattern of human freedom. It is true he gained freedom, but only freedom *from* something, not liberty *to do* something. Apparently, he gained freedom to do anything – because it was purely negative – but in fact he was without directive, without any definite and determining content.[3]
>
> (2005 [1900], p. 405)

As was already outlined, contemporary positivist economics avoids normative analysis and complex reasoning. Rationality is perceived by economists as inner consistency of choice or maximisation of agent's utility.[4] This redirects us to the very crucial feature of instrumental reason – value-neutrality. Adorno and Horkheimer explains that bourgeois society is ruled by equivalence – it reduces things to abstract quantities to make them comparable. The irreducible is illusion; consigned to poetry. The fated enlightened necessity, which is today manifested in market imperatives, evolved as the logical conclusion and predominates every rationalistic system – as myths entail enlightenment, the more deeply enlightenment entangles in mythology. In such a rationalistic system, all births are paid for with deaths, fortunes with misfortunes:

> While men and gods may attempt in their short span to assess their fates by a measure other than blind destiny, existence triumphs over them in the end. Even their justice, wrested from calamity, bears its features; it corresponds to the way in which human beings . . . looked upon their world from within a society of oppression and poverty.

As authors conclude, "for both mythical and enlightened justice, guilt and atonement, happiness and misfortune, are seen as the two sides of an equation. Justice gives way to law" (Adorno and Horkheimer 2002 [1944], pp. 11–12). With regards to value-neutrality of the methods of reason, authors claim that equivalence is thus the instrument which regulates rewards and punishment, and by its equal valuelessness conceals the hierarchy, urgency, justice and *subjective* values, which means that it does not originate in freedom in the end: fetishes had been subject to the law of equivalence; now, equivalence itself becomes a fetish. As adopted by Gorz (1989), quantitative measurability substitutes rational value judgments. All knowledge is thus false, and true only when the question of good or evil does not apply.

According to Kosík (1976), science by obeying this imperative excludes value judgements and rationally justifies only the effectiveness of the means. The appropriateness of the goals when dealing with human behaviour remains outside science, for otherwise science would lose its scientific character, and scientific reasoning reduces itself to mere issues of action *techniques* (K. K.), radically divorced from "subjective" human values and goals which are abandoned to unreason and irrationality. Humans are therefore provided with instructions on how to use resources efficiently to reach a *given* goal without confronting rationality of the goal itself. Contemporary "scientised" economics has set the goal, currently taken as *given*, which is based on von Neumann and Morgenstern (2007 [1953]) who established a new perspective on microeconomics. Economic agents' goal is to achieve maximum benefits with minimum costs which constitutes the very bottom of agent's rational and efficient behaviour. On the other hand, the "cunning of reason", the "intention of nature" or the wisdom of the "invisible hand" do not sufficiently grasp the fact that the result of interacting individuals differs from what they had originally intended – the result of conflicting interests, performed by individuals themselves, does not coincide with their former intentions; intentions which might be originally "reasonable".

Leppin's axiological theory (1968) inspired by Kant nevertheless posits that development of value consciousness stems from the difference between "what *is*" and "what *should be*", by which he follows the outlined discourse of the descriptive and the normative. Here we come to the three concepts of value. Firstly, the subjective concept recognises the source of value in personal motives. Secondly, the objective concept sees the source of value in the essence and qualities independent on man. And lastly, relational concept describes relations between objective world and the subject. It is claimed that subject assigns the world a value character, and therefore objective qualities cannot be assessed without subject. The subject however discerns contradictions of intersubjective value systems which leads him to a quest for objectivity. This subject then becomes lost in "subject-objective value antinomy". Further, it inevitably leads to distinction between final and instrumental values: for instance, satiating hunger is final value, while the process of obtaining bread represents instrumental value. The possible threat then occurs when man succumbs to the reign of instruments; when the society is pushed to produce more and more bread while it stays still hungry – when the intentionally reasonable production ceases to be "reasonable". The idea is observable even earlier. Horkheimer adds on this account that the activity of society is "blind and concrete in the bourgeois economic mode, that of individuals abstract and conscious", based on the proposition that tools are prolongations of human organs to state that the organs are also prolongations of the tools (1972 [1937], pp. 200–201). Adorno (1998) continues that objective institutions in the present society (late 1960s) have attained such an overwhelming power over the individual that individuals became functionaries of the predominant forces beyond their control.

In any case, instrumental reason requires an intertemporal frame. For Kosík, an individual in the world of procuring is always in the future (similarly as for Adam Smith) and turns the present into a means for individual's ends. An individual thus lives in the future, neglects that-which-is and anticipates that-which-is not, therefore lives in nothingness and inauthenticity. Such "Cartesian" reason is in its consequences subordinated to its own unreasonable and irrational products. The reason ceases to be independent and reasonable, while its products manifest themselves as the very seat of reason and autonomy. The reason becomes unreason outside the individual reason. Cognition of these transcendent laws is called science, subjecting to them is being called freedom in the sense of freedom as "the recognition of necessity". The reason leaves aside what is irrational and simultaneously establishes the irrational as a form of its own existence. To put it with Adorno and Horkheimer (2002 [1944]), reason turns into faith whose fanaticism is the mark of its untruth. The paradox of faith degenerates into fraud and faith's irrationality into rational organisation in the hand of the enlightened who steer society toward barbarism.

Despite expanding the potential of freedom, tolerance to superficial diversity is connected with incomparability of values which consequently leads to inability to formulate any objective or universal direction. The principle of tolerance may support the oppressors in society that is already repressive and unequal – tolerance metamorphoses into indifference and injustice. Adorno and Horkheimer (2002 [1944]) posits that despite each party receives its due in an exchange, economic reason results in social injustice. The reign of the universal reason, however particular it is, serves as the instrument of privilege within equality. Clever people become dunces; reason turns into unreason; reason acts as an instrument of adaptation. "Means and end are inverted", says Adorno (2005 [1951], p. 15) when describing reduced and degraded man who powerlessly resists the magic which transforms him into a façade. The façade consists of the subjugation to the production process that is presented as the result of our free choice. Although "the nearer the sphere of immediate, physical existence is approached, the more questionable progress becomes, a Pyrrhic victory of fetishized production" (2005 [1951], p. 117). Reason is silent about ends and is reduced to a tool for calculating means. Valueless instrumental reason consecrates technological advance as the highest humanity and serves uncritically the institutions that objectify it in routines, processes and products (Antonio 1983). Reason is the organ of calculation, neutral to any end and its element is coordination. There are no substantial goals for reason, all affects are equally remote to it and stand against mythology. If all affects are of equal value, Adorno and Horkheimer say, then self-preservation offers the most plausible maxims for action and dominates the form of the system. Rationally enforced self-preservation thus had become the reified drive of each individual on the one hand, and destructive natural force on the other – pure reason become unreason; a procedure free from any content. Society as the permanent and organised compulsion then perpetuates the threat from nature by reproducing itself in individuals' systematic self-preservation (Adorno and Horkheimer 2002 [1944]).

Instrumental rationality was always present but did not reign society. It is also worth to note that instrumental reason will be always needed to secure reproduction of society.[5] Critical theory has been arguing with poetical reason or normativity. Today, most of such arguments are already absorbed by instrumental reason. Hauser (2013) concludes that truly rational and emancipated society should use instrumental reason to avoid pressure of "internal nature".

## Rational Attitude Towards Self-Preservation

With reference to the previous subchapter which dealt with instrumental reason, the present subchapter reveals that such a form of reason by consequence drives rational agents towards self-preservation. For Adorno and Horkheimer, the system is the form of knowledge which deals with facts, while facts consequently assist the subject in mastering nature and self-preservation becomes the constitutive principle of science. Even the ego, by the authors referred to as "the synthetic unity of apperception", to which Kant assigns the whole of logic, is both the product and the condition of material existence (2002 [1944], p. 68). "The system's principles are those of self-preservation" (2002 [1944], p. 65). A close interrelatedness between methodological positivist's attitudes and self-preservation has high theoretical importance.

Reason, "the legislating authority of any action" (Adorno and Horkheimer 2002 [1944], p. 22) derives from the materialistic moment of physical[6] violence (Adorno 1967). Natural components of humans are inseparable from any analysis related to human behaviour. They are always present, in any time and at any place. By this, we exceed phenomenal aspects of any particular space-time or epoch, also a fixation of Marxist tradition on class division etc., which has at the end prevailed in Marxian theory over Marx's postulates on constancy of hunger and sex. The first inspirational dualism (for Marx and especially for Freud) of this kind might be found in Schiller: "*Hunger and love* are what moves the world" (in Cotti 2007). For Kalivoda (1968), who combines Marxian and Freudian approach, these materialist instinct layers of human existence are the essential factors of natural existence of man – his "biopsychic energy"[7] which drives him to a permanent conflict with reality. Dissatisfaction of these essential factors decomposes formerly dualistic concept of *Éros* as the instincts are sexual and self-preserving.

In Marx's (2007 [1844]) work, it is read that the subject of human instincts exists beyond and independently of human himself. Thus, man must turn to "the Outside" in order to reconcile his instincts and desires. Economic activity of man, which is perceived as the base, is for Kalivoda the "superstructure" of the biopsychic forces. Economic activity is therefore secondary, a mere social projection of man's instincts, or as Machovec (2006 [1983]) similarly explains, "internal nature" leads to utilitarian action in "external nature". Attributes of these instincts were also captured by surrealist André Breton:

> In the clamor of crumbling walls, among the songs of gladness that rise from the towns already reconstructed, at the top of the torrent that cries the perpetual return of the forms unceasingly afflicted with change, upon the quivering wing of affections, of the passions alternately raising and letting fall both beings and things, above the bonfires in which whole civilizations conflagrate, beyond the confusion of tongues and customs, I see man, what remains of him, forever unmoving in the center of the whirlwind. Abstracted from the contingencies of time and place, he truly appears as the pivot of this very whirlwind as the mediator par excellence.
> (1997 [1934], p. 138)

Everyone has to play the game regardless of conditions he faces: "In the woeful idiocy they practice, their empty horror, they are able to vent their impracticable woe, their crass fear of death, and yet continue to repress it, as they must if they wish to go on living" (Adorno 2005 [1951], p. 241). Successful are "[o]nly those who subject themselves utterly pass muster with the gods" (Adorno and Horkheimer 2002 [1944], p. 5). Agents are subjugated to market forces, while they experience success to the extent to which they follow market rules. Objective necessity stays beyond control of agents and rationality based on exchange detaches itself from the idea of reason. On the other hand, economic laws are for critical theorists socially constituted and these laws only manifest themselves as laws of economic nature. In Lukács's (1978) language, economic laws have established themselves as "a second nature". Bonefeld, however, reminds that the fact that man has to eat says nothing about the mode of subsistence and what it entails. Therefore, the society, not nature, is the point of critical departure. Agents are compelled to sacrifices (in the broadest possible sense) in order to gain access to the means of subsistence for which they compete on the market. Agents face over-determining structured framework. Such an agent is an investor, an entrepreneur of labour power who seeks for access to the means of subsistence. Legal equality masks the fundamental inequality – as put by Bonefeld: "economic compulsion is a form of freedom that is experienced in and through a constant struggle to secure her living existence" (2014, p. 106). That is to say, known from the very Marxian (2015 [1867]) times, that each agent has to expand her capital, so as to preserve it, only by means of progressive accumulation.

A rational whole serves the self-preservation to the dominated social whole. The immanent reason inevitably turns into a means of enforcing the particular interest and the individual is confronted by universal power: "The power of all the members of society, to whom as individuals no other way is open, is constantly summated . . . in the realisation of the whole, whose rationality is thereby multiplied over again" (Adorno and Horkheimer 2002 [1944], p. 16). Authors follow that individual's behaviour is standardised as the only natural and rational one – individuals become things of success and failure whose criterion is their self-preservation – "successful or unsuccessful adaptation to the objectivity of their function and the schemata assigned to it". Those who act "without any rational reference to self-preservation, revert to the realm of prehistory" (Adorno and Horkheimer 2002 [1944], pp. 21–22). The subject is allegedly free from mythical thought and ambiguous meanings and reason become a universal instrument to the all-encompassing economic apparatus. The exclusivity of logical laws, authors claim, stems from the compulsive character of self-preservation as it constantly magnifies into the choice between survival and doom. It touches existentialists' "existence precedes essence" – the essence is constructed when human beings are already in the world. The essence can be made only when human beings are able to remain in the world. Man, therefore, exchanges essences by "abandoning one's own soul to the supporting and nurturing life of the world" (Klages 1932, p. 1409). The whole reproduces itself by imposing its universality on man whose self-preservation corresponds to his subordination to the whole. Sanction of economic praxis has been internalised and became a "second nature" of the individual (Adorno 1967).

Famous interpretation of Homer's *Odysseus* by Adorno and Horkheimer (2002 [1944]) depicts the correspondence of the main character and economics based on self-preservation, illustrating the intertwinement of myth and rational labour. For Odysseus, the realms of time have been namely transformed into the tripartite division in order to combat a mythical prehistory and to liberate the present moment from the power of the past by reviving the irrecoverable past. In doing so, the past is placed as usable knowledge in the service of the present: ego as the bearer of the divine substance owes its existence to the sacrifice of the present to the future. The sacrifice is a behaviour pattern drilled into the subjugated, "by which they reenact against themselves the wrong done to them in order to be able to bear it" (2002 [1944], p. 41). The self remains trapped in the clutches of the natural, seeking for preservation through overcoming one another. Read through economic lenses, savings represent materialised activity of the past which come back to life in the present, actualised in the competitive struggle motivated by self-preservation. A common denominator with Kosík's (1976) three-dimensionality of time is also detectable. Based on traditional Hegelian dialectics, the difference between animal and human craving is that the latter interpose a mediating element – labour – which is an elementary model of dialectics itself. Except the fact that man lives in a world of his own artefacts and the animal is tied to conditions of nature, the humanised craving forms the three-dimensionality of human time: it transcends the nihilism of its animal craving and in this act of restraint uncovers a future as a dimension of its being. The animal is controlled by time, whereas man controls time through his ability to resist immediate satiation: man sets the present as a function of the future while making use of the past. Hence, man's preconditions are rooted in the past, conditions of his action are anchored in the present, and consequences of his action reach into the future. Man, thus, sees nature in a double light: as a power and objectivity that has to be respected independently of him and as a mere material in which human intentions and meanings are realised.

Anyone who wants to survive must not listen to the temptation of the irrecoverable. Odysseus, in contrast to his comrades who have plugged their ears with wax, is able to hear tempting calls. Workers concentrate to look ahead and ignore the rest; Odysseus is bound to the mast and denies the happiness the more the closer it approaches. Adorno and Horkheimer conclude that workers reproduce the life of the oppressor as a part of their own, while Odysseus cannot step outside his social role. The bourgeois stoicism eases the privileged to see suffering as a possible threat for themselves. Adorno says in one of his aphorisms, commenting the privileged who seem to spare the pursuit of their own interests, the following: "But the possibility [of doing so] is purely formal, for the privileged are precisely those in whom the pursuit of interests has become second nature – they would not otherwise uphold privilege" (2005 [1951], p. 31). Therefore, not only workers but also capitalists are bounded to conditions of their reproduction, while neglecting these conditions means losing capitalists' privileges and their extinction.

Odysseus, free of practical cares, is allowed to build up self-mastery: "Precisely the strength which is detached from self-preservation benefits self-preservation: in the struggle with the feeble, gluttonous, undisciplined vagabond or with those who have basked in idleness" (Adorno and Horkheimer 2002 [1944], p. 44). What is not used to serve self-preservation actually serves to self-preservation – the more an individual has above what he needs, the more likely he will keep himself alive – the superiority of nature in the competitive struggle is confirmed and only adaptation to it is a way to self-preservation – asceticism has always been glorified as a social precondition of becoming wealthy. It is the principle of bourgeois disillusionment – the external schema for the internalisation of sacrifice which makes survival virtually dependent on death. An individual in his *apparent* freedom is a product of society's economic and social apparatus – the harshness of competitive society. Individuals succumb to the universal mechanism of competition in their "petrified otherness", with a "subtler means of adaptation from weakness"; individuals' personalities are levelled out. And since all the content of the self comes from society, the self-sufficient individual has become "a mere receptive organ of the market", a shell without content (Adorno 2005 [1951], pp. 135–136, 149).

"The individual as a rule must simply accept the basic conditions of his existence as given and strive to fulfil them" (Horkheimer 1972 [1937], p. 206). Such adaptation to conditions of production external to man causes him deformations. Nevertheless, such deformations are not a sickness in man but in the society and mode of production itself. The will to live becomes dependent on the denial of the will to live: "self-preservation annuls all life in subjectivity". The living has made itself a mere thing, equipment of the production: "The ego consciously takes the whole man into its service as a piece of apparatus. In this re-organization", Adorno continues, "the ego as a business manager delegates so much of itself to the ego as business mechanism, that it becomes quite abstract, a mere reference point: self-preservation forfeits its self". The separation of character traits both from their instinctual basis and from the self, causes man to pay for his inner organisation with increasing disintegration. In the light of this duality, all the achievements of adaptation described by social psychology or cultural anthropology are mere epiphenomena (Adorno 2005 [1951], pp. 229–231). The pressure of adaptation annuls subjectivity and dominates the insights of specialised sciences from its meta-position. The next subchapter follows the pressure of adaptation in more details.

## Metamorphosis of the Subject and Its Objectification

The term "subject" designates a variety of things and interpretations, ranging from psychoanalysis, through ethnology, to semiotics backgrounds. In its simplest variation it is synonymous with the "individual". In psychoanalytical discourse, which has played an important role to critical theory, the "subject" is found in the unconscious layer as "the self". It encompasses both private and collective, conscious and unconscious aspects of being. But for the purpose of this book most importantly, "subject" can be understood as the subjected object of various social and historical determinations (see e.g. Smith 1988; Silverman 1983). In any case, the subject and related subjectivity account for a certain autonomy which is, according to critical theorists, undermined in the modern capitalist socioeconomic system.

Adorno and Horkheimer (2002 [1944]) maintain that individuals are overwhelmed by demonstration of freedom of choice and the charm of not belonging to the system. However, in both cases, they remain mere objects – self-preservation of the particular depends on conditions of the objective.

Economic success is the function of subject's adaptation to the objective. Under the threat of the natural, animal and vegetative existence is back in play. The success in market capitalist society is based on providing countervalue, which means that the subject must perform in the market. Hauser (2005) interprets Adorno's understanding of self-preservation with implications to subjectivity as follows: individuals obey laws of capitalist economy as long as they are interested in their self-preservation. "Rational" attitude towards self-preservation led to the conquest of nature, while individual's subjectivity springs out right from the conquest. On the other hand, "rational" attitude towards self-preservation leads to the acquiescence to capitalist economy and individual's subjectivity disappears. In other words, individual pays for minimising the risk of extinction with his subjectivity. As the result, man became the object of exchange since man had subjected himself to the principle of reality – man is the object of changing external market forces which form subject's fluidised selfhood, ending up in "reflexively controlled self-presentation" (Luhmann 1970) or "reflexive conformism" (Voswinkel 2011). The pioneer of this idea, except for Marx, was Lukács (2000 [1923]) who labelled the subject adapting on autonomous systems of calculation as "reified". A reified subject is overdetermined by the proliferation of the commodity form which furnishes social production. The products are seen as routinised dehumanised reality. Such adaptation finally causes a decay of subjectivity. Honneth (2009), inspired by Lukacs's concept of reification, deciphers physiognomy of capitalist organisation of society through Adorno's understanding of relationship between exchange and reason. It is claimed that as individuals are forced to behave according to the scheme of exchange in still more spheres of their lives, the richness of their rationalities is reduced to egocentric utilitarian calculation.

For Kosík (1976), *homo oeconomicus* is exactly the subject who objectifies himself. The subject becomes integrated in a trans-individual whole. The subject abstracts from his subjectivity and then metamorphoses into an object, a mere element determined by the system. A man becomes an abstract, analysable, and mathematically describable unit, the real metamorphosis of man performed by capitalism which establishes and develops economics as a *science*, where the individual becomes the general, the stochastic, the lawful. To make such transformation, contemporary economics stands over individual purposes, becomes independent of them, and the social relations among individuals transform as an autonomous natural force over them. *Homo oeconomicus* is thus a functioning element of a system whose essential features were defined to make the system running – a reified moment of praxis.

Human beings are being averted from the principle of the self – species are becoming identical to one another through isolation within the compulsively controlled collectivity. The oppression of collectivity affects all human beings regardless their social status: "It is the servant which the master cannot control at will" (Adorno and Horkheimer 2002 [1944], p. 29). The market appropriates humans' capacities to make them fit to the production. Despite humans have been endowed with an individuality, they are forced to behave the same way. The platform for human interaction forces them into conformity and negation of each individual. The triumph of repressive *égalité* degenerates the equality of rights into the wrong inflicted by equals, where "[a]ny attempt to break the compulsion of nature by breaking nature only succumbs more deeply to that compulsion" (Adorno and Horkheimer 2002 [1944], p. 9). Human beings are therefore reduced to mere objects of administration which conjures up an illusion of objective necessity before which they feel powerless. "Poverty as the antithesis between power and impotence is growing beyond measure, together with the capacity permanently to abolish poverty" (Adorno and Horkheimer 2002 [1944], p. 30). The power of the system over human beings increases as they rationally endeavour to escape the compulsive power of nature.

Despite the discussed receptivity, man will always find himself in a network of relationships through his existence. The entanglement of the individual in the network confronts him as the practical-utilitarian world. Objective relationships thus manifest themselves as a world of procuring – a world of means and ends. The individual exists in a "ready-made system of devices and implements" and procures them as they in turn procure him and penetrate his entire life: "The everyday appears as the anonymity and tyranny of the impersonal power which dictates every individual's behaviour, thoughts, taste and even his protest against banality" (Kosík 1976, p. 46). Procuring expresses itself in the phenomenally alienated form, in the environment of everyday manipulation and ready-made "things" in which man himself is transformed into an object of manipulation. The world of procuring is the ready-made and given surface of reality which does not appear as the world formed by the man himself but as a ready-made impenetrable being.

In this world, things acquire meaning only insofar as they are manipulable. The world of objectivity (manipulation and procuring) might engulf an individual so completely that his subjectivity disappears and objectivity exposes itself as the real subject: "[m]an might disappear in the "external" world because his is the existence of an objective subject which exists only by producing a subjective-objective historical world" (Kosík 1976, p. 47); the content of subjectivity itself becomes "a mere function of the production process"[8] (Adorno 2005 [1951], p. 214). Man is real only when he develops those abilities that are required for the operation of the system. The rest of abilities are private and romantic, irrelevant and unreal. The man is real only as an element of the system (Kosík 1976). Adorno reacts that the more the subject adjusts himself to external relations, the more he becomes a thing for himself. The subject is divided into two parts – as a continuation of the machinery of social production and as a residuum opposing "rationality" and perishing into curiosity (1967). Bonefeld adds that economic progress requires a constant adjustment from the agents: "Man receives from society what she puts into society" (2014, p. 220). The person is then objectified in the economic thing, while the economic thing subjectifies itself. Under the compulsion of the *unintended* (R. M.) universal, individuals are mere character masks of economic forces (Adorno 2004 [1966]). This has a common ground with Freudian "death impulse" – instead of active engagement in things man inclines to be dominated by objectivity.

To conclude with the epiphenomenal role of specialised sciences, it can be seen that, for example, psychology-based behavioural approaches in economics, suggesting an elaboration and objectivation of psychology,[9]

> uncritically accepts the phenomenal form of reality as though it were reality itself. . . . Not theory, but reality itself reduces man to an abstraction. Economics is a system and a set of laws governing relations in which man is constantly being transformed into the "economic man".
>
> (Kosík 1976, pp. 51–52)

Subjectivistic economics is ideological: it explains market processes through psychological moments which can be, however, classified as mere randomness accentuating phenomenon instead of the essence (Adorno 1967). Also, Kosík (1976) criticises "psychologization of economics" which strives to present economic laws as objectivation of psychology. Behavioural and experimental "opposition" to mainstream economics, famously advocated, for example, by Orrell (2012), accuses economics of pythagorianic ideologism (i.e. cosmos composed of numbers). Nevertheless, Orrell's critique relies on a naïve idea that the difference between the essence of being, unknowable for Kant, and phenomenological appearance, is seen in what has not been yet recognised in the empirical world. The suggested solution then obviously relies in advanced methods of description which better align to the observable world. Such an approach reveals that economists cannot avoid what Sartre called "Stalinist statistical fetishism". Behavioural and experimental economics therefore rely on a naïve idea that summation of various facts constitutes truth about the whole, which was labelled by Kosík as "false totality". As has been shown, it is impossible to gather all relevant facts – a claim posited not only by critical theorist. Secondly, a sum of particularities does not constitute the whole.

*Homo oeconomicus* therefore does not answer "What is man?" but rather how the man should be to keep the system of economic relations in motion. Economics transforms, subjugates, and adapts individuals to its objective mechanisms – methodology gets ontologised (Kosík 1976). Incorporating critical insights should remind us that human behaviour cannot be reduced to a single-factor explanations, may it be psychology, sociology, economics, or rational choice. Instead, we should understand all these scientific branches as subsumed within a concept of totality, which enables to see human behaviour in complex, unreduced and dialectical relationships.

## Notes

1 Nevertheless, many doubts have been raised concerning the viability of the normative notion of objective reason that Marcuse and Horkheimer in particular employed to oppose instrumental rationality and positivist empiricism. An excellent elaboration on this issue in the wider historical context can be found in Jay (2016). Jay's book also vividly presents the aforementioned paradigm of Jürgen Habermas who rejects the substantive theory of

rationality in favour of enlightened proceduralism. The goal of his philosophy is to specify the conditions for a rational discourse in which substantive claims are authenticated via dialogue between the participants. It should also be noted that particularly critical theorists influenced by postcolonial studies remain sceptical concerning theories of rationality as such; they consider the appeal to reason to be thoroughly Eurocentric.

2 Simmel uses the term "peasant".

3 This concept of freedom was retaken by another critical theorist Erich Fromm. Similar resolution of freedom, nevertheless in a wholly different context, can be found in libertarian thinker Nozick (2001 [1974]). His distinction recognises "negative" and *agreement-based* (R. M.) "positive" rights. The first claim autonomy which cannot be intervened by others, while the latter relate to rights to receive something. The concept of positive and negative freedom was famously delivered by Berlin (1958).

4 Critique on these concepts of economic rationality was already elaborated, for example, in Sen (1991).

5 There are, however, various opinions on the issue. For the differences, see, for example, Machovec (2006 [1983]) and Adorno and Horkheimer (2002 [1944]).

6 Biological aspects of the phenomenon were raised by Maslow who refers to homeostasis – an automatic mechanism of all living organisms which strives to preserve their natural living conditions. To be concrete, his first finding says that "physiological drive" is the strongest motive in human action. The second finding explains that unsatisfied physiological needs make other needs non-existing (1943, pp. 373–374). Valuable philosophical foundations of the biological drive were also put by Spinoza: "Conatus sese conservandi primum et unicum virtutis est fundamentum. [The endeavor to preserve oneself is the first and only basis of virtue]" (1677). Plattner, for instance, summarises Hobbesian bourgeois view on human nature as follows:

> All men are governed by selfish passions, above all the desire for their self-preservation, and no man has a greater right to what is necessary for his own preservation than does any other man. Each man is the sole judge of the best means to his own preservation; therefore, all men are naturally free. But men's selfish passions put them into perpetual conflict with one another. It is in this sense that Hobbes's natural man is evil. . . . [F]or object of men's strongest desire, self-preservation, is threatened by their very efforts to achieve it.
>
> (1979, p. 128)

7 Similarly, another Czech philosopher Mukařovský used the term "anthropologic constant". Despite similarities of these two terms, both insist on different nuances.

8 In a similar way, Horkheimer posits that masses "act as mere functions of the economic machine" (1972 [1937], p. 237).

9 Fisher (2009) for instance, criticises biochemisation and hence individualisation of psychic diseases which consequently lead to their depolitisation.

## References

Adorno, T.W. (1967). Ke vztahu mezi sociologií a psychologií. In: *Dialektika a sociologie*. Praha: Svoboda, pp. 36–71.

Adorno, T.W. (1998). Scientific experiences of a European scholar in America. In: *Critical models*. New York: Columbia University Press, pp. 215–242.

Adorno, T.W. (2004 [1966]). *Negative dialectics*. London and New York: Routledge.

Adorno, T.W. (2005 [1951]). *Minima moralia: reflections on a damaged life*. London and New York: Verso.

Adorno, T.W. and Horkheimer, M. (2002 [1944]). *Dialectic of enlightenments: philosophical fragments*. Stanford: Stanford University Press.

Antonio, R.J. (1983). The origin, development, and contemporary status of critical theory. *The Sociological Quarterly*, 24(3), pp. 325–351.

Berlin, I. (2016 [1958]). Two concepts of freedom. In: Blaug, R. and Schwarzmantel, J.J., eds. *Democracy: a reader*. Edinburgh: Edinburgh University Press.

Bonefeld, W. (2014). *Critical theory and the critique of political economy: on subversion and negative reason*. London: Bloomsbury Academic.

Breton, A. (1997 [1934]). *Communicating vessels*. Lincoln: University of Nebraska Press.

Cotti, P. (2007). Hunger and love: Schiller and the origin of drive dualism in Freud's work. *The International Journal of Psychoanalysis*, 88(1), pp. 167–182.

Fisher, M. (2009). *Capitalist realism: is there no alternative?* Winchester: Zero Books.

Gartman, D. (2012). Bourdieu and Adorno: converging theories of culture and inequality. *Theory and Society*, 41(1), pp. 41–72.

Gorz, A. (1989). Critique of economic reason. In: *Critique of economic reason*. London and New York: Verso, pp. 107–180.

Habermas, J. (1987). *The philosophical discourse of modernity: twelve lectures*. Cambridge: MIT Press.

Hauser, M. (2005). Adornovo nenormativní osvícenství. In: *Adorno: moderna a negativita*. Praha: Nakladatelství Filosofického ústavu AV ČR, pp. 9–52.

Hauser, M. (2013). Instrumentální rozum. In: *Kritická teorie společnosti: Český kontext*. Praha: Nakladatelství Filosofického ústavu AV ČR, pp. 497–548.

Honneth, A. (2009). *Pathologies of reason: on the legacy of critical theory*. New York: Columbia University Press.

Horkheimer, M. (1947). *Eclipse of reason*. New York: Oxford University Press.

Horkheimer, M. (1972 [1937]). *Critical theory*. New York: Herder and Herder.

Horkheimer, M. (2012 [1949–1967]). *Critique of instrumental reason*. London and New York: Verso.

Jay, M. (2016). *Reason after its eclipse: on late critical theory*. Madison: The University of Wisconsin Press.

Kalivoda, R. (1968). *Moderní duchovní skutečnost a marxismus*. Praha: Československý spisovatel.

Klages, L. (1932). *Der geist als widersacher der seele, III/2*. Leipzig: Johann Ambrosius Barth. Cited in Adorno, T.W. and Horkheimer, M. (2002 [1944]). *Dialectic of enlightenment: philosophical fragments*. Stanford: Stanford University Press.

Kosík, K. (1976). *Dialectics of the concrete: a study on man and world*. Dondrecht: D. Reidel Publishing Company.

Leppin, Z. (1968). *Filosofie hodnot a naše doba: úvod do problematiky axiologie*. Praha: Svoboda.

Luhmann, N. (1970). Reflexive mechanismen. In: *Soziologische aufklärung 1: aufsätze zur theorie sozialer systeme*. Köln: VS Verlag für Sozialwissenschaften, pp. 92–112.

Lukács, G. (1978). *Marx's basic ontological principles*. London: Merlin Press.

Lukács, G. (2000 [1923]). *History and class consciousness: studies in Marxist dialectics*. Cambridge: MIT Press.

Machovec, M. (2006 [1983]). *Filosofie tváří v tvář zániku*. Praha: Akropolis.

Marx, K. (2007 [1844]). *Economic and philosophic manuscripts of 1844*. Translated by Martin Milligan. Dover Books on Western Philosophy. New York: Dover Publications.

Marx, K. (2015 [1867]). *The capital: a critique of political economy*. Vol. I. Moscow: Progress Publishers.

Maslow, A.H. (1943). A theory of human motivation. *Psychological Review*, 50, 370–396.

Nozick, R. (2001 [1974]). *Anarchy, state and utopia*. Oxford and Cambridge: Wiley-Blackwell.

Orrell, D. (2012). *Economyths: how the science of complex systems is transforming economic thought.* London: Icon Books.

Plattner, M. F. (1979). *Rousseau's State of Nature: An Interpretation of the Discourse on Inequality.* Dekalb: Northern Illinois University Press.

Sen, A. (1991). *On ethics and economics.* New York: Wiley-Blackwell.

Silverman, K. (1983). *The subject of semiotics.* Oxford: Oxford University Press.

Simmel, G. (2005 [1900]). The philosophy of money. Abingdon: Taylor & Francis e-Library.

Smith, P. (1988). *Discerning the subject.* Minneapolis: University of Minnesota Press.

Spinoza, B. (1677). Ethics, 4, prop. 22, cor [online]. Available from: https://en.wikipedia.org/wiki/Ethics_(Spinoza_book).

von Neumann, J. and Morgenstern, O. (2007 [1953]). *Theory of games and economic behavior.* Princeton: Princeton University Press.

Voswinkel, S. (2011). Admiration without appreciation: the paradoxes of recognition of doubly subjectivised work. In: Smith, N. and Deranty, J.-P., eds. *New philosophies of labour: work and the social bond.* Leiden: Brill, pp. 273–299.

Weber, M. (1978). *Economy and society: an outline for interpretative sociology.* Roth, G. and Wittich, C., eds. Berkeley: University of California Press.

# 5 Immanence and the Transcendence of Contemporary Inequality

## On the Worthiness of De-ontologised Positivism

In order to ensure that the insights of critical theory are compatible with contemporary economics, it is important to address a number of ambivalences. The aim is not to synthetise these two "irreconcilables", but to consider selected topics of critical theory that are, at least partially, interrelated with economic thought and which contribute towards surmounting the aforementioned problems that face contemporary economics, as well as towards revising the strictly anti-positivist standpoints of critical theory itself. Therefore, the role of critical theory is inspirational rather than dogmatically constitutive. Reading critical theory through the economic lens, incorporating new professions into established orders, is thus in line with the traditional Smithian (who might be labelled a "critical theorist" of his time) claim that

> systems which have universally owed their origin to the lucubrations of those who were acquainted with one art, but ignorant of the other; who therefore explained to themselves the phenomena, in that which was strange to them, by those in that which was familiar; and with whom, upon that account, the analogy, which in other writers gives occasion to a few ingenious similitudes, became the great hinge on which everything turned.
>
> (Smith 1982, p. 51)

Contemporary economics is based, to a great extent, on a mathematical apparatus through which economists formulate relationships between the various relevant variables. Conversely, critical theorists[1] remain sceptical about expressing social relations via mathematical symbols that are aimed at their representing rational relationships between quantifiable elements. It can be argued that despite the present chapter not operating with agents in formal mathematical language, their behaviour is quantifiable and mechanistic. And this is partly true. The aim, however, is also to reconsider the perception of the agent as an isolated mathematical point and to encompass the agent's antagonistic[2] character with concern to the Outside – his/her dialectical totality – which

DOI: 10.4324/9780429273841-6

does not automatically serve to disqualify more analytical (or generally positivist) procedures. By so doing, we fulfil the notions of numerous critical theorists. For example, Antonio (1983) criticises extreme anti-positivism which ignores the techniques and ideas that are critical to the empirical dimension of any form of critical research. Kilminster (1979) similarly called for the harmonisation of positivist methods with dialectics in order to capture the empirical moment of the immanent critique. Among others, Kellner (1990) also urged critical theory to develop new perspectives and to re-politicise existing political struggles and, incidentally, to stop neglecting the political economy and empirical research. Lastly, Kosík (1976) also recognised the "pluses" of positivism in terms of its opposition to metaphysical concepts via its understanding of *materia* as objects and processes rather than as something transcending behind phenomena. Undoubtedly, doctrinaire anti-positivism and hostility to systemisation (primarily to its artificial and unscientific forms) occasionally assumed somewhat dogmatic forms, which, occasionally, created dilemmas for critical theorists. The anti-positivist debate was held mainly from the 1940s to the 1960s due to the fact that the leading intellectuals of critical theory were forced to flee to the United States where, at this time, the dominance of empiricism in the social sciences was strong. Despite the debate having been concluded, it is still worthy of a brief methodological elaboration.

Firstly, it is crucial to understand the origin of the anti-positivism of critical theory. Crucially, critical theorists in fact opposed the *ontologisation* of positivist methods rather than positivist methods per se. Critical theorists attacked positivism as a *paradigm*, as an interpretative direction towards the truth, as the approach to deciphering the substance and as the fundamental approach to the problem itself. Such an orientation, according to critical theorists, resulted in multi-level naivety. In the first instance, the ontologisation of positivist methods pushed researchers to make extrapolations based on empirical findings. The naïve positivist approach hence relied entirely on existing facts. An example is provided by David Hume: despite his opposition to the institution of slavery, Hume expressed his conviction of the inferiority of "negroes" (2011 [1777], p. 372, 452). Of course, the empirical notions of the 18th century supported Hume's claim that no civilised nations, arts or sciences had been established by black people. This opened the way to ontologised positivism interpreting these facts in the sense that black people were principally unable to reach a certain level of civilisation. That is to say that such an approach accepts existing facts as being absolute and automatically rejects broader social, political, economic and historical conditionalities. This inevitably acts to pass off images of reality as reality itself. The critical theory dialectical critique of positivism thus focused on how facts *came to be* and not only what the facts *are*.[3] This does not mean that observable facts are irrelevant or that the general validity of factual knowledge is negligible. On the contrary, they *mediate* the substance of social reality. Nevertheless, they do not *fully represent* the substance. Any true attempt to penetrate the substance – an activity immanent to all dialectical research – therefore devaluates the *idea* (rather than the methods) of positivist descriptivism as the *only source* and *criterion* of truth.

It is important for critical theorists to reject precisely this element of positivism. On the other hand, the increasing complexity of the issues researched enhances the importance of the application of positivist analytical methods, of which the most important and challenging concerns their restriction to their instrumental function. These methods must serve as methods of numerous means that serve to uncover the social reality. In this way, it is possible to apply positivist value-neutral methods to already-defined (and thus value burdened) problems from the viewpoint of critical theory. Critical theory argues that defining the problem itself comprises the manifestation of values. Based on this conviction, critical theory sees positivist drawbacks not in the utilisation of positivist methods for partial analysis purposes, but rather in terms of relying on them when defining the problem itself. During an interview, the famous economist and Nobel Prize laureate Thomas Sargent was asked why it is better for students to acquire the tools before being introduced to questions. His answer was emblematic of the criticised positivist fallacy: "[L]earning tools actually teach you what the good questions to ask are" (Shi 2019). Is it possible to find a better example of how to instrumentalise reason? With difficulty. Scientific exploration originates in curiosity in that which exceeds the already known. Such an ontologised form of positivism therefore serves scientists with the tools, and the only remaining question is: "What else can I find when using the provided tools?" The truly scientific procedure, in cases where the question demands the invention of new tools which, finally, still serve the "greater cause", becomes a part of prehistory.

But why not make use of positivist analytical constructions if they are subordinated (as a supportive element) to dialectical analysis? This is crucial for complex modelling situations and non-linear dynamic systems for which mere essayist and narrative approaches are insufficient. In our particular case, the positivist moments should comprise the clarifying elements that enable the structurally genetic (dialectical) analysis to be more transparent and ensure smoother communication between critical theory and economics. In this way, these positivistic elements remain mere instruments; they do not instrumentalise reason as criticised by critical theorists and, hence, they are not ontologised. The *supportive* role of positivism potentially enables the mediation of the immanent relations of the subject. In addition, we might obtain more reliable results by grounding these methods within a defined theoretical context (in this particular case the non-positivistic framework of critical theory) and, as a result, operate with positivist methods more successfully than positivists do themselves.[4]

Here we approach analytical Marxism, which is easier to connect with popular agent-based modelling in modern economics. Still, the microeconomic foundations of Marxian thought were overlooked for many years. Authors intentionally ignored the subjective aspects of Marxism, even though they have occupied a central position from early times: "In place of the old bourgeois society, with its classes and class antagonisms, we shall have an association, in which the free development of each is the condition for the free development of all" (Marx and Engels 2008 [1848], p. 26). Elster (e.g. 1982) was one of a number of authors to finally resurrect these microeconomic foundations. By considering game theory, Elster focused principally on questions of how capitalist mechanisms work at the individual level. For him, traditional Marxist assertions of macrostructures and long-run trends were, without reflecting on the individual component, mere speculation. Roemer (1982) shares Elster's views and posits that methodological individualism should not necessarily be linked exclusively to bourgeois social sciences. Rather Marxist analysis should be reconciled with this approach so as to manifest itself, for example, in the aforementioned game theory, so as to enable the further development of the microstructure thereof. Sensat (1988), conversely, aims at the proponents of methodological individualism. He opines that they should not disregard Marxian theory simply because it is not primarily equipped with an individualistic microstructure. The potential reconciliation of Marxism and methodological individualism was addressed as a part of the ongoing debate in *Theory and Society*. Weldes (1989) acknowledges Elster's focus on the importance of micro-foundations for macro-social theory; however, Elster's call for micro-foundations should not be allowed to reduce the subject matter to methodological individualism (as criticised e.g. by Wolff 1990). Weldes underlines that social science ought to be methodologically anti-reductionist. Table 5.1 serves to clarify the distinction.

The second objection of critical theorists to positivism is that the positivist approach does not reflect subject-object dialectical unity and isolates the agent as an independent mathematical point. However, subject-object dialectical unity recognises the fact that objective conditions, external to and uninfluenceable by the subject, penetrate subjective consciousness since the subject is forced to act within these objective conditions. On the other hand, the subject actively changes and forms these objective conditions through subjective action. Since the dialectical totality of critical theory understands determinative forces in their wholeness, we deduce that economic agents must exist in subject-object dialectical unity. Economics, on the other hand, is notoriously narrow in its understanding of human action and social phenomena, which is manifested in its general neglecting of the conditions of the action: as Bonefeld (2014) reminds us, just as objectivity does not exist without a subject, subjectivity does not exist without an object.[5] In our understanding, the personal motives of agents relate to the subjective while the specific action of the agent happens within (and, at the same time, is at least partially subordinated

*Table 5.1* What is explanatory of social phenomena?

| | | *Properties of and relations between aggregate social entities are irreducibly explanatory* | |
|---|---|---|---|
| | | *Yes* | *No* |
| Relations between individuals are explanatory | Yes | Anti-reductionism | Methodological individualism |
| | No | Radical holism | Atomism |

Source: Weldes (1989)

to) historical objective conditions that independently exist beyond the agent's control. The resultant action of the agent is then the vector of both subjective and objective forces and, hence, the theoretical enrichment must depict an interplay of macro-social determinants, universal instinct structures[6] and individual motivations. Unequal economic distribution can be – and in terms of economic research usually is – easily explained through individual properties. Distribution can be attributed to education, skills, individual effort, luck, initial endowments (which precede the production process) and so on. However, if we wish to inspect the *systemic* forces behind the phenomena – how structurally genetic objectivity drives inequality – we have to abstract from these particularities and neither free choice nor preferential ranking are able to play this role at the defined level of abstraction. This means that if we reformulated Table 5.1 (individual determinants vs. social determinants), we would not end up with methodological individualism, which is somehow recognised in both contemporary economics and cited papers by analytical Marxists, but a general methodological approach that respects that, from this perspective, the dialectical totality of critical theory rather tends towards anti-reductionism. Methodological individualism, which continues to be advocated within traditional economic circles, is insufficient since it interprets individual and social phenomena *only* through the properties of individuals – social changes are explained through a summation of observable individual behaviour. This means that the individual and social being is determined neither exclusively by subjective capacities nor by objective external conditions, but only by both. In the context of critical theory, it should not be seen as a sin to consider selected aspects of methodological individualism since it has played an emancipatory role over the course of history, for instance when Adam Smith formulated "spontaneous order" where the expediency of an individual's action is realised via causal processes. Nevertheless, in the following parts of this book, causal processes must be placed in context with the uninfluenceable determinative power of external forces (market imperatives), which bestows a new dimension on the action of the agent. While respecting the long history of economic thought from Adam Smith (1776) to Robert Lucas (1986), the implementation of such a theoretical-historical approach requires a knowledge of both the known principles of human nature and the circumstances of their external situation and interaction.

This closely approaches what constitutes the dialectical totality of the action of agents. Our examination of distributive questions in economics must accommodate "the decisive substantive elements" (Horkheimer 1972 [1937], p. 234), the base of the unchanging factors of the capitalist market production process that is immanent to any particular phenomenon of the process; a structured dialectical whole from which any particular fact can be rationally comprehended (Kosík 1976).[7] Is this so unique in the context of economic thought? Let us continue with Adam Smith. Stewart (Smith 1985, p. 22) interprets the Smithian approach as follows: In the absence of direct evidence, "when we are unable to ascertain how men have actually conducted themselves upon particular occasions" we must consider "in what manner they are likely to have proceeded, from the principles of their nature, and the circumstances of their external situation". He follows that "[t]he known principles of human nature"; "the natural succession of inventions and discoveries"; "the circumstances of society" – these are the foundations on which Smith's thinking rests whatever the nature of his subject: astronomy, politics, economics, literature and language. "In most cases, it is of more importance to ascertain the progress that is most simple, than the progress that is most agreeable to fact; for . . . the real progress is not always the most natural". The connection between economics and critical theory can be built upon these shared principles with one exception: Smith, despite being a pioneering scholar in questions of competition accentuated a form of mutuality among rational agents, while the perspective of critical theory exposes their irreconcilable conflict. Pavlík further develops Stewart's interpretation: the simplest/general direction of progress does not necessarily have to correspond to facts since these facts (immediate reality) are co-determined by incidents which may not occur again, and which are not a part of the general measures and tendencies in society. Simply put, Smith strives to explain general motion through a single causal principle. The result is a uniform interpretation of all the teleological aspects of the order without being reductionist or making simplifications, where the unifying causal principle arranges incoherent phenomenal *materia* and establishes its unity in diversity (2001, pp. 915–917, 922). In other words, the "exclusion of final causes from the theoretical image of the functioning of the market economy was necessary in order to grasp its functioning as the spontaneous order" (2001, p. 917).

Unfortunately, most economic models follow the ontologised form of positivism and, thus, seek truth in a set of statements that accurately describe selected fractions of reality. The economic model then becomes a descriptive tool for which the reduction of reality should be to the lowest possible extent, that is, with a minimum of unrealistic assumptions. In order to provide an insight into general distributive patterns, we need to develop an "epistemologically diagnostic" tool which strives to grasp decisive abstract market forces: the unifying causal principle that serves to structure incoherent phenomenal *materia*. These abstract forces represent the Real (Lacan) which, in other words, is the intangible force that establishes the abstract logic of motion. Our understanding of distributional dynamics in economics may seem to be too reductive; however, this is due to the higher level of abstractness. As was already noted, Kosík (1976) reacted by positing that reality is what reduces man.[8] The aim of the thinking of the model *is not* to describe *reality*, concerning which we have already conducted extensive research, but to examine the abstract market logic – *the Real* – which lies behind our empirical reality.

The following sections will focus on providing an explanation of distributional patterns as the function of systemic powers. Here, it is important to remind the reader that the economic agent is not fully dominated by structurally genetic market forces. The agent is apparently objectified by these external forces, which affect his/her actions and within which the actions occur. However, at the same time, the agent modifies the conditions of structurally genetic market forces through his/her actions. Therefore, we do not praise one-sided dominance – nor the dominance of the subjective or the objective – rather, we must insist on subjectively objective dialectical totality which opposes the Cartesian rationalisation scheme of subject and object duality. Although the aim is to transcend the particularisms of the immediate empirical world, we should be able to formulate general systemic forces which render the immediate empirical world explainable. Assuming this perspective, the opposite is true: empirical economic models may minimise their assumptions about reality, but their interpretation is reduced to this immediate reality with a problematic external validity. On the other hand, adopting reductive assumptions on the immediate reality emphasises and isolates the abstract logic of motion, which allows for the explanation of a broad range of behaviour in terms of immediate reality. In other words, the confrontation between critical theory and economics should act to uncover the abstract structurally genetic patterns that lie behind the law of substantial motion.

The more conventional methodological perspective of the rationalist tradition provides a certain amount of inspiration, despite the various substantial differences. This perspective is also useful for another reason, that is, it encompasses traditional thought in both economics and, partly, critical theory. Both disciplines assume that the world is explainable through an underlying logic. Traditional economic thought, in contrast to the scepticism of critical theory, is convinced that the world can be understood by means of thought and logical reasoning. After putting aside current trends towards economic empiricalisation, both disciplines agree that our senses are overwhelmed with a non-processable amount of data so that our ability to register reality is limited only to a certain fraction of reality. It is, therefore, believed that the "substantial law of motion" is detectable through theoretical reasoning (which exceeds pure logical reasoning in the case of critical theory). Of course, it is then more difficult to define the criteria for the validity of the theory, which is based on the consistency between the logical order of economic reality and the logical structure of the proposed theory.

The methodological component, which differs from the traditional rationalist point of departure, is connected to the dialectical nature of critical theory. The dialectical approach recognises the mutual interdependency between empirical reality (senses) and theoretical grasp (thought). Based on this critical-theoretical methodological correction, we cannot confront formulated theory only with empirical facts, which would reduce our activities to mere empiricism, neither can theory be compared to a single explanatory principle, which would slip into mere rationalism. Critical theory, therefore, stands in opposition to both the methodological concepts of "truth" in economics.

## Heteronomous Agents and the Transcendence of the Market Economy

According to Jevons (1888), the market is a place in which two or more agents deal in two or more commodities with the intention of their exchange. Agents, with their private interests, must act within perfectly competitive markets so that they can switch to another agent if it is advantageous for them. Jevons continues that, for instance, farmers cannot withhold all their corn from the market since consumers, due to their purely biological necessities, may deviate the price of corn away from the optimal relationship to existing supplies. In this view, competitive markets ought to positively contribute to the choice of the consumer and the resulting outcomes. Naturally, if the agent voluntarily exchanges a commodity for another commodity, it necessarily implies, at least when evaluating the situation as a phenomenal act of freedom, that both agents gain from this exchange. Agents thus enter the market with their private interests and with the foresight of a personally perceived better state of the world. Freedom in economics is thus reduced to its subset, to a form of freedom of choice or contract. It is obvious, however, that this subset, with its more fundamental and holistic interpretation of "freedom", has no substance and refers to mere formal procedures. As was demonstrated previously, the goals of agents, formally embedded in their utility functions, have no substantive background. In order to prevent a complete dissolution into particularity, economics "technocratically" exploits the reason to optimise means to attain ends. This singular focus excludes any meta-individual dimension and normative relationality concerning the ends. Less obvious, however, remain questions on whether such exchange is genuinely free; whether agents freely enter the market arena and what forms of distributional outcome markets finally tend to produce. Naturally, as markets do not serve only for the trading of *surplus* production, rather, production as such is aimed at markets as the very essence of the capitalist production process, the question of free exchange becomes more complex.

These questions should be introduced in the context of general categories. The traditional view sees the production process as the transformation of the raw natural world into products that satisfy human needs. Economic distribution is given by the share of individual participation in production; the institute of exchange then enables the trading of an appropriated share of production for other products that reflect individual needs, which are mirrored by consumption preferences. In this way, human needs appear to comprise the main driver behind production – production creates products which are allocated via exchange mechanisms to final consumption and the satisfaction of human needs. Distribution based on the share of individual participation is the social moment of distribution, while consumption reflects the individual moment. Subsequently, production objectivises the individual and consumption individualises the product; and while distribution follows generally applicable distributive principles between production and consumption, exchange mediates the particularity of individual contributions and interests. Finally, economic inequality stems from this dynamic process as the immanent moment of social reproduction.

Let us start with certain details concerning consumption. Following on from the self-preservation of every living organism, it is common that such organisms must look beyond themselves so as to obtain the necessary resources for their elementary reproduction. Humans, animals and even plants appropriate resources from their external environment for their homeostatic purposes, that is, they actively perform in the external environment in order to maintain the conditions necessary for their survival, that is, to preserve their "first nature". The act of the appropriation of resources is an internally motivated process which accommodates the effects of the external and internal environments so as to ensure the constant re-creation of equilibrium conditions. Such instinctual acts have been studied over the long term by a number of scholars from Thomas Hobbes and Baruch Spinoza to Abraham Maslow and Theodor Adorno, who attributed such acts to various thoughts on natural laws, ethical conduct, psychological drivers and principles of the socio-economic system. Thus, a part of the resources of agents is necessarily consumed so as to ensure their mere existence, which – since it replaces already existing but depreciated elements of the agent's reproduction repertoire – can be referred to as *reproductive* consumption.[9]

Conversely, *productive* consumption refers to resources that can be used in the production process. The allocation of these resources is intentional rather than instinctual. This is in accordance with Smith's *Theory of Moral Sentiments* where the sacrifice of immediate pleasures in favour of long-term personal interests (i.e. future consumption and long-term self-preservation) comprises a significant feature of the capitalist system with moral connotations.[10] Smith, therefore, sees "capital accumulation" not only as a necessary condition of the origins of capitalism, but also as an essential systemic condition for the reproduction of its germ cells. Scholars who posited that economic questions arise only when surplus over the subsistence level is generated might deduce that instinctual action to secure one's very existence is, due to the lack of relevant alternatives and preferential ranking, of no general interest to economics. However, one particular interest potentially arises through the transformation to the simple problem of constraint optimisation, concerning which the target function – which reflects reproduction consumption based on subsistence requirements – is subject to given constraints, and so that the agent is forced to optimise resources with respect to the given subsistence requirements. A broader application in economics, nevertheless, relates to the intentional action of productive consumption. Alternatives are no longer related to the use of means in order to attain *pre-established* ends, as was the case of reproductive consumption, but are also, formally related to the attainment of the agent's particular ends. These alternatives are ranked according to individual preferences and the agent, who operates in the market, enjoys the freedom to translate these preferences into consumption patterns.

Production, as the mirror category to consumption, primarily supplies the market with products for both productive and reproductive consumption. The question here is how to incorporate economic growth into the context of general market forces. In order to provide an alternative, the production process and the final aggregate output depends on consumption patterns. If all the agents in the economy follow only subsistence purposes, that is, their first nature, the level of production will be more or less the same and the potential for growth *per agent* will be limited, exactly as humankind experienced in its earlier stages of development. The growth of production is, thus, interlinked primarily with productive consumption. Their relationship is as follows: production at the aggregate level is the sum of individual resources; a part of these resources is consumed for subsistence reasons (reproductive consumption), and the rest refers to productive consumption. Since productive consumption represents resources which can be used to enhance the production process, the greater the productive consumption, the greater the overall production tends to be. Alternatively, the productive consumption of an individual agent represents a productive potential which subsequently enhances the aggregate productive potential of the whole economy. If the agent, after securing his/her own subsistence, utilises the remaining resources that vary from physical products, free time, social contacts, money or just human energy as such, in order to perform an activity which – more or less directly, but still immanently – contributes to the quantum of knowledge, skills and competencies which are deliverable to the market, then the agent also increases the growth potential of the whole economy. While reproductive consumption finds its purpose in satiating immediate self-preserving requirements, productive consumption encompasses surplus resources whose purpose is embedded in the future – potentiality.

Naturally, there are clear limits to this binary concept of consumption. If the agent is not under serious competitive pressure, which means that the agent has a certain monopolising power to appropriate new resources in the market, then not all the resources that have not been consumed for reproductive purposes are necessarily allocated to future productive purposes. In such a case, the agent is not forced so strictly by other competitors to continue to participate in the production process. This theoretical vacuum, which might be termed "hedonic consumption",[11] occurs only in imperfectly competitive markets. Under lower competitive pressure, agents with surplus resources (resources above their subsistence level) are allowed to dedicate a certain amount to purely hedonic purposes – to their immediate pleasures, which neither serve their immediate reproduction nor their necessity to succeed in the long-term competitive struggle. The difficult question is therefore (albeit beyond the scope of this book) what type of consumption activities in fact do not contribute to future (re)production, since any type of immediate pleasure can, in some way, be interpreted as a factor that supports the mental, physical or social abilities of the individual.

These general categories become increasingly undistinguishable – consumption is production and vice versa, in a similar way that neoliberal subjects are simultaneously capitalists and employees (see e.g. Prusik 2020, p. 154). Individuals consume food and water to reproduce themselves, while the consumption of professional literature contributes to the production of mental abilities and the consumption of art produces aesthetic sensitivity. On the other hand, consumption necessarily presupposes production. The process of production entails the procuring of food and water, the writing of professional books and the painting of an artwork. Under certain circumstances, consumption drives production while, under different circumstances, production drives consumption. Hunger drives individuals to enter the production process in order to procure food, while the final products of technological progress drive consumption only because individuals are taught to develop the need to consume technologically advanced products. While the production process thus creates and shapes consumers, consumers also initiate and shape production.

The general principles of distribution and exchange are interconnected with the mentioned categories. Distribution works in the form of an objective law of the "second nature" which co-determines consumption patterns, thus the position of individuals within the production process. In general terms, market distribution is based on providing a countervalue which also unifies the problem with the category of exchange. It is believed that the agent appropriates his/her share of aggregate production based on his/her contribution to the production process. This is usually connected with marginal productivity (or revenue from the marginal product) which measures the value added by the agent to production. The agent therefore exchanges his/her capabilities for a share of aggregate production. Those who appropriate a greater share of aggregate production, it is believed, contribute to production with their capabilities to a greater extent than those whose share is lower. The decisive aspect of distribution is, therefore, the agent's competitiveness, which is transformed into the agent's ability to appropriate resources in the market. Sources of competitiveness, be they unique knowledge, increased personal effort, exclusive social connections, pure monetary power or enough time to devise an innovative solution, denote materialised activities as the result of productive consumption. In other words, the agent builds up his/her competitiveness through productive consumption which entails all the individual resources that have not been consumed for elementary reproduction (and for hedonic consumption in the case of non-competitive markets). In this sense, productive consumption, which is equivalent[12] to what a representative agent *delivers* to the market, thus comprises activity that contributes to the agent's competitiveness at the individual level as well as – by adopting simplifying summative logic – activity that stimulates the growth of production at the aggregate level. Moreover, distribution is the result of exchange relations. The agent *appropriates* resources in an amount that is equivalent to the agent's share of the production process, that is, to what was delivered to the market by the agent. Here we see once again the dialectical totality of productive consumption – it is the source for *taking from* the market, as well as it is for *delivering to* the market. Rather than suggesting that the aforementioned sub-processes are the same, it is proposed that they are differing elements of a unifying totality.

Although this publication focuses on unequal distribution, it is worth considering a further important critical perspective of market exchange. Adorno (1967) posits that the exchange value is, in contrast to the "use value", merely imaginary: exchange reigns over usefulness and imagination reigns over reality. The fact is that the triumph of subjective reason can consider the truth solely in the context of exchangeable relationships. This is, however, an a priori condition of marketable production which prevents the spontaneous need to appear within the thing in itself: "Everything has value only so far as it can be exchanged, not in so far as it is something in itself" (Adorno and Horkheimer 2002 [1944], p. 128). Marx (2015 [1867]) informs us that the value is represented in exchange – a lack of exchangeability means a lack of value and everything valueless is discarded. Elsewhere, Marx (1973 [1939–1941]) notes that world trade is exclusively driven by the needs of the seemingly transcendental power of money, whereas money itself merely renders it visible. Thus, is the "hand" really "invisible"? The principle of countervalue represents the *conditio sine qua non* – the condition without which the market is unable to function. The agent maximises utility firstly through reproductive consumption, via which his/her first, internal nature is manifested. If the resources that satisfy mere reproduction are subjected to market conditions, that is, to the agent's second nature, the agent's first step is to become objectivised according to the needs of the second nature. In other words, the agent must be able to provide the desired countervalue to what the agent necessarily needs from the market. On this account, Adorno reminds us of a German commercial jargon which refers to someone who is able to pay via the saying "the man is good" (2005 [1951]).

In summary, the agent appropriates resources that are equivalent to what the agent delivered to the input market, and exchanges the reward for goods and services in the output market. The agent therefore enjoys goods and services to an extent that corresponds to the countervalue provided, that is, the agent's performance in the input market. If the agent does not provide the necessary countervalue in the input market, no matter how urgent the agent's needs are, these needs become irrelevant under competitive market distribution conditions. For example, 5 litres of potable water can be used for life-saving purposes in various parts of the world or can be used for flushing the toilet elsewhere. This example demonstrates the incomparable difference in the use value in favour of thirsty people in poor regions. On the other hand, the poor may not be able to provide a sufficient countervalue to the market, which means that their needs are not backed by a sufficient exchange value. People in rich regions, conversely, do not generally care about the quality of the water used to flush the toilet, thus their use value in this case approaches zero. But, unlike the poor, the rich are able to provide a countervalue for potable water which generates the potential for the realisation of the exchange value. Now, let us consider the problem from the perspective of the supplier of water. Does the supplier in a competitive market have any reason to supply poor regions with potable water for a lower exchange value? If the supplier does so, the competitive market will punish him/her by decreasing the amount of his/her disposable resources, which then negatively affects the supplier's productive consumption – the supplier's competitiveness. Competitive market imperatives are oriented uncompromisingly towards the exchange value; thus, the 5 litres of potable water is provided in rich rather than poor regions. The institute of exchange, therefore, also plays a role in the market for final products – it serves to both transfer and sustain previous distributional inequalities from the input market and, through a single criterion, that is, purchasing power, it leads to the dismantling of any reasonable hierarchy of needs. Individual agents are then reduced to interchangeable exemplars of a false subjectivity.

In addition, the market economy has a further feature that serves to reinforce the dialectical totality of production, exchange, distribution and consumption. One may ask why those resources that are not consumed for mere reproduction are returned to the market for further appropriation. Why do they not serve to provide spontaneous joy, with no economic ends as outlined via the example of hedonic consumption? The answer is simple: competitive pressure. The production process generates a limited output which all agents in the economy have to compete for since their lifetime reproduction depends on the resources appropriated in the market. Market agents reflect Bourdieu's "distance from necessity" and so they instinctively – and subsequently also rationally – pursue the greatest possible difference between their disposable resources and their reproductive consumption. Hence, all the resources that do not serve immediate reproduction take the form of productive consumption via which agents compete for additional resources in the market. This perspective demonstrates aspects which transcend individual agents, whose only rational behaviour comprises adaptation to external market conditions for the sake of their own survivability. A strictly competitive market system provides space for individual preference expressions, but only *within* the framework of this second nature. This fact reduces agents to receptive elements of the socioeconomic system, whose freedom is limited to choosing between alternatives concerning how to enhance individual competitiveness. Resignation to competitiveness as such is not an option since a lower degree of competitiveness threatens resource appropriation, thus the agent's long-term reproduction. The agent's freedom is instrumental as is the agent's reason.

Moreover, agents are unable to escape from such confinement in the context of pure economic theory, according to which their freedom is reduced to mere "freedom of choice". During the first stage, one has merely the choice of conforming or being consigned. Fundamentally understood freedom however only manifests itself when necessity is transformed into possibility – when freedom of choice is transformed into freedom to change the very conditions of choice. It renders transcendental determination redundant and frees human action from the pressure of self-preservation. Conversely, subjugation to the ruthless principle of reality confirms the agent's non-being, and his/her autonomy is increasingly denounced the more adaptation to the mechanism of instrumental rationalisation is disseminated. The mechanism offers freedom but within a given action vector direction. Freedom in economics is the freedom of Sophie Zawistowski: the main character of William Styron's psychological novel is confronted with a series of choices of which the most notorious relates to having to choose between her two children – which child will be saved and which one will be de facto sentenced to death in the Brzezinka extermination camp in Poland under the Nazi occupation. Sophie, unlike the Jews and communists, was "favoured" by being given the choice of whether to save her son or her daughter. While no-one was forcing her to decide between Jan and Ewa, refusing to choose meant the sacrifice of both. In other words, she was offered the survival of one of her children and it was her decision and hers alone as to whether Jan or Ewa should be spared. Contemporary economics favours the same kind of freedom – freedom that offers alternatives under the repressive power of the second nature. However, the consideration of the second nature – the socially constructed logic of interaction between humans and between humans and nature – is precisely that which can potentially reveal the determining force behind human action. Thus, behaviour cannot be classified as free insofar as the action is, in terms of its fundamental direction, determined by the pressure of inescapable necessity.

Contextualising this account in a coherent way within the history of ideas, from Hegel, through Dewey, to Honneth, freedom takes the form of realisable potentiality which requires a higher degree of consensus. It cannot be reduced to a mere processual feature of a solitary subject. Competitive pressure for scarce resources serves to cancel the intersubjective exercise of freedom as holistic individualism – others are perceived as an obstacle to our freedom, that is, as a threat which acts to reduce the amount of resources available for reproduction; a threat that potentially intervenes in a singular dimension of ourselves. Does freedom in economics as freedom of contract presuppose that both sides of the contract must enjoy sufficient economic independence to be able to decide on the contract freely? No. For instance, a worker accepts an unfavourable contract in the labour market not because of his/her free will, but because of the conditions of both the first and second natures, both of which exist independently of the worker. In this case, subjective preferences and their free fulfilment play a role only in the form of a specific circumstance of the labour market – the worker can do whatever s/he wants, but only within a defined circle of market conditions and with no reasonable or acceptable alternative course. In this case, one might consider the option of becoming self-employed. Depending on the power of the market, self-employed agents do not need to adjust to the labour (inputs) market but to the product (outputs) market. The point is that in each position, all agents – except for market-makers in non-competitive markets – must firstly adjust to conditions that have been established by others. These conditions are beyond the agent's control and, due to competitive markets, which provide the impression of impenetrable objectivity, agents face limitations in terms of questioning these conditions. Conversely, critical theory sees society, at least in the previously outlined historical tradition, as the potential for the full realisation of individual freedom. The critical theory perspective would classify the reduced concept of freedom as superficially liberating at the individual level and collectively oppressive at the societal level.

Clearly, the problem of freedom is not a stand-alone issue; inter alia, it implies various imbalances and difficulties related to individual responsibility. Both imaginable and historical socioeconomic systems have assumed a part of the responsibility in selected areas of social life, be it the nation state, political party or trade unions, or the family, tribe or local community. However, such pillars do not form a part of highly individualised market societies. The example of Sophie Zawistowski illustrates how difficult it is to bear the burden of forced decisions. Responsibility for "free choice" is imposed on agents who are destined to act under conditions which they did not choose, which they cannot reliably control, and which co-determine the final outcome of the agent's action, which cannot be easily predicted. Attributing the final outcome solely to the empirical dimension of the agent's action is fallacious. Since responsibility and consequences, which both spring from the agent's scope of action, should be on a par, this suggests that attributing full responsibility for the agent's action raises serious questions, primarily with respect to how to isolate and evaluate the effect of the agent's action on the final outcome. Due to such discrepancies, agents face situations in which the less privileged are exposed to greater responsibility than their scope of action allows, and the more privileged enjoy a greater scope of action for which they usually do not take full responsibility. It is no surprise that under the weight of responsibility, Sophie finally committed suicide. Another literary character, Josef K. in Kafka's *Trial*, was arrested, dragged to court, interrogated and accused of serious, although unspecified crimes. The character symbolises powerlessness against the second nature, and the most illustrative aspect is that he is unable to enter the conditions that determine his life (and, subsequently, his death). How can I be fully responsible for an outcome that I do not control; an outcome which I can barely influence? This is the question of agents who face a complex impulse-response socioeconomic system. Unlike the brutal authorities of the 20th century as experienced by Sophie Zawistowski, which were identifiable and directly mediated, the power of the authority of the market is abstract and indirectly mediated. Josef K., although left at large in the tradition of liberal freedoms, which meant that formally he could do anything, in fact restricted by the given limited number of alternatives, was sanctioned for *unknown* wrongdoings by an *unknown* authority. Uncertain about the consequences, each step towards improving his case usually made his situation even worse without any chance of effectively managing his case – to enter the conditions of his fate.

This is not to suggest that liberal freedoms have not played a liberating role over the course of history; on the contrary, they comprise an essential component of human liberation. We only point out their limits since their relevance arises primarily in *directly* oppressive contexts. But such freedoms, when taken alone, turn out to be insufficient in terms of tackling the market imperatives which agents are forced to internalise, or complying with them – the potentially free behaviour of the agent is open to contamination from the pressure of external forces. From the critical perspective, the freedom, responsibility and general powerlessness of economic agents are similar to the situations of Josef and Sophie – the principles of the market economy on the one hand provide enough means for potential liberation, but on the other they simply transcend the agent's free will in an oppressive manner. As a reflection of their status, Günther (2007) observes that humans often escape to masochism with a common purpose – they voluntarily accept conditions of subjugation under which they are not responsible for what they do. Participants in this research then described the loss of responsibility as liberating – freedom is experienced through obedience and compensated for through the *voluntary* act of entry.

Economic agents behave according to their preferences, and their actions should principally lead to individually perceived better states of the world than is the *status quo*. The needs of agents can be satisfied through resources which exist beyond them. Agents pursue their ends in an environment of scarce resources; hence, they are forced to compete for these resources in the market. There are various ways in which to enhance competitiveness, and agents choose between the alternatives available in the market. As regards their mere reproduction, since this depends on the appropriation of market resources, which effectively constitutes their heteronomy, agents face a fake "choice" between unconscious internalisation, conscious adaptation and starvation. But the more agents pursue the mitigation of the pressure of self-preservation by maximising the distance from the critical level of reproduction – that is, to comply to the first nature – the more they are forced to adapt to current market conditions – that is, to comply to the second nature. Rationality, as an effort to primarily escape the pressure of the first nature, is no longer the liberating tool of enlightenment, rather it paves the way to another form of subjugation. The ends of agents are reduced either to a stimuli-response action or to subjective calculation. These reified agents become instruments of their socially constructed powers on the one hand, and objects of their biological conditionality on the other. Freedom of choice is reduced to superficial differentiation between consumer goods or the means of enhancing competitiveness. As rationality has become strictly subjective and tied to the mere optimisation of means, the rationalisation process is being taken over by proceduralism, according to which the objective-dominated subject is no longer needed – the agent as a rational autonomous subject is decaying.

Unlike early utilitarians, who ignored differences in individual preferences, contemporary economics took a contrasting approach, that is, the fetishisation of such differences which, unsurprisingly, ended up in relativism and ignorance. The falseness of the current approach is that agents share at least the basic preconditions for their reproduction, and so they are predetermined towards a common basket of goods. It is not a question of preferential ranking whether one prefers to eat, drink or have a place to sleep. The true freedom to give up societal conventions and sleep on the street necessarily presupposes the availability of housing, just as sacrificing one's life in support of higher noble goals is brave only when there is the possibility of staying alive. Market allocation evens out all the fundamental differences – institutions under the rule of the market, be they universities, firms or hospitals, are exempt from their specific contents since they are subject to universal market imperatives. On the other hand, the markets offer various individualised features *within* the operation thereof; hence, actors in the market have the option to be *superficially* differentiated as compensation for their fundamental uniformity. Agents close to the threshold of their reproduction usually do not reach this position as the consequence of their free will. However, economic behaviour starts with individual preferences, and thus every inequality between agents can be explained through individual preferential rankings. The fundamental critique should, therefore, be conducted as an accusation of tautology.

## The Immanence of Unequal Distribution

The dialectics of critical theory stresses, among others, the process of reciprocal interaction between "superstructural" and "base" phenomena. However, at the same time, we should bear in mind that the typical emphasis of critical theory on totality challenges the isolationism of either the base or the superstructure as being reductive and simplistic. Hence, the following subchapter does not pursue the reconciliation of the concept of totality with the reductionist idea of base and superstructure – dialectical totality should act against this artificially structuralising binarity. Nor does the subchapter slip into economic determinism and reductionism while omitting the "cultural" aspects of social reproduction, as it might appear at first sight. The aim is to outline a simple model which captures unequal distribution as the immanent feature of contemporary socioeconomic totality, where all the determining factors are only *operationalised* and *interpreted* from this reduced perspective. The dialectic nature of the model defines how structurally genetic market forces govern individual behaviour, as well as how individual behaviour shapes those structurally genetic forces. The resulting inequality does not stem from a unidimensional determinist model which sees the economic base as the sole causal factor of socioeconomic dynamics, rather it is rooted in complex relationships between the various aspects of society which are structured by market imperatives. Unlike the previous subchapter, which underlined how the laws of the market economy transcend the individual agent, this subchapter demonstrates how unequal distribution is immanent to the interaction of agents governed by market principles, which penetrate all spheres of human life.

Contemporary economic research, due particularly to the behavioural upsurge of recent decades, reflects all the habitual, egoistic, altruistic, bigoted, logical and other motivational elements in human behaviour. However, research that focuses on the very basic principles of the reproduction of economic agents practically no longer exists. The theoretical analysis of inequality resulting from these basic principles of social reproduction is not a privileged phenomenon to which the dialectical critique is applied. It is not an incomplete, partial or one-sided perspective which applies the causality of economic categories to a particular segment of social reality. On the contrary, the process of inequality penetrates right to the essence of the production process, that is, to the process of the creation and distribution of wealth in its all-embracing sense. Kosík (1976) posits that theoretical analysis exposes social being in the system of economic categories once they are conceived as an expression of people's *objective praxis* in their interconnected *social* relations as a particular *historical* stage of development. Inequality is, therefore, explained as a system of repetitive regularities followed by rationally behaving agents, where the agent's subjectivity, randomness and idiosyncrasies play no role – due to the decay of their subjectivity, agents perform as objectified entities. This implies that divergence can be captured even between agents with the same preferences and decision-making processes, which allows for inequalities to emerge directly from the production process itself. If we assumed heterogeneous agents, we would be able to attribute the inequalities between them primarily to their heterogeneity, that is, there would be only hypothetical chance of inequality resulting from the principles of their interaction. Although we do not follow a unidimensional approach to inequality, the reasoning presented here might appear to be totalising economism – every single step of the agent is explainable in economic terms since every single step occurs in a space-time with a certain degree of scarcity and opportunity costs. Firstly, this is because we want to make critical theory and economics communicate on common ground; secondly, we intend to demonstrate that even when accepting neoclassical assumptions, socioeconomic systems might report the opposite dynamics than that suggested by the traditional neoclassical approach.

Starting with the neoclassical perspective on economic distribution, inequalities may have the following causes; bearing in mind the aforementioned principles of distribution, the main differentiating factor comprises productivity. Agents who contribute to production with lower productivity, be it low-skilled labour or less productive capital, should expect correspondingly low rewards. Their share of the final output, that is, their reward, depends, simply, on the resources they provide for production. The second reason for unequal distribution is that barriers exist to the pursuit of individual interests in the market. One such type of barriers is of an individual nature; agents may have different mental and physical capabilities in terms of dealing with the factuality and uncertainty of the world. Neoclassical economics also admits to barriers that stem from the operations of markets, which are linked mainly to market imperfections such as monopoly power that displaces competition and subsequently distorts market outcomes. It must, however, be noted that these non-equilibria, which deviate from perfectly competitive outcomes, simply reflect the real nature of the world. Finally, unequal distribution may result from individual preferences. One option is that an individual may choose leisure over participation in input markets, which necessarily leads to a lower reward. A further option is that the agent prefers current consumption over savings; as a consequence, lower savings undermine investment and, therefore, weaken any potential flow of future gains.

If one abstracts oneself from individual barriers and their role in market allocation, a number of options exist in terms of how to move upward within the economic distribution. This commences with the disposal of high-productive inputs that are deliverable to the production factor (input) market. Boosted by education, professional training or, for example, highly fertile land, the more productive inputs the agent provides, the greater the reward. Secondly, the greater the reward, the greater the preference for participating in the input market over leisure – or more generally, the more the agent maintains his/her production factors (labour, capital and land) in productive use. Finally, as mentioned previously, the greater the intertemporal preference for savings over current consumption (*ceteris paribus*), the greater the reward. From the opposite perspective, the roots of poverty are simply ignorance, laziness and excessive impatience in consumption. If we continue to consider natural barriers, rational government is supposed to eliminate only those market imperfections that are caused by barriers in competitive markets. In other words, inequality stems from individual choice, techniques and pre-existing resource endowments; thus, the principles of economic distribution provide the impression of desert-based allocation with a flavour of protestant virtues and the natural and unavoidable differences in conditions that we face.[13]

In simple terms, the production process represents a function which transforms inputs into outputs. Inequality in the distribution of outputs is a dynamic process which results from the creation and appropriation of economic wealth. The intrinsic features of the production process and, concurrently, the most influential attributes of the researched inequality relate to the imperative for resource maximisation and a level/form of competition. As Horkheimer (2012 [1949–1967]) acknowledges, production in a competitive market leads to innovations. However, no *too* profitable industry or *too* productive employee is possible in the quantified world. Economic rationality knows "more" and "less", but not "enough", which consequently implies infinite goals. Any slowdown or stagnation results in destruction. As we have learned in the previous chapter on the self-preservation and objectification of the subject, the constellation of such attributes means that every single agent who is ruled by market forces has to adjust his/her behaviour to them, that is, to maximise the amount of disposable resources due to competitive pressure. If an agent does not accept these imperatives over the long run, then he/she loses his/her competitiveness edge and is excluded from the market. Every agent whose reproduction depends on resources from the market thus obeys the set rules, and the agent's behaviour is beyond any form of preferential ranking – the agent is assigned by the prescribed agencies of power.

At the macroeconomic level, these infinite goals lead us to seek inspiration from the Schumpeterian growth theory, which allows for the capture of "infinite" growth driven by the innovation strategies of microeconomic constituents. The so-called theory of "creative destruction" is compatible with the dialectical character of economics as seen by critical theorists; with "[t]he dual nature of progress, which always developed the potential of freedom simultaneously with the reality of oppression" (Adorno 2005 [1951], p. 146). Reflecting the totality of the production process, infinite growth is neither a matter of our preferences nor one of alternatives that we are offered in the market economy, nor is it the normativity to which society or individual agents are teleologically attached. Market dynamics force every single agent into enhancing competitiveness, which positively affects the production function of the whole economy. Growing production is the inevitable result of perpetually competing individuals who pursue – for their own reproductive purposes – still greater productivity. Impotent complaints about the negative aspects of an ever-growing economy without confronting its cause – competition for privately appropriable scarce resources – merely indicate a fundamental misunderstanding of the driving forces of the capitalist economy. Economic growth as the materialisation of individual instrumentalised rationality faces its own perversion – initially a means to greater ends, it has suddenly become an end in itself. Under such settings, it is obvious that growing production does not necessarily eradicate basic scarcity among people; paradoxically, it creates a new scarcity of a higher order for those who are able to provide a countervalue.

Such progress is, however, far from being a smooth process. Already a century before Schumpeter, the *Communist Manifesto* stated that old industries are destroyed and replaced by new industries due to the motive to survive (Marx and Engels 2008 [1848]). This destructive element of the production process thus illustrates one of the determinants of long-term business cycles. Taking such a macroeconomic perspective, we see that new technology – the aggregate result of the innovation imperative – gradually destroys existing technology even though the new technology has not yet been widely adopted. During this phase of the business cycle, the negative effect of destruction prevails over the positive effect of a higher productivity level and, consequently, the output of the economy falls. During the next phase, the new technology becomes widely adopted, the effect of higher productivity dominates over the effect of destruction and the output of the economy exceeds that of the previous system. Such productivity shocks occur stochastically (usually modelled at the Poisson rate $\lambda$) with various levels of intensity and serve to generate a "monopolistic rent" for those who successfully introduced the new level of productivity. This macroeconomic perspective is depicted in Figure 5.1.

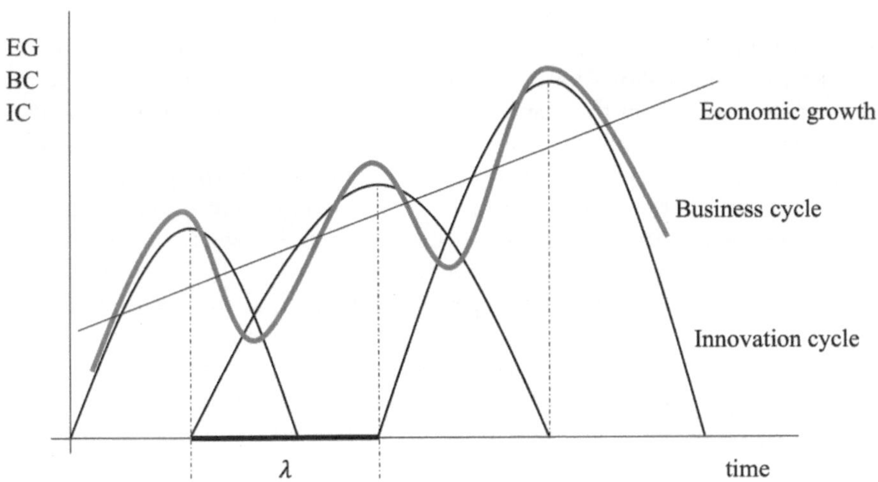


*Figure 5.1* The Productivity-Enhancing Process as the Source of Economic Growth

Source: *Own elaboration*

Hence, we obtain a non-stationary framework in which "innovations" (or "new combinations" in Schumpeterian language) activate economic progress. In summary, the innovation process absorbs all the individual productive consumption simply because everything that has not been consumed for immediate reproductive purposes tends to be allocated to strengthening the agent's competitiveness; the extent depends on the competitive pressure – the greater the pressure, the more of what has not been consumed for reproduction is allocated to productive purposes. Perfectly competitive markets therefore imply that the difference between disposable resources and reproductive consumption is allocated in full to productive consumption. Productive consumption thus represents the materialised activity of the past which is rejuvenated in the present and aims towards the future; or – as Adorno and Horkheimer (2002 [1944]) posit – the past is placed as usable knowledge in the service of the present. This materialised activity of productive consumption occurs within the competitive struggle motivated by lifelong self-preservation. It includes *all the activities and resources* that are aimed at strengthening competitiveness after the agents have secured their immediate reproduction.

The crucial question with concern to unequal distribution relates to the identity of the successful "innovator". From the microeconomic perspective, we refer to an agent who successfully utilises productive consumption, which means that the agent successfully appropriates additional resources in the market. However, both the Schumpeterian and neoclassical traditions consider significant de-monopolising tendencies. Despite the example of the *Aluminum Company of America* provided by Schumpeter (2008 [1942]), which demonstrates how even monopolists must innovate due to competitive pressure, Aghion and Howitt (1992) remind us that the most successful agent has the lowest motivation to innovate since innovation potentially leads to the destruction of the agent's own monopolistic rent. Even if we moderate the aforementioned destructive power, that is, if we consider lower barriers to the appropriation of resources in relation to the previous (pre-innovation) level of productivity, which allows lower competitive agents to continue to be able to appropriate resources in the market, the neoclassical argument shares a similar reasoning with respect to the profitable motivation of agents. The fact is that an agent who most successfully appropriates resources in the market is least motivated towards the further advancement of productivity of all the agents present simply because the positive marginal effect is lowest: the difference between an assumed new potential level of productivity and the current level of productivity is the lowest for the agent with the highest current level of productivity. Thus, the agent who most successfully utilises productive consumption, and hence appropriates the greatest share of resources in the market, will potentially experience the lowest marginal benefit from his/her productivity-enhancing process and will become the least better-off in the case of the successful advancement of productivity of the other agents present.

Both traditions, therefore, impose barriers to monopolising tendencies and the concentration of resources. These perspectives presuppose that there will always be an agent who is more motivated to occupy the leading position and, thus, successful appropriators rotate in the market over time. The salient moment here is whether the agent who has greater economic *motivation* to appropriate resources also has the corresponding economic *ability* to appropriate them. This ability should be scrutinised as a probabilistic process via which agents utilise their productive consumption, which enhances their competitiveness, in order to attain additional resources in the market. According to the rule of competitive markets, agents divide their disposable resources into reproductive and productive consumption. We can intuitively assume that reproductive consumption is not constant; rather it increases at a decreasing rate with the availability of disposable resources. The reason here is that the more the agent has at his/her disposal, the more the agent needs to consume for mere reproduction purposes. In any case, productive consumption under competitive market conditions, given as the difference between disposable resources and reproductive consumption, must increase with the amount of disposable resources at an accelerating rate. Agents who are initially successful in terms of appropriation in the market, whether it is due to a higher level of competitiveness or just good luck, are *able to* concentrate relatively more resources in productive consumption than their competitors. Consequently, more successful agents have more resources that can be used in the competition struggle (in the form of productive consumption) for the appropriation of additional resources. From the agent's perspective, these resources are appropriated based on his/her relative competitiveness compared to other agents, which is given by the share of the agent's productive consumption of the productive consumption of all agents. In sum, more successful agents enjoy a higher probability of additional appropriation and their success tends to accumulate over time. The same logic applied vice versa thus implies that poorer agents are forced to consume relatively more on their reproduction; the share of productive consumption of their disposable resources is lower and agents have fewer resources with which to increase their competitiveness. With lower competitiveness, agents eventually suffer from a lower probability of the appropriation of resources in the market, which implies the lower availability of disposable resources.

It is evident that this perspective on competitive markets reduces the agent's behaviour to an "animal-like process of biological survival" (Matthaei 1983). Freedom as spontaneity does not coexist with the agent's natural causation – the agent reproduces not only his/her physical and intersubjective dimensions but also the socioeconomic order which exists beyond his/her control and which conditions the agent's survival through his/her obedience – freedom has ceased to be a regulative idea of reason. Some agents are forced to exchange their labour for means of subsistence, while others are not allowed to enjoy their full profit due to the need for continual investment as the result of competitive pressure. "Economic and social forces take on the character of blind natural powers that man, in order to preserve himself, must dominate by adjusting himself to them" (Horkheimer 1947, p. 97). Hence, reproductive consumption transforms the fallacious trade-off between labour and leisure, which came to

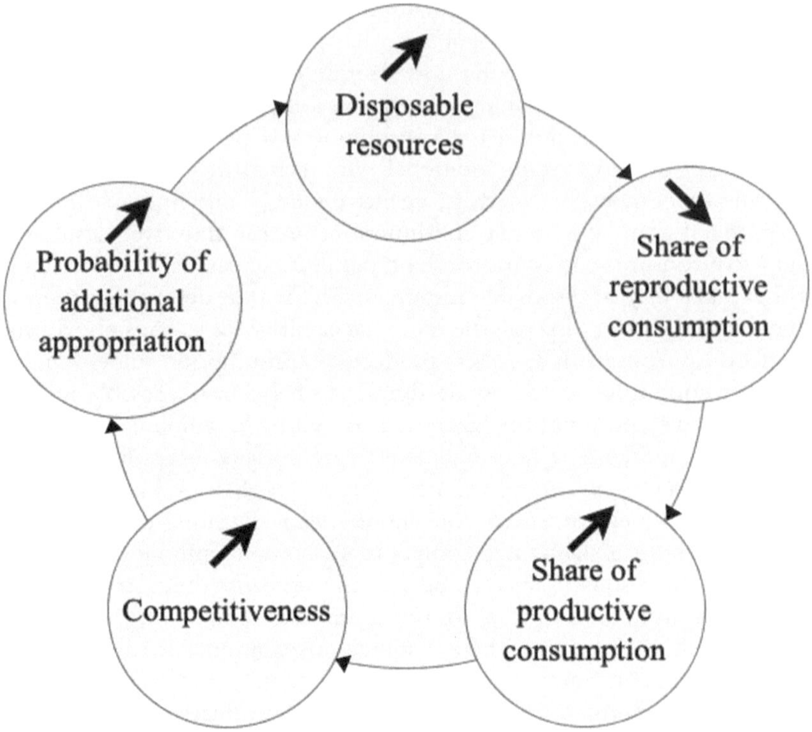


*Figure 5.2* Inequality Loop
Source: *Own elaboration*

be so typical for microeconomic optimisation, into the choice between labour and starvation. The consideration of reproductive consumption has a transformative implication since it is not a necessary condition only for leisure but also for the agent's existence as such.

It is important to emphasise that our economic agent is not an independent mathematical point, as economic agents are usually considered by critical theorists, but an element that absorbs the contradictory imperatives of the first and second nature on the one hand, and which drives and shapes the second nature through the behaviour of the agent on the other. The historically conditioned agent behaves with respect to socioeconomic dynamics and rationally anticipates the behaviour of other agents. For instance, economic models frequently apply the *subjective* discount factor $\beta \in (0,1)$ which signifies how strongly the agent prefers the present to the future. The lower the value of $\beta$, the more impatient is the agent, and the fewer the resources, the agent tend to transfer to the future. A lower subjective discount factor is then interpreted as an intertemporal *preference* which indicates that the agent is less willing to transfer a part of his/her disposable resources to the future and, subsequently, benefit from their valorisation, simply because the subjective value of present consumption is greater than the present value of the valorised future consumption. But what if the agent's disposable resources are so small that they barely cover reproductive consumption, and the agent naturally cannot transfer more resources for their future valorisation in the form of productive consumption? What if the agent's truly subjective mindset pushes him/her towards future consumption, but the pressure of reproductive consumption cancels out any forward-looking mental drivers concerning resource allocation? Economic categories such as the subjective discount factor are not only unable to detect these ambivalences, but they also hide their immanent insufficiency under an ideological veil.

Economic agents, who stand before a "permanent economic tribunal" which establishes those "deontic powers" that lie behind the phenomenal side of human action, have no other option than to join the competitive struggle for scarce resources. Markets, which – poetically said – provide an impression of the agent's free expression, are presented to the agent as impenetrable objectivity. This objectivity takes the form of natural selection – stronger agents are able to successfully usurp resources for their reproduction, while weaker agents balance on the edge between survival and extinction. Market inequality, however, does not issue from unequal or selective treatment – all agents are treated equally despite their immanent heterogeneity. However, this formal equality masks the fundamental inequality surrounding the decision on which *principles* of distribution should apply.

And, just as astronomical objects bind more mass the greater their mass, economic agents find themselves in a similar state of objectivity in which distribution follows the natural "law of the stronger". Praising unequal market distribution represents a step back to naturalness – it is a clash between civilisation and barbarism. Civilised society is characterised by the fact that natural forces are under the control of reason. This "suppression of the natural" is restricting and liberating at the same time and objective civilised reason – as a counterweight to subjective "barbaric" reason – decides what is worth sacrificing for what goals. This "success-breeds-success" mechanics, the natural law of power as the contraposition to civilisation, renders the supposed normativity of the Pareto optimum nonsensical. Any intervention in perfectly competitive markets aimed at equalising the agents must necessarily take place at the expense of the prosperous agents and, therefore, in contradiction to Pareto-optimality. The hidden normativity behind the Pareto optimum serves as a shield for those who benefit from the *status quo*. This "argumentation shield against civilisation" protects privileges from emancipatory tendencies, may it be the French Revolution, the abolition of slavery or the prohibition of child labour. All this progress towards a more civilised society happens at the expense of those who hold privileges – the aristocracy, the slave-masters and the early capitalists. The progress of humankind *is* about abolishing privileges, while advocates of these privileges only abuse the Pareto optimum for their own particular ends.

These principles are linked not solely to economic distribution but also to the distribution of power as such. The concentration of the economy in the hands of the few translates into unfair social contracts and various social inequalities. The reality of inequality becomes both the obstacle to a more civilised society and a necessary condition of the evolution thereof. The Real – a void beyond capturable existence which absorbs all the meanings, reasons and justifications of all practical conducts – follows the logic of conflict theory: self-interested agents operate under a perpetual scarcity of resources and their pervasive conflict is unavoidable both within and between social groups. This quest for resources in competitive markets drives the output of the economy and the principle of competitiveness as the decisive distributional criterion drives economic inequality. Under the rule of the free market, these two are inseparable, but under political rule, they are controllable. The market mechanism therefore immanently contains diverging distributional patterns which are more observable the more perfectly markets allocate.

## Notes

1 For instance: "The subject is no mathematical point like the ego of bourgeois philosophy; his activity is the construction of the social present" (Horkheimer 1972 [1937], pp. 210–211). Or alternatively, that

> [f]or any datum it must be possible to deduce all its determinations from theoretical systems and ultimately from mathematics; thus all finite magnitudes may be derived from the concept of the infinitely small by way of the infinitesimal calculus, and this process is precisely their "production".
>
> (Horkheimer 1972 [1937], p. 198)

2 Social antagonism is understood as the general propensity of individuals to want to be distinct from others, that is, the recognition of oneself in society based on the pursuit of one's own interests and needs. In this sense, social antagonism is reflected in the competitive relationships between agents as a result of the natural drive of individuals. Such a Kantian-Hobbesian perspective also encompasses individual freedom as autonomy from the determination of the "internal nature" (i.e. the pressures of instincts) and from the determination of the "external nature" represented by social relations. In a more general sense, relationships between agents are antagonistic because their interests in the market are irreconcilable in principle. Similarly, in biology, competition is a form of indirect antagonism, that is, two and more organisms compete for the resources necessary for survival (for instance for oxygen or nutrients in the soil), which is mirrored in the proposed idea of competitive struggle at the societal level.

3 It also is possible to find a number of "hypocritical" and "dogmatic" examples in critical theory. Despite the justifiable insistence on the resolution of the base and superstructure and, hence, on the fact that everything is ruled by production relations, it is still necessary to consider the obvious limitations. For instance, the cultural decay evident in Adorno's critique is frequently associated with the capitalist structure. Although this is undoubtedly relevant, selected phenomena that have little in common with the capitalist mode of production (e.g. Adorno's critique of jazz music) may have different decisive factors that are related to the 20th century in general or to specific local conditions. Nevertheless, in general terms, we observe that more and more elements of the superstructure are becoming increasingly common to all countries as the capitalist mode of production spreads. Naturally, this "levelling" is taking place in spite of previously very different historical, economic and cultural backgrounds.

4 An extended discussion is also provided in Rozental (1962).

5 Adorno would certainly have problematised the relationship to an even greater extent – as a complicated balance between collective subjectivity, individual subjectivity and objectivity.

6 Despite instinct structures being intrinsically linked to the agent, instincts remain uncontrollable by the will of the agent, and they manifest themselves as external to the agent. This clarifies why agents, despite the innerness of determinative instinct structures, can be classified as heteronomous.

7 It is obvious that no single model is able to provide a detailed explanation of the multitude of all stochastic particularities. By "any particular fact" one should understand any fact that is explainable as a systemic in the sense that it derives from the natural propensity of men – in Smith, for example, "the propensity to truck, barter, and exchange one thing for another" (1776); "the known principles of human nature".

8 Abstraction, however, does not mean that the "intangible" whole stands above its 'real' parts, but that it is important to depict the mutual dialectical interdependency of these two spheres: the whole creates the parts and the parts create the whole.

9 Harris similarly defines necessary consumption as a "quantity required for consumption in order that a unit of labour may be maintained in production" (1978, p. 55).

10 The normative aspect of deferred consumption even promotes the proposed procedure. The fact that the agent's disposable resources are divided into two parts, that is, one dedicated to immediate consumption and the second to the securing future income, was also referred to by Raphael (1995, p. 65).

11 See, for example, Hirschman and Holbrook (1982).

12 Since we focus on inequality that stems directly from the mainstream perspective on the production process, the problem of such equivalency is not considered further.

13 Clearly, such a view is asserted predominantly by neoclassical economists and it does not cover the whole range of economic theories – Keynesians would certainly incorporate the institutional and structural framework of the macroeconomic environment; Marxists would be opposed in a more radical way by considering class affiliations and so forth.

## References

Adorno, T.W. (1967). Sociologie a empirický výzkum. In: *Dialektika a sociologie*. Praha: Svoboda, pp. 19–35.

Adorno, T.W. (2005 [1951]). *Minima moralia: reflections on a damaged life*. London and New York: Verso.

Adorno, T.W. and Horkheimer, M. (2002 [1944]). *Dialectic of enlightenments: philosophical fragments*. Stanford: Stanford University Press.

Aghion, P. and Howitt, P.W. (1992). A model of growth through creative destruction. *Econometrica*, 60(2), pp. 323–351.

Antonio, R.J. (1983). The origin, development, and contemporary status of critical theory. *The Sociological Quarterly*, 24(3), pp. 325–351.

Bonefeld, W. (2014). *Critical theory and the critique of political economy: on subversion and negative reason*. London: Bloomsbury Academic.

Elster, J. (1982). Marxism, functionalism, and game theory: the case for methodological individualism. *Theory and Society*, 11(4), pp. 453–482.

Günther, K. (2007). Mezi zmocněním a disciplinováním: odpovědnost v současném kapitalismu. In: Honneth, A., ed. *Zbavovat se svéprávnosti: paradoxy současného kapitalismu*. Praha: Nakladatelství Filosofického ústavu AV ČR, pp. 145–174.

Harris, D.J. (1978). *Capital accumulation and income distribution*. Stanford: Stanford University Press.

Hirschman, E. and Holbrook, M.B. (1982). Hedonic consumption: energizing concepts, methods and propositions. *Journal of Marketing*, 48(Summer), pp. 92–101.

Horkheimer, M. (1947). *Eclipse of reason*. New York: Oxford University Press.

Horkheimer, M. (1972 [1937]). *Critical theory*. New York: Herder and Herder.

Horkheimer, M. (2012 [1949–1967]). *Critique of instrumental reason*. London and New York: Verso.

Hume, D. (2011 [1777]). *Essays: moral, political and literary*. Miller, E., ed. Carmel: Liberty Fund.

Jevons, W.S. (1888). *The theory of political economy*. London: Palgrave Macmillan.

Kellner, D. (1990). Critical theory and the crisis of social theory. *Sociological Perspectives*, 33(1), pp. 11–33.

Kilminster, R. (1979). *Praxis and method: a sociological dialogue with Lukács, Gramsci and the early Frankfurt school*. London: Routledge & Kegan Paul.

Kosík, K. (1976). *Dialectics of the concrete: a study on man and world*. Dondrecht: D. Reidel Publishing Company.

Lucas, R.E. (1986). Adaptive behaviour and economic theory. *The Journal of Business*, 59(4), pp. 401–426.

Marx, K. (1973 [1939–1941]). *Grundrisse: foundations of the critique of political economy*. Harmondsworth: Penguin Books in Association with New Left Review.

Marx, K. (2015 [1867]). *The capital: a critique of political economy*. Vol. I. Moscow: Progress Publishers.

Marx, K. and Engels, F. (2008 [1848]). *Communist manifesto*. Oxford: Oxford University Press.

Matthaei, J.A. (1983). Freedom and unfreedom in Marxian economics. *Eastern Economic Journal*, IX(2), pp. 71–78.

Pavlík, J. (2001). Teoreticko-historický přístup a dějiny astronomie. In: Smith, A., ed. *Pojednání o podstatě a původu bohatství národů*. Praha: Liberální institut, pp. 913–930.

Prusik, C.A. (2020). *Adorno and neoliberalism: the critique of exchange society*. London: Bloomsbury Publishing.

Raphael, D.D. (1995). *Adam Smith*. Praha: Argo.

Roemer, J. (1982). Methodological individualism and deductive Marxism. *Theory and Society*, 11(4), pp. 513–520.

Rozental, M.M. (1962). *Principy dialektické logiky*. Praha: Nakladatelství politické literatury.

Schumpeter, J.A. (2008 [1942]). *Capitalism, socialism, and democracy*. New York: Harper Collins.

Sensat, J. (1988). Methodological individualism and Marxism. *Economics and Philosophy*, 4(2), pp. 189–219.

Shi, J. (2019). *Interview with Thomas Sargent on the PhD and elite MA programs at PHBS* [online]. Available from: https://siqef.phbs.pku.edu.cn/en/2019/ONews_0719/12.html.

Smith, A. (1776). An inquiry into the nature and causes of the wealth of nations. In: *History of economic thought books from McMaster university archive for the history of economic thought*.

Smith, A. (1982). *Essays on philosophical subjects*. Wightman, W.P.D. and Bryce, J.C., eds. Vol. III of the Glasgow ed. of the works and correspondence of Adam Smith. Indianapolis: Liberty Fund.

Smith, A. (1985). *Lectures on rhetoric and belles lettres*. Bryce, J.C. and Skinner, A.S., eds. Vol. IV. of the Glasgow ed. of the works and correspondence of Adam Smith. Indianapolis: Liberty Fund.

Weldes, J. (1989). Marxism and methodological individualism: a critique. *Theory and Society*, 18(3), pp. 353–386.

Wolff, R.P. (1990). Methodological individualism and Marx – some remarks on Jon Elster, game theory and other things. *Canadian Journal of Philosophy*, 20(4), pp. 469–486.

# Conclusion

If one considers a truly emancipated society, one must problematise the relationship between essence and appearance in the understanding of social reality. This requires grasping the various systemic features in their dynamic forms, as well as in their internal and external processual contexts – to derive knowledge of the essence that is behind the scene of our immediate reality. On the other hand, we should not rely on the artificial separation of factual and evaluative claims, nor on the separation of the subject and the object. And economics plays a crucial role in this effort. Its approach, with its strong elements of essentialism and determinism, which subsequently absorbs all thinkable economic phenomena, renders the economic "hard core" – and with it the conditions of the capitalist economy – untouched. Profit, utility, (counter)value and competition are examples of the various constituents that form a conceptual whole which, when examined by economists, finds its meaning in statistical regularities and logical inference, in sum in a descriptive preservation, in contrast to the value-driven transformation pursued by critical theorists. However, economic theory insists that rational economic agents maximise their utility, which is difficult both to evaluate and to disprove. The only measure comprises the way in which the agent actually behaves, which implies no guarantees that individual rationality is transformed into the rational behaviour of the whole. The truth, in fact, is valueless, embedded in its observable existence – positivist in its purest form.

The essential, systemic socioeconomic laws are mirrored in distributional patterns. The quantitative criteria of the production process, as enforced by deeply embedded competitive pressures, result in the fact that the rapidly increasing output in market economies is not aimed principally at eliminating fundamental deficiencies, and nor do they exert primary emancipatory effects. Increasing output is driven by systemic forces that are blind to any qualitative differences. Impersonalised equal treatment and structural potentialities then suffice to preserve the illusion of equal opportunities, which, subsequently, finally favour and advocate unequal distribution. The behavioural confrontation with the mainstream neoclassical framework only replicates the perverted idea of neoclassical dogmas – this confrontation is drowning in its own inability both to disprove the established concept of rationality, as composed of the

DOI: 10.4324/9780429273841-7

maximisation of the target functions under constraints and the consistency of choice, and to formulate generalisable theoretical insights.

Conversely, viewing socioeconomic phenomena as principally dialectical, that is, from the perspective from which the antagonisms of conflicting actors, whether they be employee and employer or producer/seller and consumer, perpetually proceed to new qualitative changes in mutual interaction, may provide significant support for the economic context. The pure division of cognition and the senses is then discarded: critical theory not only postulates that objective material conditions form our thoughts and knowledge but also acknowledges that cognition and theory may determine our perception of the objective world. Consequently, the subject is constituted by objective conditions, while, at the same time, the subject acts to form these objective material and historical conditions. The subject has the full emancipatory potential, yet it remains powerless. The dominating power of the objective is propelled by the power of repetition over existence. Rationality, reduced to its instrumental form, dictates obedience to repetition and regularity – to the objectified economic laws to which agents are bound for subsistence reasons; any form of insurgency is a sign of suicidal imprudence. Despite being the creators of these laws, economic agents have become their imprisoned functionaries. Inspired by dialectical reasoning, I aimed to decipher the extent to which Reason is unreasonable and the victim of these unmastered forces.

The book also attempts to explain how individual rational behaviour constitutes the irrational dynamic of the system and, conversely, how these macro-level forces determine the behaviour of the micro-level constituents thereof. In order to exhaust the whole of the essence of the phenomenon rather than its mere constitutive facets, I focused on the inescapable economic laws that govern human action and, in the final instance, the whole of society: the lawful character of the contradictory interactions of agents constitutes the dialectical totality of production. In order to condense the internal movement of the production process and to demystify the randomness of inequality in economic distribution, I came to the following conclusion: the survival of agents depends on the limited amounts of resources available in the market. Agents are, therefore, forced to compete for these resources due to mere reproduction purposes. The surplus of resources over their reproductive consumption is then further invested due to competitive pressures that act to strengthen the agent's competitiveness, which then serves to enhance the chances of subsequent appropriation compared to those of lower-level competitive agents. In line with traditional economic assumptions, agents are supposed to appropriate the amount of resources proportional to their competitive power. Market competition, as a widely promoted equalising tendency, also results in more competitive agents becoming even more competitive and, hence, successful in terms of their appropriation of resources, while exactly the opposite trend is experienced by initially less competitive agents. Inequality is, therefore, being reproduced over and above the regular functioning of the production processes in the market economy, and becomes an inseparable phenomenon thereof.

These "success-breeds-success" system dynamics, anchored by the "rational instinct" for self-preservation and applied in competitive markets, cancel out the autonomy of agents, reify their existence, and lower them to an instrument of their socially constructed reality.

The dichotomy of the agent's existence is experienced as violence: the reproduction of agents is derived from their *natural* relations to the world, which are not subject to change. However, the market mechanism as the predominant mode of production serves to administer the reproduction of agents via social, *exchange* relations, which are, conversely, subject to change. In order to emancipate man, unlike the original enlightened *cogito*, which was aimed at escaping from subjugation via the mastering of the conditions of man's life, contemporary *cogito*, with the same purpose, dictates exactly the opposite – adaptation to the dominant conditions of market distribution. It would be too naïve to praise the superficial differentiation of agents as a means to success in the market, and to remain blind to their fundamental uniformity. Echoing the primitive, uncivilised mode of reason, the success of agents up to the present day is the greater the better the agent adapts to the external environment. The difference is that this adaptation is not aimed directly at the immediate nature, but is instrumentally bound to social relations. As long as the agent's self-preservation is tied to the market, he/she has no other option than to follow market imperatives. However, market allocation evens out all the urgency; its criterion comprises the consideration provided. The agent pays for his/her survival with subjectivity, and hence this subjectivity comes into conflict with the existential conditions of his/her being.

Undeniably, ostracised individuals in much of the world could well lose more than their chains – loyalty to the *status quo* is due not only to the false consciousness of the brainwashed masses; the current state of affairs, from various perspectives, should not be seen only in its darkest forms. The source of obedience is not only in the pressure of nature – for instance, wages are often not suppressed to the reproduction minimum. But in the light of the aforementioned, economics is able – due to its all-embracing scope and the fact that every human action occurs in an environment of scarcity (at least that of space and time) and, in most cases, with various alternatives – to consider and explain all social phenomena within its theoretical framework. On the one hand, this monistic approach raises the risk of presenting a tautology since there is no chance that a thing can be otherwise, on the other hand, it allows one to see economic inequality as the immanent product of the production process with its serious consequences for socioeconomic reality.

This book comprises a modest attempt at contributing towards the frequently held but underdeveloped discussion on the relationship between critical theory and economics. I attempt to develop an argumentation that positions economic inequality in its systemic entirety, in which it is seen as a result of systemic determination based on the self-producing impulses of the system itself – unequally competing agents who rationally avoid economic misery, thus constitute a society that must constantly increase its wealth in order to preserve its mere existence.

# Index

Note: Page numbers in *italics* indicate a figure and page numbers in **bold** indicate a table on the corresponding page.

abstractness 113–114, 133n8
Adorno, T. W. 6, 11, 13, 15, 93, 116, 128; on aesthetics and cultural and art critique 20–21; on bourgeois society 95; on dialectics 79, 81, 94; on division between sociology and economics 20; on exchange value 118–119; on human emancipation 17–18; on individuals as objects 101; on instrumental reason 96; on positivism 70, 71, 75; on self-determinism 18; on self-preservation 99–101; on social injustice 97; on social totality 85–87; on subjectivity and objectivity 76–77, 133n5; on universalism of human needs 22–23
aesthetics and cultural and art critique 20–21
agent-based models 80, 98–99, 110–111; heteronomous agents in 114–124; market conditions and 120–121
aggregability of feelings of individuals 31–32
Aghion, P. 128
Akerlof, G. A. 61
Allais, M. 45
*Aluminum Company of America* 128
anthropologic constant 105n7
Antonio, R. J. 7, 77, 109
Ariely, D. 61
Aristotle 54
Arthur, C. J. 80–81
Barone, E. 44
Becker, G. S. 51
behavioural economics 44–63, 136–137; empirical evidence in natural sciences and 45–49; optimism and pessimism in **60**, 60–61; public policy and 59–60; rationality in 50–52, 56–57, 61–62; retirement savings and 58–59; satisficing behaviour and 55–56; self-interest in 50–55; status quo bias and 61; systematic movement of phenomena and 45–46; utility in 51–56; *see also* economics
Benartzi, S. 45, 59
Benjamin, W. 6, 11
Bentham, J. 42; on pleasure and pain 30–31, 33; on utility 32
Bernardelli, H. 71
Birnbaum, M. H. 61
Blaug, M. 43
Bolton, G. E. 53
Bonefeld, W. 24, 79, 81, 103, 111
Bourdieu, P. 20, 120; on popular culture 21; on social inequalities 22
Brain, A. 31
Braunstein, D. 21, 70
Breton, A. 98
Bruhin, A. 60
Buzgalin, A. 16

Cairnes, J. E. 34
*Capital* 23, 24

capitalism 132n3; global 24; social contradictions in 19–20; state 23, 24, 25n8
Cartwright, N. 49–50
Chernoff condition 56, 62
Chetty, R. 61
Chytilova, H. 59
Clark, A. 33
Clark, J. B. 41
Cobb-Douglas utility function 53–54
*Communist Manifesto* 127
Congdon, W. 45
Connerton, P. 7
consumption 115–118, 120, 128–130, 133n10
critical theory: abstract determinations in 17; within aesthetics and cultural and art critique 20–21; constructing a developing picture of society 7–8; defined 5, 25n1; dialectical approaches in 74, 79; dialectical totality and the pseudoconcrete in 84–90; difficulties in mapping and grasping 6; domination-free society and 8; economics and 1–2, 16–25; empiricism and 74; focus on human emancipation 8, 17, 39; Frankfurt School and 6–7; history of 5–11; internal tensions in 11; Marxian categoric imperative and 9; materialism and 9–10, 12–13; as materialist content of idealist concept of reason 8; not seeking harmony 81–82; positivism and (*See* positivism); pseudoconcreteness and 86–90; refining the relationship between the base and superstructure 10; traditional theory and 11–16
critical thinking 89
*Critique of the Gotha Programme* 40
cumulative destructive process 23

Darwin, C. 71
death impulse 103
Deaton, A. 49–50
Debreu, G. 38
deductive chain of thought 73
deferred consumption 133n10
DellaVigna, S. 50
deontic powers 74
de-ontologised positivism 108–114, **111**
despotism 72–73
determinism 10
Dewey, J. 6
dialectical-critical (D-C) logic 84
dialectical totality 84–90, 108–113
*Dialectic of Enlightenment* 6, 72, 77, 88, 94
dialectics: negative 81; as reaction to positivism 78–84; reductionism and 83
*Die Grundlagen der ökonomischen Theorie* 71
disjunctive syllogism 79
distributional theories 37–44, 118–119; based on diminishing marginal utility 42; equalisation 38–39; exploitation 40–41; immanence of unequal distribution 124–132, *127*, *130*; individual income 39–40; modern demand theory 43; neoclassical theory and 37–38; Pareto-optimality 43–44; reward for talent 41–42
Di Tella, R. 33
domination 8
Doucouliagos, C. 55–56
Druckman, J. N. 47
Dubiel, H. 10
Dupuit, J. 32

Easterlin, R. 33
economics: abstract determinations in 17; aesthetics and cultural and art critique and 20–21; agent-based models in 80, 98–99, 110–111, 120–121; aggregability of feelings of individuals in 31–32; behavioural "critique" in (*see* behavioural economics); consumption 115–118, 128–129; critical theory and 1–2, 16–25; distributional theories in 37–44, 118–119; division between sociology and 20; dominant class in 22; exchange value in 34–35, 118–120; foundations of contemporary 29–36; heteronomous agents and transcendence of the market economy and 114–124; immanence of unequal distribution in 124–132, *127*, *130*; individual perception of pleasure and pain in 30–31, 33; instrumental reason and contemporary 93–101; Keynesian theory 36; laws of 98–99; market prices 30; mathematical

models in 46–47, 108–109, 130–131; monetisation of society and 94; monopolising tendencies in 128–129; neoclassical 35–36, 37–38, 41, 45, 47, 50–53, 62–63, 125; popular culture and 21–22; production process 115, 126–127; profit maximisation in 33–34; psychologization of 104; rationality in (*see* rationality); relationships to other social sciences 36; social contradictions in capitalism and 19–20; social inequalities and 22; state capitalism and 23, 24, 25n8; technology development and 18–19; universalism of human needs and 22–23; utility in 32–33, 42–43; value of labour in 29–30; variety of economic theories in 35; *See also* capitalism
economism 10, 20
Elster, J. 110–111
emancipation 8
empirical evidence: economic theory based on 49–50; in natural sciences 45–49
empiricism 73–74, 87–88
Engel, C. 54
Engels, F. 10, 79
equalising policies 38–39
*Essays* 47
exchange value 34–35, 118–120
exploitation 40–41

facts: gatherable *versus* non-gatherable 75; totality of 87
faith and rationality 96
false totality 87, 104
Farr, A. 19, 81
Fehr, E. 53
Fleurbaey, M. 42
formalism, mathematical 72
Frank, R. H. 33
Frankfurt School 5–7, 9–10, 16, 24; economists of 23; social totality and 85
freedom 4, 14, 105n3, 115; capitalism and 22–23; of choice 120–122; consumption patterns and 116; equality and 25n7; in high and low cultures 21, 22; market system 120–124; Marxian economics on 36; philosophy and intellectual 76; political 24, 39; responsibility and 123; in simple exchange 19; from something 94; as spontaneity 129; tolerance and 96–97; unfreedom and 82; value-neutrality and 95
"free riders" 51
Freud, S. 5–6, 103
Friedman, M. 47, 52
Fromm, E. 6, 105n3
Fuchs, C. 8
fungibility 21

Gartman, D. 20, 21, 22, 94
Gechter, M. 46–47
Geuss, R. 7
Goodwin, N. 51
Gorz, A. 21, 95
Gossen, H. H. 32
Gramsci, A. 13
Grossman, H. 23
Grünberg, C. 6
*Gründrisse* 24
Gul, F. 53
Günther, K. 122
Gutierrez, R. J. 61

Habermas, J. 6–7, 9, 72, 93, 104–105n1
habitus 21
Hamermesh, D. 46
Hammond, P. J. 42
Harbaugh, W. T. 60
Harsanyi, J. 44
Hauser, M. 97, 102
Hayek, F. 47–48, 86
hedonic consumption 117, 120
Hegel, G. W. F. 6, 10–11, 14, 79, 81, 86, 90n10
heteronomous agents 114–124
heuristics 36
*History and Class Consciousness* 85
history of critical theory 5–11
*History of the Human Sciences* 16
Hobbes, T. 116
*Holy Family, The* 10
homeostasis 105n6
Homer 99
*homo oeconomicus* 51, 71, 102
Honneth, A. 6–7, 25n10, 81, 102
Horkheimer, M. 6, 9–16, 85, 93, 128; on abstract determinations 17; on

agent-based models 80; on bourgeois society 95, 132n1; on individuals as objects 101; on instrumental reason 96; on materialism *vs.* idealism 94; on positivism 70, 71, 75; on production 126; on role of economic relationships 16; on self-preservation 99–101; on social injustice 97; on unemployment, precarity and economic crises 18
Houser, D. 54
Howard, D. 8
Howitt, P. W. 128
Hrubec, M. 9, 15
human emancipation 8, 17, 39, 135; *See also* freedom
human instincts 98, 105n6, 133n6
Hume, D. 109

*Institut für Sozialforschung* 6, 85
instrumental reason 93–101, 104–105n1
*Introduction to Sociology* 20
*Introduction to the Principles of Morals and Legislation* 30

Jay, M. 8–9, 104–105n1
Jevons, W. S. 29, 51, 70; on exchange value 34; on the market 114–115; on utility 30–32, 43, 57

Kafka, F. 122
Kahneman, D. 33, 45
Kaldor, N. 44
Kalivoda, R. 19, 98
Kam, C. D. 47
Kant, I. 5–6, 8, 13–14, 96, 97, 104
Keller-Allen, C. 45
Kellner, D. 9–10, 84, 109
Keucheyan, R. 9
Keynesian theory 36
Kilminster, R. 77, 109
Knetsch, J. L. 56
Kolganov, A. 16
Kosík, K. 19, 20, 48, 51, 79, 90n6; on dialectics 83; on facts 87; on historically conditioned man 83; on inequality 124; on objectification of self 102, 104; on one-sidedness 81; on positivism 75, 77–78, 109; on procuring 96; on pseudoconcreteness 86, 88–90; on reality reducing man 113; on three-dimensionality of time 100; on value judgments 95

labour value 29–30
Lakatos, I. 36
Lazarsfeld, P. 78, 89
Lee, L. 50, 56
Leigh, A. 47
Leppin, Z. 96
Lerner, A. P. 42
Levine, D. K. 53
Levitt, S. 50
Li, R. M. 45
List, J. 50
logic: analytical-descriptive (A-D) 83–84; dialectical 82–83; dialectical-critical (D-C) 84
Löwenthal, L. 6, 7
Lucas, R. 112
Lukács, G. 8, 16, 85, 99, 102
luxury, theory of 21

Machovec, M. 98
Madrian, B. 45
Maialeh, R. 38, 45, 56
Mandel, E. 80
Mandler, M. 51
Marcus, L. 73
Marcuse, H. 6, 19, 80, 81–83, 85
marginalist revolution 29
marginal utility 42
Marshall, A. 42, 48
Marx, K. 5–7, 10, 16, 24, 70–71, 102, 119
Marxism 5–10; agent-based modelling in 110–111; conscious rationality and 17; on economic distribution 40; on exchange society 19; on exploitation 41; on human instincts 98; normative realism in 17; pseudoconcreteness and 86; totality concept in 85
Maslow, A. 116
materialism 9–10, 12–13
*Materialism and Metaphysics* 10, 12
McCloskey, D. 17
Mead, G. 6
mechanical materialism 10
Menger, C. 29
Michňák, K. 72

Mill, J. S. 30, 34, 40, 52
Miller, S. M. 38
monetisation of society 94
monopolising tendencies 128–129
Morgenstern, O. 95
Munro, A. 59
Murray, P. 71
Myers, D. G. 33

natural sciences 45–49
negative dialectics 81
negative heuristics 36
neoclassical economic theory 35–36, 37–38, 41, 125; behavioural economics and 45, 47, 50–54, 62–63
Neumann, F. 23, 24
Ng, Y. K. 33
*Nicomanchean Ethics* 54
normative judgments 74–75
*Note on Dialectics, A* 82

objectivity 76–77, 80, 104–105n1, 136; subject 101–104
Ockenfels, A. 53
*Odysseus* 99–100
Oliver, A. 59
optimism and pessimism **60**, 60–61
Orrell, D. 104
Oswald, A. J. 33

Pareto, V. 42
Pareto-optimality 43–44, 131
Parsons, T. 87
*Pascalian Meditations* 22
Pavlík, J. 113
Pearson, G. 7
Persky, J. 52
Pesendorfer, W. 53
*Phenomenology of Spirit* 11
philosophy 76, 89
Piccone, P. 8
Pigou, A. C. 42
pleasure and pain 30–31, 33
Pollock, F. 6, 23
popular culture 21–22
positive heuristics 36
positivism 14, 16, 135; advocating the status quo 72; critique of 70–78; deductive chain of thought and 73; de-ontologised 108–114, **111**; dialectics as reaction to 78–84; Marx on 70–71; ontologisation in 109–110; subjectivity and objectivity in 76–77; value judgments in 71–72
Postone, M. 10, 14–15; on Frankfurt School 24; on social relations in capitalism 19–20
poverty 103
"Prisoner's dilemma" 51
production process 115, 126–127
productive consumption 116, 120, 128–129
profit maximisation 33–34
Prusik, C. A. 16
pseudoconcreteness 86–90
public policy 59–60
Pugh, M. 16
Pullmann, M. 9

Rabin, M. 53
Rainko, S. 9
randomised controlled trials (RCTs) 47
rationality 50–52, 61–62, 135–136; abstract reality and 113–114; as consistency of choice 56–57; faith and 96; instrumental 94, 95, 104–105n1; retirement and 58–59; self-preservation and 97–101, 102
Real and the Symbolic 90n9
*Realpolitik* 22
reason: contemporary economics and instrumental 93–101; metamorphosis of the subject and its objectification 101–104; and rational attitude toward self-preservation 97–101, 102, 104–105n1
*Reason and Revolution* 86
recognition 25n10
reductionism 83
Rein, M. 38
reproductive consumption 116, 129–130
Resnick, S. A. 35, 37–38
retirement savings 58–59
Ricardo, D. 24, 37
Robbins, L. 29, 43, 48, 56
Robinson, J. 40
Robinson, W. I. 24
Rockmore, T. 16
Roemer, J. 111

Rosenbaum, E. F. 43
Ross, N. 75
Rothschild, M. 61
Rowntree, S. B. 39
Rusche, G. 71

Samuelson, P. 70
Sargent, T. 110
Sartre, J.-P. 104
satisficing behaviour 55–56
Schmidt, K. M. 53
Schumpeter, J. A. 127–128
Schunk, D. 54
Searle, J. 74
self-interest 50–55
self-mastery 100
self-preservation 97–101, 102, 123
Sen, A. 39, 42, 44, 50–51, 56
Sensat, J. 111
Simmel, G. 94
Simon, H. A. 45, 55, 56
Simon, J. L. 33
Smith 108
Smith, A. 17, 24, 38–39, 96, 112–113, 116, 133n7
social antagonism 132n2
social injustice 97
*Social Science and Social Policy* 73
social totality 84–87
Sohn-Rethel, A. 24
Spinoza, B. 116
state capitalism 23, 24, 25n8
status quo bias 14, 61–62, 72, 82, 123, 131, 137
Steigerwald, R. 9
Stiglitz, J. E. 61
Styron, W. 120
subject, metamorphosis of 101–104
subjectivity 76, 80, 136
Sunstein, C. 45
systematic movement of phenomena 45–46

Thaler, R. 45, 59
*Theory and Society* 111
*Theory of Moral Sentiments* 116
Thompson, M. J. 7, 11–12, 74–75, 78–79, 83–84
*Time, Labor, and Social Domination* 24
tolerance 96–97
totality: dialectical 84–90, 108–113; false 87, 104
"Traditional and Critical Theory" 13
traditional theory 11–16
*Trial* 122
tripolar theory of justice 24
Tversky, A. 45, 61

unequal distribution 124–132, *127*, *130*
utility: in behavioural economics 51–53; Cobb-Douglas utility function 53–54; diminishing marginal 42; individualisation of 43; instrumental reason and 95; maximisation of 55–56; theory of 32–33

value, exchange 34–35, 118–120
value consciousness 96
value judgments 71–72, 95
value-neutrality 95
Veblen, T. 21
Veenhoven, R. 33
von Bertalanffy, L. 87
von Heiseler, H. J. 9
von Neumann, J. 95
vulgar hedonism 51, 53

Walras, L. 29
Weber, M. 20, 73, 93
Weil, F. 85
Weiss, A. 61
Weldes, J. 111
Winkelmann, L. 33
Winkelmann, R. 33
Witteloostuijn, A. 55–56
Wolff, R. D. 35, 37–38
Wolff, R. P. 51

Zawistowksi, S. 120, 122
*Zeitschrift für Sozialforschung* 71